JEREMIAH
and God's Plans of Well-being

STUDIES ON PERSONALITIES OF THE OLD TESTAMENT
James L. Crenshaw, Series Editor

JEREMIAH

and God's Plans of Well-being

BARBARA GREEN

The University of South Carolina Press

© 2013 University of South Carolina

Published by the University of South Carolina Press
Columbia, South Carolina 29208

www.sc.edu/uscpress

Manufactured in the United States of America

22 21 20 19 18 17 16 15 14 13   10 9 8 7 6 5 4 3 2 1

Library of Congress Cataloging-in-Publication Data

Green, Barbara, 1946–
    Jeremiah and God's Plans of Well-being / Barbara Green.
        pages cm. — (Studies on personalities of the Old Testament)
    Includes bibliographical references and index.
    ISBN 978-1-61117-270-6 (alk. paper) — ISBN 978-1-61117-271-3 (epub)
    1. Bible Jeremiah—Criticism, interpretation, etc. 2. Jeremiah (Biblical prophet)
I. Title.
    BS1525.52.G74 2013
    224'.206—dc23

                                                        2013007825

This book was printed on a recycled paper with 30 percent postconsumer waste content.

CONTENTS

SERIES EDITOR'S PREFACE

Critical study of the Bible in its ancient Near Eastern setting has stimulated interest in the individuals who shaped the course of history and whom events singled out as tragic or heroic figures. Rolf Rendtorff's *Men of the Old Testament* (1968) focuses on the lives of important biblical figures as a means of illuminating history, particularly the sacred dimension that permeates Israel's convictions about its God. Fleming James's *Personalities of the Old Testament* (1939) addresses another issue, that of individuals who function as inspiration for their religious successors in the twentieth century. Studies restricting themselves to a single individual—for example, Moses, Abraham, Samson, Elijah, David, Saul, Ruth, Jonah, Job, Jeremiah—enable scholars to deal with a host of questions: psychological, literary, theological, sociological, and historical. Some, like Gerhard von Rad's *Moses* (1960), introduce a specific approach to interpreting the Bible, hence provide valuable pedagogic tools.

As a rule these treatments of isolated figures have not reached the general public. Some were written by outsiders who lacked a knowledge of biblical criticism (Freud on Moses, Jung on Job) and whose conclusions, however provocative, remain problematic. Others were targeted for the guild of professional biblical critics (David Gunn on David and Saul, Phyllis Trible on Ruth, Terence Fretheim and Jonathan Magonet on Jonah). None has succeeded in capturing the imagination of the reading public in the way fictional works like Archibald MacLeish's *J. B.* and Joseph Heller's *God Knows* have done.

It could be argued that the general public would derive little benefit from learning more about the personalities of the Bible. Their conduct, often less then exemplary, reveals a flawed character, and their everyday concerns have nothing to do with our preoccupations from dawn to dusk. To be sure, some individuals transcend their own age, entering the gallery of classical literary figures from time immemorial. But only these rare achievers can justify specific treatments of them. Then why publish additional studies on biblical personalities?

The answer cannot be that we read about biblical figures to learn ancient history, even of the sacred kind, or to discover models for ethical action. But what remains? Perhaps the primary significance of biblical personages is the light they throw on the imaging of deity in biblical times. At the very least, the Bible constitutes human perceptions of deity's relationship with the world and its creatures. Close readings of biblical personalities therefore clarify ancient understandings of God. That is the important datum which we seek—not because we endorse that specific view of deity, but because all such efforts to make sense of reality contribute something worthwhile to the endless quest for knowledge.

James L. Crenshaw
Robert L. Flowers Professor of
Old Testament, Emeritus
Duke University

ACKNOWLEDGMENTS

As I complete and present this book, I think gratefully of the students I have taught at San Domenico School, Dominican College of San Rafael (now Dominican University), the Graduate Theological Union. I am deeply appreciative of colleagues who have taught me a great deal and in so many ways. I have gained immeasurably from the many opportunities I have been given to present my work before professional audiences and lay groups as well, each helpfully supportive and critical as called for. Much of the material in this book has received such attention. As libraries become in many ways increasingly anonymous, I want to thank all those working behind the scenes to make research as easy as it can be and to name the librarians I have known best at the Graduate Theological Union: Robert Benedetto, Oscar Burdick, Phillippa Caldeira, Clay-Edward Dixon, Marie Hempen, Mary Mead, David Stiver, Kris Veldheer.

CHART OF THE BOOK OF JEREMIAH ASSUMED

Chapter 1: Call
    superscription: 1:1–3
    call proper: 1:4–10
    call enacted: visions: 1:11–12, 13–19
Chapters 2–10: Overture
    • **2:1:4:4:** toggled quoted speech
    • **4:5–6:30:** 4:5–14; 4:16–31; 5:1–9; 5:10–19; 5:20–31; 6:1–15; 6:16–30
    • **7:1–8:4:** 7:1–15; 7:16–26; 7:27–8:3
    • **8:5–9:25:** 8:4–12; 8:13–23; 9:1–10; 9:11–25
    • **10:1–25:** 10:1–5; 10:6–10; 10:11–16; 10:17–18; 10:19–22; 10:23–25
Chapters 11–20: Prose Ministry (in lowercase letters) and Soliloquies (numbered for prophet and deity); they are additionally grouped into seven units (upper case letters)

• *One: #a, 11:2–14, is a covenant speech:* **unappreciated past**

    Y: #1: **fire and the green olive** (11:15–17)
    J: #1: **the trusting lamb** (11:18–23)
    J: #2: **sheep for the slaughter** (12:1–6)
    Y: #2: **heritage destructive and destroyed** (12:7–13)

• *Two: #b, #c, #d*

    #b, 12:14–17 is a YHWH resolution: **uprootings**
    #c, 13:1–11 is a sign-act, functioning as an analogy: **loincloth**

• The numbers spelled out refer to the blended sets.
■ The prose narratives of deity/prophet partnership are represented by the # lowercase letter used above.
○ 'God's prophetic soliloquies by number.
• Jeremiah's prophetic soliloquies by number.

#d, 13:12–14 is a proverb, presented and then twisted to surprise: **wine jugs**

Y: #3: **the flock-whisperer** (13:15–27)

Y: #4: **wandering feet** (14:1–10)

- *Three: #e, 14:11–16, is a reported dialogue:* **on intercession**

  Y: #5: **tears amid drought** (14:17–22)

- *Four: #f, 15:1–4, is a pronouncement:* **on intercession**

  Y: #6: **grieving women, whining sons** (15:5–14)

  J: #3: **tasty words** (15:15–21)

- *Five: #g/h: 16:1–13 and 14–18, is directions for a set of sign-acts, interpreted and then explicated as to cause when queried, then finished off by a shifted proverb:* **prophetic identity** *and* **worse fate**

  Y: #7: **hearts indelible, irrevocable, gone off** (16:19–17:13)

  J: #4: **reluctant shepherd** (17:14–18)

- *Six #i, 17:19–27, is a dictated preaching on gate options:* **teaching regarding Sabbath**

  #j 18:1–12, is a demonstration of process, the narrative of a sign-act: **potter parable**

  Y: #8: **provocative anomalies** (18:13–17)

  J: #5: **the pits** (18:18–23)

- *Seven #k: 19:1–13, is a denunciation with an illustrative prop:* **parable of potsherd**

  J: #6: **enticing deity** (20:7– either 13 or 18)

  Chapters 20–39: Heartland Ministry

- *A hinge: Jeremiah imprisoned: 20*

- *B warnings to kings and other leaders: 21–23*

  ○ 21:1–14: wistful wish flattened

- *C demonstrations of alternative outcomes: 24–26*

  - Figs
  - Cup of Wrath
  - Temple Sermon

- *D prophetic words interpreted, contested: 27–28*

  ○ 27:1–22: yokes contested

- *E timing and true liberation: 29*

- *F words of hope: 30–31*

- *G land deed needed: 32*
  - ○ 32:1–44: *land deed needed*
- *F' words of hope: 33*
- *E' timing and false liberation: 34*
  - ○ 34:1–22: *slave reprieve revoked*
- *D' prophetic words contested: 35–36*
- *C' liberation contested: 37–38*
  - ○ 37:3–21: *disputed departure*
  - ○ 38:1–13: *in and out of Malchiah's mud*
- *B' the end of monarchic Judah: 39*
- *A' hinge: Ebed-Melek released: 39*

Chapters 39–44: Finale
  - 39: four immediate fates
  - 40–41: roads taken and not taken
  - 42–43 Jeremiah's last words in Judah
  - 44: stranded in Egypt

Chapter 45: Word to Basuch

Chapters 46–51: Oracles to or regarding the Nations
  superscription: 46:1
  regarding **Egypt**: 46:2–28: 46:2–12; 46:13–26; 46:27–28
  regarding **Philistia**: 47:1–7
  regarding **Moab**: 48:1–47
  regarding **Ammon**: 49:1–6
  regarding **Edom**: 49:7–22
  regarding **Damascus**: 49:23–27
  regarding **Kedar**: 49:28–33
  regarding **Elam**: 49:34–39
  regarding **Babylon**: 50:1–51:58
  colophon re **Seraiah**: 51:59–64

Chapter 52: Final Events
  summary of Zedekiah's reign: 52:1–3
  the capture of Jerusalem and aftermath: 52:4–27
  summary of exiles: 52:27–30
  release of Jehoiachin: 52:31–34

INTRODUCTION

Scope and Stipulations

> Modern Western thinkers do not believe that either divine anger or human
> sinfulness fully explain disaster. We understand both national and personal
> catastrophes to come from complex webs of cause and effect.
>
> Kathleen M. O'Connor, "Reclaiming Jeremiah's Violence"

Scope

Can a responsible, coherent, compelling book on biblical Jeremiah be composed
from the vast complexity of issues that must be addressed in it? How can a classic,
gathering shape from the sixth century B.C.E. and then thriving under interpreters for more than two thousand years, be freshly addressed? Can such an ancient
religious document pose issues for twenty-first-century readers? I am confident
that such a project wants doing and offer it here, challenged by the series in
which it appears to construct familiar biblical figures in ways that are fresh, clear,
and scholarly but also readable, interesting, provocative, and valuable.

To produce such a book, we must proceed with discipline and care, omit-
ting from the discussion certain issues long beloved of Jeremiah scholars. Chief
among those will be precise historical reconstruction, both of events presumed in
the prophetic book and also of processes of the book's composition, various links
between the book of Jeremiah and other biblical material. Missing as well will be
specific engagement with postmodern methodological issues currently absorbing
professional Jeremiah scholars that tend to highlight the book's incoherence and
contemporary reception. This volume will also sideline certain theological and
religious issues of its day and will not claim to read characters' psychology.

What is left, you may be asking? Jeremiah is available to us as a literary
construct, emerging from the pages of the extant biblical book, specifically here
from the Hebrew edition.[1] We will engage textual Jeremiah and present from our
negotiation the literary features of the book bearing his name. Jeremiah language
abounds, some fifty-two chapters of it, where the prophet is offered in various
ways and from diverse angles. Jeremiah speaks and is spoken with, acts and is

acted on. He fails mightily, once succeeds. He is loved, feared. There is literary texture aplenty and no lack of controversy. Jeremiah as a biblical character, perhaps overlapping generally but not coinciding closely with a historical personage, is well-sketched, and becomes a vivid and viable character living on in the tradition. Though likely a good deal of the prophet's life as presented is fictive, the narrative world against which it is projected—adequately known and generally agreed to by scholars—will suffice for our needs. I will construct rather than claim to retrieve Jeremiah and challenge you to do the same.[2]

Useful literary methods are not particularly arcane but demand attentive discrimination. We will need to note consistently who is talking—often but not always clear—and appreciate overlapping but not coinciding perspectives. We will attend to other features of character speech: rhetorical choices, imagery, stock and distinctive language. We must watch especially for characters' constructions of others, opponents in particular. We will track choices of the book's "outside" (extradiegetic) narrator. We are offered rich detail, more than we can see or use. But without losing the forest for trees or leaves, we will try to catch what we can of the careful etching available if we are skilled, with method made more explicit as we proceed.

To be more specific, the narratological model most helpful to guide us is adapted from Jerome Walsh and modified slightly.[3] Consider a set of frames, the outer edges being the real authors and real readers. These two sets include actual persons involved in the writing or production of the book and also in its reception, stretching from those for whom the book was intended—that is, postexilic readers whose situation is often and appropriately discerned—through history to ourselves. The frame within that of real authors and real readers marks implied author and implied reader, important here for one main reason: it is easy enough to recognize that the implied author is the book-of-Jeremiah writer, a subset of the real author(s); an implied reader by definition understands that author's words completely, transparently. Walsh notes, perceptively, that it is precisely the gap between such a wholly compatible implied reader and our less competent real selves that opens points for negotiation and provides the rich range of semantic possibilities.

In a third frame, positioned inside the two just named, the narrator voice tells the contents of the book to the one narrated to, most familiar to us, perhaps, from listening to books on tape. We recognize a familiar and generally reliable voice and know it is not quite the same as the author. Finally, within these three frames is the story world, comprising plot, characters, setting, and so forth. Story events are by definition fictive but generally plausible, reliant on the world of the tellers and hearers of the events. Good reading, in my view, calls on this entire model, situating particular interests specifically and proportionately within it.

With awareness of the importance of real authors and readers, of the innumerable pockets of uncertainty that rise when we are not fully in the know, desiring to be as accurate as possible about persons, events, and settings contributed by the real world, our interest is in the fictive story world that the book projects.

Having reduced the role historical studies usually play and promoted the contribution of literary language, we consider now the appropriate role of reader interpretation. Assumed and to be demonstrated here is that readers/hearers are crucially involved in the making of meaning. As contemporary hermeneutics makes clear, the process of interpreting is not exact and objective but crucially perspectival. Interpreters—whether Jeremiah's intended audiences, later editors of the material, other biblical writers borrowing from the material, artists and others who have drawn on it, myself as writer of this book, or you as reader— bring particular interests to their task. These lenses will be operative, and so we want to anticipate them.[4] Please expect to encounter a Jeremiah deeply affected by the circumstances of his life, struggling consistently at his most urgent task of persuading his hearers to choose a path they mostly resist. I will draw him to be learning as he goes and thus able to offer insight as he speaks. I aim to show him convincingly as a figure from whom readers struggling with analogous issues can gain insight. Jeremiah is important not simply because he may once have lived but because his literary characterization is instructive for ourselves, reading. In order for this strategy to work effectively, we must engage the text with such dialogical possibility in mind. Of course, you may choose to resist my interpretation.

I will show how the shape and function given to the character Jeremiah is to mediate God's plans of well-being for the people of Judah. Jeremiah must first intuit what such a possibility entails, come to understand and accept it. This part of his ministry is filled with resistance and struggle, since the plans are not preferred and unpalatable—all but unimaginable as what God could desire and consider good. But once Jeremiah comes to accept his learning, he must articulate and communicate it both positively and negatively, offering incentives and disincentives, must find ways of enacting his insight with and without words. Though Jeremiah succeeds with one group—though perhaps only partially and tentatively—he continues to labor with others, ultimately failing to persuade most of his hearers and thus entering "negative space" to demonstrate what is *in*compatible with God's plans even as it is selected by various groups in diverse ways. The communication continues broadly effective as Jeremiah lives on, both in the biblical and extrabiblical materials.

Consider an analogy for understanding the nuanced character of this construction: There comes a point in the lives of many when they must leave their familial and familiar homes to enter a care facility. Rarely does anyone *want* to make this move, given its implications of loss and change, its signaling the end of one long era and the beginning of another, likely shorter. The choice rarely feels good, even if, at the rational and theoretical level, it is indicated. Ways of resisting are multiple, with main strategies being to deny the necessity or to delay action until it is too late. In consequence "refusers" devolve into either a condition so serious as to disqualify admission or else death intervenes. But what occasionally happens is that individuals learn that to walk with some of their possessions into a facility is better than arriving by ambulance and without belongings. To move with grace into some good years can seem preferable to being taken off to an urgent-care ward or dying in a heap on the floor at home. In such cases, the people who go "willingly" may even come to see that positive good comes out of their move, not simply negative good (less bad than the worst alternatives). This is deep and experiential learning, not quick or easy.

Jeremiah's challenge is to see, say, sell the idea that to choose to resettle in Babylon, counterintuitive though it is that God should desire such a thing, is not only better than the alternatives (delay, deny, seek allies) but *may*—eventually—be an experience of profound well-being. To go to Babylon will always be a painful choice, but it can be accepted as necessary, even potentially fruitful. Jeremiah is thus charged both to show a specific painful need and also to suggest and catalyze a deeper and beneficial synchronicity with the mysterious ways of God: plans of well-being.

This general frame is relevant for us—not because we are deciding whether to walk to Babylon or not—but because we in our era are faced by many huge choices that overwhelm and paralyze us. You will not have trouble naming such scenarios, but let me hold up simply the question of climate change. Shall we, as some urge, radically change our way of living to accommodate looming threats? Some dismiss the claims. Others accept them tentatively but without making substantial changes in their lives, hoping that enthusiastic recycling and driving a hybrid car may address the threat. Few of us, in my view, have accepted the profound implications for how we must live if the scientists who believe in global warming are correct. Fewer still imagine how it might actually be better than our present situation. The point here, of course, is not about climate and lifestyle change but to help us understand more deeply what operates when impending circumstances demand radical and deep conversion. We will better appreciate the prophet's challenge of effective persuasion and the resistance he meets.

Stipulations

Three sets of general information require dropping into place now, against which we will hear the prophet cast his language: the general and then more specific historical circumstances facing Judah as the seventh century gave way to the sixth (that is, as the 620s and 610s shade into the 590s and 580s); a pertinent understanding of worship; and a brief note on prophecy. Since we need this information for general backdrop rather than for demonstrating historicity, it can be "stipulated to," as lawyers say when agreeing that certain pertinent issues neither will be contested nor need demonstrating. Those wishing more precise detail or engagement with the many controversial points will not lack resources in materials referenced throughout this book.

Jeremiah's people, as we meet them in the Bible, are descended from Abraham and Sarah through twelve tribes. Faced with a crisis urging them into Egypt, they escaped from there to make a painful journey back to their land, resettling and eventually choosing to be ruled by kings, notably by those descended from David, an arrangement in place from around 1000 B.C.E. We must envision the "land of promise," situated between the Mediterranean Sea and the Jordan River and extending roughly from the Dead Sea in the southeast to the promontory of Mount Carmel in the northwest. Think of Israel/Judah as the center of a large X whose arms can be envisioned as four imperial beasts, alternatively ravenous and powerful or weak and napping. To the northwest of Israel-and-Judah lay the land of the Hittites—hungry for conquest in the mid-second millennium (before our story begins) and eventually known to us as Greece (later than our story extends). To the southwest of Judah sat Egypt, powerfully if intermittently stretching a paw upward, envisionable as a sort of absentee landlord struggling to control rowdy tenants as the second millennium gave way to the first. To the northeast of Judah crouched powerful Assyria, whose appetites ranged along the Mediterranean coast irregularly but relentlessly from the ninth until late in the seventh century. The prelude to the life and ministry of Jeremiah was the collapse of Assyria and the apparent kindling of Judah's hope to wriggle freer of imperial control than had been the case for some time. And finally, more to the southeast, sat Babylon: heir-apparent to the Assyrian empire but threatened in that aspiration by Egypt.[5] It was the location of Israel/Judah rather than its character that drew empires to venture from their corners: proffering resources for armies, offering access routes to the whole region, boasting a fertile breadbasket, promising honor and glory. Location at the center of a large imperial X determined the fate of the peoples of Israel/Judah and their near neighbors. Think of a display as if in a Jerusalem post office, changing flags and faces as one conqueror replaces the previous: Hittite overlords, then Egyptian, Assyrian, Babylonian, Persian, and eventually Greek and Roman. But a generic imperial face remains largely foreign over the life of biblical Judah, including Jeremiah's moment and beyond it.

With the big picture suggested—notably the dominating presence of imperial foes and the subsequent struggles of Israel/Judah over self-determination—we can zoom in on the immediate time of Jeremiah to understand events in the neighborhood—still in rough detail, providing a fifty-year "history-like" warp across which the literary weft of Jeremiah's persona will be strung, thus allowing our construction(s).

The waning of the seventh century saw a change in the imperial power balance, as the long domination of Assyria gave way around the year 612, with Egypt and Babylon alert to their opportunities, uncertain as to just how relationships would shake out. The turmoil and uncertainty of big power politics sent waves into the Levantine neighborhood to unsettle the smaller, nearer ethnic entities, who anticipated independence and jockeyed for it. Set amid such uncertainty and narrated biblically (2 Kings 22–23) is the reform of King Josiah.[6] As described, the reform was overtly cultic, involving the removal of non-Yahwistic items and practices from the Jerusalem temple and environs and the proscription of alien elements nearby. To change worship is to change economics, since cult requires animals for sacrifice, and acquiring these locally is not the same as obtaining them centrally. Though Jeremiah does not name the reform explicitly or allude to Josiah as a reformer, the reform's "alleged content" is of crucial importance for understanding his preaching, marking a place for us to consider the apparently deep and radical divisions about worship and other cultural issues. But before Josiah's measures seem to have "taken," the king was killed, apparently tangled between Egypt and Babylon as they jockeyed for position in a neighborhood undergoing change from the Assyrian collapse.

Into such a context of flux we have the arrival of Jeremiah, also within the context of royal Jerusalem and Judah. Jeremiah's initial date is difficult to label. He was either born or received his prophetic call in Josiah's thirteenth year, our 627 (Jeremiah 1:2). He was likely active in Josiah's reign, since even if 627 marks the prophet's birth, he would be an adult of eighteen years at Josiah's death. But the post-Josiah era is the prophet's main context, comprising the reign of three of Josiah's sons and a grandson. First named is Shallum, called by the throne name of Jehoahaz (2 Kings 23:30–34). Evidently pro-Babylonian, he was removed to Egypt after just three months, where he died. He was replaced by his older brother, Eliakim, more commonly called Jehoiakim, evidently sufficiently pro-Egyptian to be acceptable to those kingmakers (2 Kings 23:34–24:6). Jeremiah comments on these two heirs in chap. 22 and attributes events in chaps. 25, 26, 35, and 36 specifically to Jehoiakim's eleven-year rule, characterizing him as thoroughly malevolent. Third successor to Josiah was Jehoiakim's young son Jehoiachin (2 Kings 24:6–17), no sooner in position than removed to Babylon with other elites, an event known as the first exile, distinct from the removal ten years later. When the Babylonians exiled one king—Jehoiachin/Coniah—and appointed another—Mattaniah/Zedekiah (another son of Josiah [2 Kings 24:17–25:21])—there were two Davidic kings alive and heading distinct communities: one in Babylon and one in Judah. Germane here is tension between those Judahites with experience of early exile and those without it, a situation to blossom at the time of return near the end of the sixth century. Zedekiah was the primary royal partner for Jeremiah (material set in his reign includes Jeremiah 21–24, 27–34, 37–39), characterized as torn and vacillating as to options, a contrast with Jehoiakim. Zedekiah's court will have had its pro-Egyptian faction and its pro-Babylonian adherents, with each hoping that the king would successfully play one of those major powers off against the other, to the gain of Judah. The two great riverine kingdoms seesawed in relation to each other and threw their weight around in the neighborhood, which included other small entities besides Judah, notably Ammon, Edom, and Moab on the east side of the Jordan River and the coastal stubs of Philistia in the south and powerful Phoenicia in the north. Without seeking historical corroboration of the detail, we will watch royal Judah maneuvering among these several small and two large state powers—likely in faction-ridden courts—usually precipitously and foolishly and to poor result. In the last decade of the seventh century an Egyptian dominance gave way before Babylon. In the battle of Carchemish (ca. 605), Babylon defeated Egyptian forces decisively, ushering in the long rule of Babylonian Nebuchadnezzar with disastrous consequences for Judah and others in the neighborhood.

The Babylonian hegemony brought increased pressure to monarchic Judah, commencing with an intensification of military presence near Jerusalem, matched by Zedekiah's foolish hopes for relief (2 Kings 24:20 and alluded to in Jeremiah 37)—the king's minirevolt tripping off intensified attention to Jerusalem. After more than a year of siege, the city fell to the Babylonians in the year 587. Zedekiah was captured trying to escape the city (2 Kings 25, Jeremiah 39). Many people were killed, others forcibly removed to Babylon to join those that had settled there some ten years earlier. And yet a sizable population remained in the land.[7] For these a governor was appointed (Jeremiah 40–44), Gedaliah of the scribal family featuring prominently in the Jeremiah narrative. Our prophet, evidently protected by the Babylonians at the time of their victory in Jerusalem, was given a choice of either going east with the exiles or remaining in the defeated land. Choosing the latter, he survived the crisis of the assassination of the governor by a member of the Judean royal family sometime in the 580s. He disappeared into Egypt, maintaining steadfastly that it was precisely the wrong destination. This skeleton of events, substantially visible in Jeremiah and other biblical sources once they have been adumbrated elsewhere, will be assumed and operative as we talk about the prophet's life in more detail.

A second crucial issue to position involves worship. To hear Jeremiah is to learn that Israel's cardinal sin involved worship violation: neglect of what God had commanded and practice of what God had forbidden. This omission-commission blend leads to divine anger, threat of violent reprisal, eventually to massive punishment—thus claim prophets. Since the equations of apostasy-and-anger, sin-and-punishment, disobedience-and-disaster are so tightly woven in biblical discourse, we need to make its complexity clearer, deliteralizing prophetic denunciation to some extent.

The most consistent biblical datum is that the deity of Judah/Israel was one and demanded exclusive aniconic worship—called by scholars "YHWH alone"—a stance not likely grasped quickly or easily in a neighborhood where deities were multiple, and worship earthy and diverse. Customs will have varied in time and place, with later official practices not quite displacing earlier and once-acceptable customs at every site. Though the charge of "foreign" worship will be hurled at behaviors disapproved, scholars recognize from names, epithets, characteristics, and stories that the Levantine religious heritage was generally shared, rendering the epithet "foreign" uncertain.[8] Religious orthodoxy was, then as now, at least partly a matter of what was deemed acceptable, a sliding scale across time and place. In sum the charge that Israel/Judah worshiped falsely cannot simply be taken at face value. At various points cultural systems will have collided and conflicted, with deities jostled and repositioned as well.[9] Moderns, especially if accustomed to default monotheism, will read the biblical text as much flatter and more absolute than experts construe it. That is, to assume that worship of "YHWH alone" is a matter simple, absolute and obvious, will render biblical language correspondingly clear. Those aware of more variance hear a wider toleration of practice. What is *maintained* with consistency is that YHWH's worship was not to include other deities, was not to depend on embodiment of the deity. It was not to import foreign ways or to deviate from the carefully prescribed details of YHWH's cult. What those words *meant* and how they were *understood* over time and place is less clear.

We can mine discrepancy between likely reality and biblical storyline narration in three areas: First, the biblical storyline makes surprisingly punctiliar the moment false worship became a problem. The early ancestors are not shown guilty of false worship. The first idolatry narrated occurs only after—in fact right after—it was proscribed: at Sinai/Horeb (see Exodus 19 and 32 and Deuteronomy 4, 10). The primary (Mosaic) covenant was offered and the law given on the basis of God's saving action at the exodus, and only then does the idolatry sin appear, first with the golden calf and perennially thereafter. It is clear the worship issue has been schematized. The question is how and why.

Second, though we can see that certain aspects of worship (sacrifice, temple shape, priesthood, divine titles, epithets, motifs, even in some cases phraseology) share a clear heritage with "cousin religions," the biblical account proceeds as though such were not the case, stressing the gap separating rather than the bridge linking lineages. Israel's religion, once largely akin to that of the neighborhood, at some point shifted, either radically or gradually, likely a combination of the two, but with overlap submerged. Why so? How so?

Third, the biblical storyline does not stress the singularity and difficulty of the command—that one people among all others would have a unique and theretofore unimaginable demand placed on it or privilege granted it: worship of YHWH alone—no other, no images. *That* the relationship was a challenge to maintain, needing constant encouragement and threats from authorities, is clear in the Bible. But the challenge of actually shifting from many to one and from embodied to aniconic—YHWH alone—is not explicitly explored. In the story as narrated, God offered Israel something virtually unique, and though God's people are described as basically willing to enter the relationship, they slip often into the perennial idolatry. To be grasped here—extraordinary from the history of religions standpoint—is the novelty and challenge of the "YHWH alone" phenomenon. How would any ancient Near Eastern deity, YHWH included, have come to be "alone" when no other deity was so imagined and experienced? And how will a people make the shift in mindset and practice to conform? Most likely the demand and toleration of "YHWH alone" became gradually clearer over time, moving unevenly for many reasons.

With this texture suggested, we can reconsider Josiah's reform and Jeremiah's plausible endorsing of its main substance. We best understand the narrated reform as artificially comprehensive and radical, noting that it vanishes at the death of Josiah, neither pursued nor even mentioned by any of the four heirs to the throne. And what of Jeremiah? The sketch to be developed here sees Jeremiah more in favor of Josiah's reform than were Josiah's successors but not so wedded to its detail or perhaps its manner of enforcement as to invoke either reform or reformer by name. Our prophet is surely of the YHWH-alone persuasion: YHWH alone, only YHWH, not embodied. Jeremiah's condemnations of worship are more general and generic than specific, lacking some detail we might expect. Like other prophets, Jeremiah's urgency cannot risk tolerance of soft edges and hence makes God's agency effective as international events respond to the disobedience and disloyalty of worshipers. The stakes seem too high to venture anything else. But the scope of our referential uncertainty is vast.

We come now to the question of prophecy, a phenomenon widely attested throughout the ancient Near East from the mid-second millennium, allowing us to position biblical prophecy widely as well as scanning it specifically.[10] Prophets mediated between the human and the divine and functioned in both worlds. Prophecy assumes that the divine realm can and will communicate with the human and expects that humans with their cultural phenomena are adequate receivers of the divine will. Implicit as well is that the two realms, though distinct, are reciprocally responsive, thanks to the efforts of intermediaries.

The biblical deity appears to individual prophets, speaks with them, commands them, urges them to inform and persuade others the value of what they are told, repeatedly as necessary. But on closer scrutiny, divine speech and human hearing and reissue blur. What is *presented* as clear must be understood by us in a far more complex and ambiguous way. Our default needs to be the *difficulty* of communication between realms, not the *ease and clarity* of it. To discern the will of the deity is challenging, not due to any participant's fault but because the realms are not so compatible as might be desired. Discernment remains partial at best, opaque and misleading at worst. We see that prophets both disagreed among themselves and suffered disbelief. Skill was required in intermediation as was authority, whether conferred officially (as may have been the case outside the Bible) or accumulated with a given prophet's ability to speak effectively and be perceived to do so. The initiative typically was God's. To aspire to be a prophet was not viewed positively. No prophet can prove that God has initiated the encounter.

Prophets addressed individuals but were fundamentally concerned with corporate Judah/Israel—specifically with elites, since peasants were not the main offenders in the prophetic world. The range of ways by which prophets generally made tangible the will of the divine were many, with some—speech and action—widely shared. They depended on language as their primary medium for prophecy, occasionally employing physical props or mime to suggest reality more adequately. Situations and events were also mined for significance. Prophets addressed hearers consistently about worship—what was and was not to be done. They spoke of what we now call social or economic justice—relations among various members of society, usually about the injustice of rich to poor. And prophets spoke incessantly about international relations, typically excoriating efforts of YHWH's people to collaborate or cooperate with imperial powers or to imitate their ways.

With those edges sketched, let's return to the issue of how pre-exilic prophets aimed to persuade, since this framework will drive our understanding of Jeremiah. Let us posit that Judah/Israel accepted God's ultimate and effective power in the world, that God could and would, eventually, accomplish the divine purposes for them. That Babylon threatened was diagnosed as a sign of sinful behavior on Judah's part, violations of relationship with YHWH. That is, the prophet underlined the givens—God's ultimate will and effective power to effect good for Judah—read imperial pressure as divine persuasion—and named the factors causing God's unhappiness and able to resolve it—worship sins as described above. The sociopolitical framework was moralized and theologized, with the prophet insisting that in time a powerful and concerned deity would effect the outcomes desired for the people for their well-being, employing agents and tools as needed to catch attention and change hearts.

But how will Jeremiah be sustained in such a stance, understand and claim that he is speaking reliably for God? How will his intended hearers deem him worthy of belief? How will we, reading, appraise his claims? As with worship the biblical record makes more simple and straightforward what was in practice more complicated. We will hear Jeremiah struggle with this issue, but not in the most obvious ways. He will never quite say: "How do I know this is from God? Might I be mistaken in what I am claiming?" We will also see that he is more likely to accuse his hearers of malevolence than of confusion. It is not difficult to see why Jeremiah struggled and failed, mostly, to persuade his hearers of his insight, which was subtle and counterintuitive. Using every rhetorical move available, the prophet did not convince most of his hearers that he was speaking God's words of well-being. The difficulty is not simply his but rooted in the fragility of all phases of the prophetic relationship dynamics.

1

WOMB AND WORKSHOP—JEREMIAH LEARNS HIS CALLING

Chapters 1, 46–51

> Jeremiah was heir to a rhetorical tradition already ancient, one that had developed in the oldest known cultures of the Near East before it took place in Israel.
>
> Jack R. Lundbom, *Jeremiah 1–20*

Call and Commission

We meet Jeremiah as he is constituted and committed as a prophet. The narrator of the book provides words of YHWH to and through Jeremiah extending over the last forty years of the monarchy, from King Josiah's thirteenth year to King Zedekiah's eleventh year, and past it: the era from 627 to 587 B.C.E. Whether Jeremiah was born or called in 627 does not much matter, since what counts is that he was already designated from the womb, whenever it was that he first prophesied. Jeremiah narrates his prophetic identity as his call catches up to him. By the time he learns he is a prophet, it's old news for God, who called him from before birth. Jeremiah takes over from the narrator past the superscription of 1:1–3 to provide what we need to know. We hear layered speech: Jeremiah relates what God said to him, what he said in response, how he and God negotiated. Jeremiah interprets to us without telling us precisely how the information came to him, providing what we need to know—not so much the process between him and God but the result among three participants, the last set being his hearers and readers. So the layered language includes what God communicated to him, what he heard, what he tells us, all cuing our response. Focal is not his receiving but his reshaping what he heard for those who must be told it.

We get a small scene from a play we are invited to watch (1:4–10), to participate in, one way or another. It comes in a familiar shape:[1] an announcement of the assignment of prophetic identity; the demur of the recipient, who senses all too well that he will never be adequate to the task; an override from the appointing deity, who resists the inadequacy claim; the deity's counterargument: <*I'm* not inadequate, or my adequacy will underwrite *your lack*, and I am sending you and will give you as much help as you need.>[2] And, Jeremiah relates, when that reply had been given, that YHWH acted, touching the prophet's mouth saying, <My words, your mouth.> From here on their utterances will often be blended, nigh indistinguishable, shared. And, assigns God, your scope is nations and kingdoms, among whom you have six jobs to do: uproot [*ntš*], break down [*ntṣ*], destroy [*'bd*], overthrow [*hrs*], build [*bnh*], plant [*nṭ'*]. Jeremiah might be a farmer or a builder, given the spheres from which language characterizing his job as prophet is drawn. He makes no reply to that charge.

But Jeremiah at once must practice his new calling in two quick lessons (1:11–19): He is shown a first vision and asked about it; recognizing an almond blossom (*šhaqed*), he hears God pun on that image and say that God is watching (*šhoqed*) to do the word. Images are to be read carefully, read and then read more deeply as language shifts and curls. Congratulating the neophyte on his first prophetic words, God tosses him a second image to see and say: A boiling pot, turned from the north, facing southwest, apparently.[3] God agrees it is so, explaining why: religious disloyalty, forsaking YHWH, turning to others—the basic charge to be adumbrated in this book. Presumably having managed the first challenge, God amplifies that just as they have done together—with Jeremiah first shown and seeing and then interpreting divinely disclosed events to us—so he must do continually, additionally, no matter the cost. Jeremiah again falls silent, having told and shown us his call and commission to be YHWH's prophet. Jeremiah, having said <No *I* can't,> is met by God, <Yes *we* can>; he is shown how it will work: words and images shared among God, prophet, readers/hearers. And, reassures God, <Good news and bad news. I will stand by you no matter the opposition, but it will be very costly for you to stay standing—though you must do so: a fortified city, and iron pillar, bronze walls.>

The initial chapter is programmatic for the whole book—the encounter anticipating the life, we may add: a call, visions, vision reports, interpretation of what will come to be, with prose elaborating and clarifying poetry.[4] But even more programmatic is the intersection of prophet and deity, with the prophet both reporting the powerful language of the deity and also somehow letting it get away from him, manifesting that he does not quite control prophetic speech even as he wrestles it into language to hand on to hearers. That we cannot quite decide who said what, that we are not able to slice cleanly between what we and the prophet heard: That's vintage Jeremiah, with its promise and withholding. We will often have trouble distinguishing prophet and deity, and that's prophetic reality.

Before leaving our introduction to Jeremiah, we may ask whom he resembles.[5] That is, after studying the portrait we are given here, of whom in the biblical family does our prophet remind us?[6] *Called early:* Moses (Exodus 7:1), Samson, (Judges 13:1–25), the Isaian servant (Isaiah 44:2, 24; 49:1); God's people (Hosea 3:2, 13:5); *quick to refuse:* Moses (Exodus 2:7 ff.; Solomon (1 Kings 3:7); *seeming too small:* Gideon (Judges 6:15), David (1 Samuel 17:34–36); *reassured:* Moses (Exodus 3–5; 19:9; 33:14; Joshua 1:5, 9; Samson Judges 13:12, 16); *lips touched:* (Isaiah 6:6); God's *words in the human's mouth:* the prophet like Moses (Deuteronomy 18:18;). Good company. A promising heritage.

Rhetorical Workshop

Since Jeremiah is too young or small here to get started as an active prophet, the second thing we will do in this chapter is accompany him to his language workshop, as it were, to observe how he learns to speak powerfully as a prophet, to sharpen the likelihood of rhetorical effect. We need a good sense of how he distinctively speaks—as a prophet and as a particular one of that species—and how brilliant is his discourse. After offering a simple catalogue of his typical patterns, we will lift some examples from Jeremiah's oracles against the nations (hereafter OANs). We can imagine the young Jeremiah practicing on them, composing and delivering them, and appraising their impact on listeners. Carolyn Sharp calls them showcases of ancient rhetoric and artistry.[7] Lundbom tells us that Jeremiah's skill has not always been appreciated by scholar-critics: Saint Jerome calls it "*rusticor,*" and S. R. Driver classifies it as "essentially artless." Lundbom himself says the following: "Upon close inspection, Jeremiah is seen to be a skillful poet, someone well-trained in the rhetoric of his day and surely perceived by those who heard him to be an engaging orator . . . . As an orator, Jeremiah could hold rank with the best Greek and Roman rhetors, . . . anticipates them all in style and modes of argumentation."[8]

As we visit the young Jeremiah's workshop and survey the shelves, we see some well-stocked with material recognizable by template, known in the methodology of language of historical-critical biblical scholars as forms:[9] stacks of oracles; of psalm-like units classified as praise, thanksgiving, petition; piled laments, some as though by an individual and others more communal; we see letters; elsewhere are parables and smaller similitudes; we can see where the object lessons are sorted; there are wisdom sayings of various types, with proverbs in one cubbyhole, aphorisms in another; speeches abound, some addressed clearly to audiences and others more closely resembling soliloquies; there is liturgical language; prowling, we spot a wide shelf of prose narratives; we see visions, and a few colophons. These verbal forms, used by all prophets, are carefully organized, at the ready, for further reshaping. Jeremiah is unusual only in the size and depth of his repertoire.[10]

But how will Jeremiah learn to customize these stock templates, to use the strength of their standard forms while shaping them to be rhetorically effective as deployed, be freshly incisive and powerful as addressed to actual hearers? For this our guide is not the essentially historical form criticism but the more comprehensively literary rhetoric and its richness—and not classical tropes of the Greeks and Romans but those employed by Hebrew speakers, known to us now thanks to the work of Hebrew biblical scholars.[11] Though we might make lists of these component features of persuasion—to observe them abstractly—we will do better to study them as they actually function, or are shaped to do. There is no system that will allow us to examine all of them, so I offer here a simple classification: (1) those that use repetition, mark patterns, and show emphasis (chiasm, *inclusio,* repetition in its varieties, key- and catchwords, acrostics);[12] (2) those utilizing imagery (audial, such as alliteration and onomatopoeia; wordplay and euphemism; metaphor and *abusio,* allegory, parable, drama, symbolism, allusion);[13] (3) those using specific tropes for persuasion (change-up combinations of poetry and prose; conditional language; argumentation from a lesser to a greater relevance; rhetorical questions and their variables; exaggeration; contrasts);[14] and (4) those making substantial use of varieties of discourse (shared speech, quotations, intertexts, humor, and irony).[15] These features obviously overlap and collaborate, but there is a heuristic value in grouping them if we are to have some access to their impact.

The OANs are a good candidate for this project, since whatever may have been their provenance, they are gathered now at the end of the Hebrew version of the book while clearly, in some instances, referencing earlier events and presumably rising in relation to them.[16] All prophets except Hosea and Jonah use this formal trope, with Jeremiah again excelling in quantity with 231 verses of them against, at, or to nine nations or groups.[17] Form critics have sought to determine the setting (for example, holy war, treaty curses), the implied addressees (the nations themselves), the purpose (reprisal). Scholars have dismissed them as nationalistic, chauvinistic, largely valueless. Current scholarship claims that the OANs are not for opponents but for the insider group (so for Judah, not for the nations referenced), aimed to negotiate and reconstruct social identity boundaries. That is, these poems are not about "them" but about "us," with the underlying concern the transgression of "emic" boundaries. They correlate as well with Jeremiah's call where he was missioned to the nations as well as to YHWH's people and with the prophet's insistence on the sovereignty of YHWH over all nations.

In order to provide a good sample, I will focus on the relatively extensive first oracle (against Egypt, 46:2–28 [v. 1 introduces the whole set of OANs]) and then on the five smaller poems with diverse addressees (chap. 49) to note how the various rhetorical moves work together: chiasm and *inclusio* marking structure, with key- and catchwords studding the units and leaking backward and forward to other sections. We can hear sound play, see metaphor and symbolism at work—particularly in terms of water—and watch the drama of the rout of Egypt and pursuit of those unable to flee. We can appraise the impact of questions, functioning to draw our attention to contrasts, reversals, improbable scenarios; and we can appreciate the interplay of voices, with intertexts, quotations, hurried dialogue. In the five shorter oracles we will examine particular features in more detail to illustrate miniatures of Jeremiah's vintage rhetorical moves. The primary point is to note specifically how Jeremiah crafts his poetic language so that our eye becomes practiced, and secondarily to appraise impact and persuasive effect on ourselves and hypothesized other listeners.

The oracle about Egypt comes in two major sections (46:2–12 and 13–26, each with an introduction) while concluding with a short address to Jacob (46:27–28).[18] The first portion references the battle of Carchemish (v.2), where Egypt was vanquished by Babylon. The second refers to another set of catastrophic circumstances where Egypt's basic opponent is YHWH. In the whole OAN set, Egypt is the first nation addressed and Babylon the last, the pair serving both as main adversaries of Jeremiah's Judah and also as dominant alliance temptations. Brueggemann characterizes Egypt as the primal metaphor for worldly power organized against God's purposes, while Hill perceptively notes that Babylon in many ways closely resembles Judah rather than simply being an opposite.[19]

The first oracle poem running from 46:3–12 is shaped chiastically into four parts: A, vv. 3–4; B, vv. 5–6; B', vv.7–8; A', vv. 9–12.

A: The first speaker is demonstrably the deity, as commander-in-chief barking a series of seven masculine plural imperatives, urging the Egyptian fighters into battle: The commands are specific and visual, involving the readying of equipment: buckler and shield taken up, horses harnessed and pulled up at the ready, helmets at hand, lances burnished, armor donned. The implication is that the fighters are well equipped, though this impression is at once challenged, since the advice given is futile: These troops will be defeated.[20] Catchwords (rise up, warrior, buckler, shield) thread and unify the passage.

B: A second voice, perhaps the prophet or another witness—even possibly the first speaker in stunned, reflexive "redirect"— reports the unexpected, the almost unimaginable, such that the incredulous speaker breaks off: warriors terrified, falling into disarray, equipment useless. Why is the outcome unexpected, the well-armed in a narrative instant routed, turned back, also trapped and immobilized. Employing the catchwords "stumble and fall," this unit suggests that not even flight and escape are possible, let alone victory. The speaker quickly shows us the destruction of troops. Having asked a question to stimulate the imagination of hearers, the speaker also answers it (*hypophora*), describing what he has seen and then commenting almost proverbially.[21] A threefold picture is sketched: Egyptian troops first arming, then routed, finally failing to escape.

B': A short piece similarly shaped (thus contributing to a short ABB'A' chiasm) asks another question: Who is this rising like the Nile? We are shown a confrontation between the mighty Nile and Euphrates, clashing their waters. The focus is Egypt's vaunted military power, whose once-famed and swollen waters are about to recede. The image unifying this small section is unthinking, reckless overreach. We hear "the river" talk to himself, announcing plans of outsized grandeur: "I will rise, cover the earth, destroy city and its inhabitants." But we have already seen bragging as unreal, so this boast is analeptic, providing us the claim after we've seen the falseness of it, have watched the one claiming victory already fallen victim.

A': The last unit resembles the first, addressing this time Egypt's mercenaries, assigning them war tasks to perform.[22] The name of the opponent is revealed: not Nebuchadnezzar—bad enough—but YHWH-of-hosts, even more dread, whose grievances against Egypt are piled high. The sword of YHWH now feasts metaphorically, eating flesh and drinking blood, showing mixed the imagery of banquet and cult; metonymically, the sword is the deity. Egypt learns in a flash the divine identity of this most fearful foe. Another *epitrophe* occurs: Egypt is encouraged to send to Gilead for healing balm, but the speaker adds at once that no healing tissue will have time to form. The balm is judged useless before it is applied or even in hand. Responses of witnesses give us access to the deed: Nations have heard of Egypt's disgrace, its cry of pain and rage. They have seen warriors stumble off together, collapsing as a team, this description sadly reinforcing the scene of vv. 5–6, where flight is impossible.

The second poem runs 46:13–26, which I will split as having a front and back frame (after a superscription of v. 13, we have vv. 14–17 [A] and 24–26 [C]) and then a center B with three parts: vv. 18–19 [a], 20–21 [b], 22–23 [c]).

A: Again directions are given by YHWH through Jeremiah, told to order his addressees to prepare for carnage, or manage it. The feasting sword has left some unconsumed, and the hurled question is to them: "Why is your mighty bull lying flat?" The referent here, according to most, is that the bull is the emblem of the deity Apis, which of course should not be prone.[23] The speaker rushes on to provide the answer without waiting for the Egyptians to explain what has happened, saying that YHWH persisted in shoving the statue until it toppled. The statue itself shares the catchwords from the previous unit (vv. 6, 12), as it stumbles and falls. Self-talk (simulated dialogue) among Egyptian fighters is reported, as those who have fallen urge themselves and their fellows to get up and return to "our people." We sense the correlation between fallen Egyptian fighters and their toppled deity emblem. The up/down imagery of the whole Egypt-focused unit, including the basic north/south orientation and the rising of the Nile, repeats here, though feebly. Rising from collapse to run before the sword of the enemy is not very glorious. The speaker renames their Pharaoh: Loud Noise Who Lets the Deadline Pass.

B: The middle piece:

a: The first of the three centerpieces of this section (labeled as an oracle of YHWH as king) is customized to employ metaphors of praise to the deity: "like Tabor and Carmel, he will come." The metaphor is puzzling, since the promontories named, though possibly towering, are not mobile and it is not obvious what they contribute to arrival of the forces of YHWH. Power and mass, yes; speed, no. But the arrival is reinforced by its effect: Exiles must be prepared to move, so these unfortunates are urged to ready baggage so as to respond to the need for arrival and departure. Daughter Egypt, accustomed to stability and security, must be ready to journey forth, leaving her cities—here Memphis—desolate, devastated, deserted. As Jeremiah likes, an event is described in terms of its effect. The catchword in use here is *ki*/because, since: causal, emphatic.

b: The next two verses return to the bovine imagery of the frame (v. 15), picturing Egypt as a comely young heifer, but bitten by a horsefly from the north. Such had been her luxury that even her hired hands (perhaps Egypt's mercenaries) seemed stall fed, luxuriating in all they might need or desire. But they, like those fighters mentioned earlier in the first oracle section, cannot or do not stand and fight but flee, stumble, fall.[24] Their day arrives, part of Egypt's fate. The imagery stresses the inexorability of disaster for Egypt, no matter what alternatives may have seemed securely in place. Contrasts underline the change: daughter Egypt, home-dwelling, not an exile; heifer Egypt, veteran of abundant care, now forsaken.

c: A third piece of midsection adds to the effect. First, audial imagery: A snake slithers almost soundlessly away, with a slight rustle through ground cover all that can be heard. It contrasts with the powerful ones approaching noisily, cutting and grinding as with axes, locusts chomping their way through Egypt's wooden structures.[25] So numerous that they don't need reconnaissance or skill, the locusts amass and move ahead, doing damage as the snake slithers almost noiselessly ahead of them. It is a brutal image, with size and sound contrasted, devastation collaborating. In this central section we have had three sets of reversals, all picturing Egypt routed.

C: The last unit of this oracle adds the column. The speaker, presumably the prophet, pronounces daughter Egypt as shamed by her defeat, handed over to the arrivals from the north. YHWH then enters the conversation, announcing more to come. What Memphis has been shown to suffer will be visited on Amon and Thebes, on Pharaoh, on all Egypt: her gods, her kings, on Pharaoh—singled out again—on all relying on him. The foe is again named: Nebuchadnezzar of Babylon and his surrogates. But even his supremacy is not forever. Egypt will dwell once again. The unit is arranged chiastically.[26] The final portion of this set of words against Egypt both completes what was promised in vv. 14–17 and reverses it. But since the weight of the unit is on developing the disaster, the eventual words of "hope" are scarcely comforting to supposed Egyptian ears or likely to Judean ones either, for that matter. Judah may anticipate the ultimate weakness of Egypt but still shudder at the strength of Babylon. Exile, short or long, is likely before the power of a ravaging foe.

A third last short section included in the oracle against Egypt in 46:27–28 is addressed to Jacob, in fact with two parallel addresses to the character Jacob. Twice is Jacob, named as "my servant," bidden not to fear or be broken down: "I am with you. . . . I will save you . . . , your time among your captors, your situation of dispersal, I will terminate." What seems overwhelming and complete will be reversed, ended. After a time of correction you, Jacob, will be returned to you place, your oppressor thwarted. The pair of proclamations is at once hopeful and cautionary, suggesting that Jacob, like the nations, will suffer much before any reversal might be expected. But fear is not the attitude, since YHWH has the matter in hand, however long the time may be. Here the sense of internal address seems strongest: Judah's hope lies not in military might but in the compassion of the deity.

As we look more synthetically at this oracle, what can we see of the prophet's skill to shape response? What is the likely impact on the audiences we can envision? Five observations: First, we have been offered powerful Egypt sketched as massively deceived about its strength, have heard its strongest people futilely encourage each other, vaunt hollowly as they slip and fall on all fronts. If Egypt seemed strong not only in its own appraisal but in that of royal Judah, the shock is the greater. The gorging sword is not Nebuchadnezzar, we learn, but YHWH-of-hosts. The Babylonian leader, mentioned twice in narrative introductions and once in the oracle, is overshadowed by the name of Judah's deity, echoing regularly throughout the oracle. How will experiencing the weakness of a dread foe affect Judah?

Second, Judah's strength is shown lacking in quite a different way. Addressed as Jacob, offered redress, reassurance, rescue, Judah remains an object, has no words at all. If Judah can, by stretching, imagine Egypt as weak and Babylon as somewhat incidental, will such a proffered portrait have suited the aims of Davidic kings? Will it have been palatable and persuasive for figs of various conditions and vintages living abroad?

Third, YHWH is seen to use the nations—here Babylon—as tools, weapons. It seems a theological truism, but it will be the main burden of Jeremiah's prophetic ministry: the tool user is more powerful than the tool, however sharp its edge may feel. Can this portrait of Babylon, standing in YHWH's shadow, allow imaginative access to a divine wielding that is not punitive?

Fourth, and related: The rhetorical footprint of the deity is, at least until the last few verses, to be a vanquishing presence, powerful, punishing, dreaded, dire. The rhetorical column of the divine warrior added up suggests fear and shame but not consolation, not compassion. Is this an identity of YHWH that can conduce Judah to the behavior God and Jeremiah seem to want? No hint surfaces here of the struggle and ambivalence we will see shortly between prophet and deity.

Finally, fifth: Empires cannot always be avoided, but they need not be indulged, chased after, relied on. They are merely tools. This is a difficult lesson for all of YHWH's people to grasp, and we may wonder if our prophet goes about establishing that point skillfully here, yet.

Our second sampling of OANs draws on short units with five diverse addressees: Ammon: 49:1–6; Edom: vv. 7–22; Damascus: vv. 23–27; Kedar and Hazor: vv. 28–33; Elam: vv. 34–39. Our aim here is threefold: to see how each of these short oracles makes visible a particular strategy; to continue to familiarize us with Jeremiah's rhetorical repertoire for our subsequent reference as we progress; to ponder the effect on a listening Judah, that is, on ourselves listening as Judah.

The brief oracle concerning *Ammon* can be held up as an example of Jeremiah's language of *dramatic persuasion,* the language employing repetitive rhetorical tropes to achieve its effect. The main impact is reversal of the fortunes to which the Ammonites apparently felt accustomed, if not entitled, with then a reversing of the reversal. Lundbom suggests as plausible context a likely perennial—running boundary disputes as can occur between contiguous neighbors—and brief allusions to Ammonite alliances at moments of minatory Babylonian presence in their shared neighborhood.[27] In any case, the problem posed is Ammon's spilling into Judah/Israel's territory. After a brief introductory note "concerning the Ammonites," we can note several *accumulatios,* piles of repeated elements: four addressed questions, four oracle notations, four directions to the inhabitants of Heshbon.[28] The questions—either two parallel pairs or four queries—are piled on rather than each necessary, and they receive and seem to expect no answer, since it is obvious that Gad does have heirs for its own territory. The point, rather, is to stress the unreasonableness of what has happened. Is there some lack of population for Gad that Ammon has replaced Gad's people? No, it seems, though Jeremiah does not here reply to his own question directly. Rather he moves on to picture a small but intense drama, filled with the imagery of invasion: Ammon as a habitation fire licked and desolate, its soundtrack played with wailing and lamenting urged and heard rising from those suffering attack. The sound of the alarm, the noise of fire, the onomatopoeic cries of humans, the clatter of rushing feet testify to aimless and futile motion: All feature the prophet's attempt at *descriptio,* painting a negative outcome that has not yet happened. Jeremiah addresses questions to Ammon as a daughter, who thought she had amassed what she needed, had gloried in what she was not able to maintain. By use of attributed speech, daughter Ammon is shown indignant before the boldness of her attackers, regretful at the loss of what she has gathered illicitly. The irony of watching security vanish is a support beam of this small unit. But abruptly the scene is broken off, and Jeremiah's hearers—perhaps themselves feeling suddenly entitled when an opponent falls into trouble—learn that Ammon can hope for a reversal of her sudden collapse. Exile is not forever. Unjust land-grabs may reverse.[29] The overall tone of the piece is somewhat difficult to assess, the question of who feels jubilant, consoled, frightened by these words.[30]

The oracle against *Edom* is the most extensive of these small pieces and has had considerable work done on its welter of rhetorical features.[31] Like Ammon, Edom is a small and near neighbor, quasi-kin to the people of Judah in the biblical tradition. Linda Haney makes the case that this oracle is distinctive among other prophetic material against Edom in suggesting a dual identity for Edom: both the opponent behaving badly in the presence of the imperial enemy, and also Jacob's brother, sharing a covenantal relationship with a common deity.[32] The governing image is arguably that of height: security, grandeur, arrogance, all to be breached, brought low, humbled. The implied contrast between Jacob and Esau also bears a covert implication, since if Esau/Edom is to be pursued and punished for violation of covenant, his brother Jacob/Judah must anticipate the same fate.

Since it is neither possible nor desirable to offer a complete analysis, demonstrated here is the potential value of establishing a *rhetorical structure.* Commentators do not agree on the precise structure, and indeed, it is best to see that structural indicators overlap and array their orders in various ways, making the quest for a single ordering pointless.[33] Here we note the relationship between the flow of the language and the logic of the argument. Argument about what, we may ask. To what persuasive outcome is the rhetoric of the piece directed? Haney suggests that the point of this oracle is to stress the incomparability of YHWH and the breach of relationship between deity and Edom; Lundbom does not name a single main point specifically, but in his general "audience and message" sections seem to repeat the insight that the deity will reckon with opponents, no avoiding it.[34] Without disagreeing with those suggestions, we need to sharpen them. Let us suppose that these oracles are indeed for local consumption—for a Judah leadership audience aware of Edom—and ask what such ears and hearts need to be advised, are likely to hear.

A: 49:7b–11: The unit begins with three questions hinting or accusing that Edom's fabled wisdom is gone, reducing that land to three choices of behavior: flee, turn away, come down. Reason: YHWH is responding to some behavior of Edom. Two more questions intensify the situation: Jeremiah, speaking for the deity, arguing from a lesser to a greater relevance (vv. 9–10): <Gleaners leave a bit, don't they, and even thieves don't or can't remove everything, right? But I will search relentlessly in every hiding place imaginable and leave no Edomite safe,> promises the deity, putting to shame the relatively feeble efforts of grape pickers and marauders—which are, of course, not so minor as implied.[35] The image of desolation is stressed, when, after the diminishment of Edom's population, the divine destroyer offers to care for the nonsurviving orphans (v. 11). The tone is confident, chilling, even cruel. If those across the Jordan are glad to hear such threats against a sometimes troublesome neighbor and sibling, the undertone of total threat must register too.

B: vv. 12–13: Another question, similarly making use of reasoning *a minori ad maius* (v. 12): If even the innocent suffer the cup, what of the guilty? Who deserves to drink the cup and who can claim exemption? No matter, says the speaker: If some who might be considered exempt must suffer nonetheless, what about the unabashedly guilty? Edom is to count itself among those who deserve the wrath and its consequences, piled up here: a desolation and mockery, a ruin, a curse, now and forever. The themes of guilt and suffering are extended from the first unit, with cause rather than effect being stressed. But the cumulative impact is that escape is unthinkable.

C: vv. 14–18: A short dramatic image is now introduced, as though to offer the hearers (both those pictured and those addressed) a visual: A speaker, plausibly the prophet himself speaking in his own persona, reports what he has witnessed. A messenger summons the nations to a council, rallies them to form a coalition against the offender: Edom, yes; Judah also? What has been mighty will be humbled. Those who feel secure as an eagle will face fear as a group of allies draws near. Again, the scene is enhanced by reactions from other witnesses. The issue becomes not how Edom will feel but how those looking on will appraise the situation—with wagging heads and hissing mouths, seeing and saying resemblance to Sodom and Gomorrah, devastated and deserted. Resistance is implied but rendered futile.

D: vv. 19–22: And as if that were not enough, an image from hunting compounds that of human warfare: A lion emerges from the thicket to raid what had seemed a secure pasture, grabbing an animal of its choosing. <No shepherd can resist me,> boasts the divine speaker. At best, he will be able to drag what is left of the ravaged animal aside. The image is magnified to suggest a massive raid against a flock, with shepherds impotent, sheep aghast and uttering sounds heard far away. The eagle soars against Edom, and all will be reduced to fear, unable to do anything in their own defense. If Edom felt itself an eagle (v. 16), its people are about to learn what a real eagle can do. The final image, the woman in travail, revisits the reference to no survivors, or to orphans carried off into care by the predator. There is no feature of this oracle not aimed at hopelessness of escape, survival. There is not a shred of hope for any listener. Innocence, guilt matter little. If there is a question buried, a thread to be pulled, it may be how such a state of alienation between humans and deity can have come about. But in reality, it seems too late to wonder about it, at least for Edom. Judah may have time to reflect.

Damascus is spoken of, briefly, offering us access to Jeremiah's capacity to suggest deep meaning from *complex imagery*. Focal is the city of Damascus, its fate learned by two other cities of the region, Arpad and Hamath, shamed by the very experience of hearing their neighbors' plight. We learn neither the particular offense of Damascus nor the identity of the human opponent.[36] Piling up in imagery is a series of logical incompatibles, happening, as it were, simultaneously. Some are roiled like the sea, others stilled; a populated city becomes deserted; the pangs of birth presage death; loud outcry gives way to silence; those who would flee sink down, are grasped; characterized as female, the participants described are men of war.[37] Two inexorable images stand out: the impossibility of postponing or avoiding labor pains, and the futility of stopping fire once it begins to devour. Reasons for this destruction are not made explicit. This oracle warns those already in the know.

The short piece addressing the fates *of Kedar and Hazor* demonstrates multiple and rapidly shifting voicing, a technique Jeremiah will use extensively.[38] In the book's poetry, the speaker will constantly and quickly shift addressees and topics, swiveling from one addressee set to another, speaking about diverse "you"s and "them"s inserting quotations into the mouths of hearers and interlocutors—all with few markers or signals. It is not unlike being presented with a long verbatim but without roles marked: not easy to sort. This short unit seems to split into two halves, with patterns of vv. 28b–30 repeated in vv. 31–33. After the superscription with its Nebuchadnezzar reference and oracle tag, the speaker, as if addressing his own, barks three sets of orders to Kedar's foes (approach, destroy, plunder) before moving quickly to describe the outcome as experienced, still from the point of view of the attackers, encouraged to take itemized plunder: tents and flocks, curtains and gear, camels. Only now is the perspective of the victims registered, a cry of distress (one of Jeremiah's favorites): "terror all around." These characters are next addressed by the speaker, are bidden to flee, to wander, to hide themselves; but the warning self-destructs, containing as it does the information (bragging or warning?) that the powerful Babylonian foe has already anticipated and planned for such a move. To urge flight and hiding seems cruel, coming from the lips of the commander who urges the foe to move in as well.

Then a second round: Address to the raiders, encouraged by the speaker that access to the target will be easy, as Hazor and Kedar have not anticipated a need for defense. The outcome of the raid is this time pictured as though by the plundered, who are shown—wordless—watching their flocks and herds become booty and spoil. The speaker now identifies more clearly as the commander-in-chief, describing the disappearance and disintegration of all enemies, scattered to the winds and not likely to be reassembled, their former habitation given over to wild animals, who replace the domesticated ones we watched disappear with marauders. In addition to those parties spoken to and spoken of, speaking and maintaining silence, is the prophet's actual audience, presumably with similar experiences themselves at the hands of raiders—or dreading them. What these hearers are anticipated as feeling and concluding remains unclear and likely diverse.

The final short oracle spoken of *Elam,* last of the chapter and the eighth of the set preceding the words addressed to Babylon, can best illustrate Jeremiah's reuse and repetition of stock elements. Compared to the preceding units, there is little to distinguish this final oracle. Its historical referents are both clear and obscure, that is, they are plausible but uninformative, and the specific reason for Elam's condemnation remains unclear, to us at least.[39] The name Elam is called out seven times. Elam suffers five fates—(to be shattered, scattered, broken, burned, pursued), while remaining completely passive, at least as described—fates that will also fall on Babylon in the long poem following this one.[40] First-person agency is maintained ten times. The refrain "oracle of YHWH" is given three times, with two other tags provided. The verb "to bring" and the root for "turning back" are reused, though keywords in the unit are fewer than usual.[41] Audial wordplay may possibly be present in terms of the proper name Elam and the sense of "forever/'lm."[42] Hooks to other material are in evidence. Babylonian fates are rehearsed, and what we have heard against Kedar and Hazor—scattering to winds, four corners (v. 32)—repeats. So far as general position is concerned, Peels finds significant that though Nebuchadnezzar's throne had been "placed" in 43:10–13, it is most definitely YHWH's throne that is set up now, just prior to the flood of words that will tell the fate of Babylon.[43] The note of reversal that ends the oracle is similar to that given to Moab and Ammon (48:47 and 49:6). Commentators note as well what is missing here: The detail of the scene—specific sights, sounds, images of war, geographical specifics. Hence this rather bland—perhaps deceptively bland—unit may be seen as a hinge between the seven that preceded it and the one that follows it.

The raw rhetorical skill remains clear, though we may judge that these units work best with specificity and focus—the Elam poem appearing to fall apart for lack of same. It may be our impoverished reference for Elam that weakens it, but we don't know as much about the other targets as we might wish, and the poetry works better there. The oracles also have greater effect when human emotions are described rather than simply implied by general attack and loss of property. These small oracles seem, indeed, like the practice of a beginner.

Conclusions

With general information about OANs noted and "on the table," these poems of Jeremiah seem best read as suiting his own purposes rather than correlating to some hypothetical formal substrate. With some hesitation I suggest that their most powerful impact is in describing the feelings of those who suffer attack. That once-dreaded opponents can be brought to their knees is both comforting and frightening, gratifying and unsettling. That YHWH-of-hosts is the ultimate victor is similarly double-edged: That God uses now one nation and now another, leads them all to victory and defeat, deals in reversals is, again, good and bad news. I am tempted to say that these poems, which provide the speaker with rhetorical training and ourselves with practice in appreciating the poet's skill, all subtly urge hearers to avoid war if possible. Once caught, the suffering is inevitable, however long it may last. To walk to Babylon is better than to be herded there, scattered to the winds, swept away. But the time for beginnings is over, and we must meet Jeremiah in full cry.

2

OVERTURE—PROBLEMS AND RESOLUTIONS REHEARSED

Chapters 2–10

> Death, cultural death, is the concern of Jeremiah.
>
> A. R. Pete Diamond, *Playing God*

Having encountered Jeremiah's persona at his calling and initial prophetic speech and considered some of his classic language regarding Judah's neighbors, we are now ready to meet him in what are plausibly early days of ministry.[1] We will now examine chapters 2–10 as an overture, hearing characters' voices both tangled in complex discourse and drawing on classic imagery. The intersection among speakers and the play of imagery will provide us a sense of Jeremiah's role as God's prophet, a rehearsal for the larger book.

The Unit

For the unit proposed, there is less disagreement about span than about component parts. We will follow Joseph M. Henderson, who wants to read what is present rather than to excavate small pieces to reassemble something else, and who insists that that material in chapters 2–10 is not simply a pile of repeating pieces but demonstrates action, progress.[2] Hence arises my insight that this unit functions as an overture precapitulating the story about to be represented in the fuller narrative of the whole book, with both overture and "symphony" stretching from the long and sorrowful past of Israel and Judah, centering on the crisis faced during the final days of the Davidic/Judean monarchy, contemplating more briefly the aftermath and the perennial choice of how the future is to be faced—in a word, exodus to exile.[3] In the manner of overtures, themes to appear later in the book are previewed, alerting us to anticipate and recognize them when we hear them again.

   Consider division into five subunits: A. 2:1–4:4 (66 vv.); B. 4:5–6:30 (86 vv.); C. 7:1–8:3 (37 vv.); D. 8:4–9:25[4] (46 vv.); E. 10:1–25 (25 vv.). In addition to plot progress, the

dominant rhetorical feature is dialogue among characters, with the main speaker—
the deity—peppering his talk with quotations and questions of various sorts. A
common root metaphor—Judah as ancestral heritage—holds the material together,
makes it coherently effective, allows room for a variety of hosted imagery without excluding the occasional wild card subimage. Articulated is the long story
of infidelity of YHWH's people and the deity's concomitant disappointment in
and reproach for this past, detailing God's efforts to conduce better behavior by
threat and punishment. The final chapter of the unit poses an open future: better
behavior as a result of invasion, defeat, and journey to the east—or not?

A note about narration: We will hear, briefly (7:1), from the book narrator, but
to a surprising extent, the prophet and deity take over the recital and introduction of speakers: themselves, each other, and other characters, steadily attributing
quotation to such others.[5] In all five sections, dialogue occurs, involving God,
Jeremiah, and God's people (Lady Zion, constructed as a feminine singular; men
of Judah as masculine plural persons), another unnamed agent—so five character
sets—with details and proportions varying as noted below. The voices are distinguishable much of the time, derived from formal characteristics (inflection),
content, or tone. Where there is uncertainty (confusion about whether deity or
prophet is speaking, or whether the deity is speaking or attributing), I will offer
a preference.[6]

Henderson's most compelling contribution is to show the discourse as
powerfully presented and dramatic dialogue, with clashing and contesting viewpoints. God and characters are in opposition, though with diverse intensity. Deity and prophet occasionally differ in angle but without contending in quite the
same way as others do or as they themselves later will do. Henderson's second
key point is that narrative progress occurs over the set of verses, with the end
position quite removed from the beginning.

Rhetoric of the Voices

For each unit of overture, I will offer a rough outline, some analysis of the voices—
with special attention to the questions—and sum up the insights.[7]

A. Chapters 2:1–4:4: This first unit is best seen as a series of God's addresses
to and exchanges with the people, a female singular alternating with male plurals.
At four points (2:1; 3:1, 6, 11) the prophet indicates that he was addressed, with the
speech in each case functioning not so much to provoke his participation as to
allow the speaker a wider platform for addressing the people. Consider the following divine addresses:[8]

2:2 to the female: no quotes;
2:4–15 to and of males: two quotes of what was not but should have been said;

2:17–25 to and about the female: three short quotes, all rebellious and
   mis-addressed;

2:28–31 to males: three quotes, rebellious;

2:32–37 to and of the female: she rejoins twice, inappropriately;

3:1–11 to and about the female: one quote, deemed wrong;

3:12 about males: no reply;

3:13 to the female: no reply;

3:14–18 to and of males: one hoped-for quote;

3:19–20 to female one hoped-for quote;

3:20–4:4 to males: one long self-excusing and accusing quote, one hoped
   for quote.

God is clearly the dominant speaker, with the prophet saying nothing in his own
voice. God's self-talk stresses the long past of infidelity, from shortly after the
exodus up until the present moment. YHWH speaks to and quotes the people
under various titles (for example, Israel, House of Jacob, my people), resulting in
language that is "generationed" and gendered variously. Reproach extends as well
across caste, including rulers, guardians of the law, prophets.

   Two trends emerge: the progress of God's self-presentation, and the excul-
pating responses of those addressed. The deity's progression can be heard as
follows: <We started well (2:2) but things went awry almost at once (2:5). Your
ancestors did not ask the questions that might have helped them (2:6, 8) and so
mistakes were made. Consequently now I accuse *you,* inform you, require you
to examine your own situation—dire and unprecedented, as the cosmos itself
might attest (2:10–12). The charge? You have spurned the good and chased the
bad—fresh springs abandoned for leaky pits—with consequences terrible (2:14).
Such deeds were not done inadvertently but in refusal (2:20), denial (2:23), determination (2:24–27). I am done with you, let other deities help you (2:28).> But
of course that concession cannot stand, and God continues to plead: <You did
not lack warning from me (2:30), and throughout the process I've tried my best
(2:32–37), but you've refused.> But then, as though again finding this approach
unprofitable, God appeals to Jeremiah, offering him a case to pronounce on: <Is a
divorced, remarried woman ever taken back by her first husband? (3:1). Of course
not! But look at my situation: a wife notorious beyond compare, going from bad
to worse (3:2–12). Not only ought she not be taken back—she doesn't seem even
to want to be back with me! I'd take her, though I ought not, and I would not
mention her past, though it's dire. This can work> (3:12–20). The eagerness with
which God projects reunion comes to overtake the language of blame, though
reconciliation has not happened, in fact the reverse (3:22). But God anticipates
reconciliation as still possible (4:1–3).[9] The trend of the asserting and quoting

divine voice is to self-exonerate and concomitantly to convict the others by words from their own mouths—except, of course, the constructions are God's and in fact those of Jeremiah-narrator and the book's narrator.

The deity's discourse moves while remaining consistent: God shows himself incredulous at the human behavior, maintaining it as incommensurate with and unprompted by divine deeds. The human antics are outrageous, pointless, fruitless; patterns are ingrained, clemency undeserved—but then offered, urged, pleaded. If we choose to hear nuance, the undertow or minor note sounded is that God is both righteous and foolish, outraged and vulnerable, decided and hopeful: in a word, conflicted. As the subunit ends, God speaks of a scenario, possibly a blend of hope and fantasy, where a fresh start can be made, the prior insistence that such a thing is impossible brushed away, for the moment. God's attributed speech for each character set, though generally consistent, varies somewhat depending on the particular role assigned: wife, son, people. The female character, quoted some seven times, refuses relationship by denying her guilt, flattering her protector, while also denying service or love. The male, also with seven attributions, countercharges reproach and accuses, admitting some wrong while claiming that all remains hopeless, a conclusion reached by the female as well. Part of the rhetorical effect is accomplished by questions, a subgenre in which the deity deals lavishly. In this section A, God hurls some twenty-two questions to the males' two that lacked (2:6, 8) and to the female's query that what the divine speaker deems is misplaced (3:5). God's questions can be restated: <What have I done wrong? Has anyone ever behaved as my people? Is there any precedent, any explanation for their behavior? Is any benefit imaginable from it? How can my people say what they say, expect what they seem to expect?> For the moment, it seems sufficient to say that both God's questions and those quoted as though by the people are composed to intensify the rightness of God's case.

We have a scene—a stage, as it were—where one main speaker, controlling the microphone, strides around, turning to address now one group and now another and within certain narrow variables. We don't actually hear them speak, but God, holding the microphone, tells us what he heard them say, or missed them saying, as the case may be.[10] Questions are hurled not to invite information but to buttress assertions, point out deficiencies. We hear the deity self-justifying while also desperate for relationship. If we were in group dynamics with him, we might suggest that such behavior is off-putting, counterproductive!

In B, 4:5–6:30, stress shifts from the extensive past to the present: The enemy approaches, then arrives, with preparations and defense offered, mostly ineffectually. I propose we consider seven subunits, each featuring God's directions to a new masculine plural agent, charging them to act as the crisis escalates. In each unit God comments on reasons for the attack, quoting the people to buttress the dual charge of ignorance and stubbornness; in each section of this unit there is intervention by the prophet or speech to him, usually both:

4:5–15: warning that the foe is coming:
 directions: announce, say, shout, say at 4:5;
 quote: agent given speech at 4:5; masculine plural personage quoted at 4:8, 13;
 prophet role: at 4:10–11 the prophet charges God misled the people to ill effect.

4:16–31: announcement that the foe has arrived:
 directions: tell, announce at 4:16;
 quote: 4:19–21, 31 the single female cries out at her experience;
 prophet role: at 4:23–26 he testifies to what others also see but he understands why it is happening, an explanation God nuances (vv. 27–31).

5:1–9: result: panic of the population:
 directions to agent: roam, see, look, note 5:1;
 quote: 5:2 they swear falsely;
 prophet role: the prophet comments on his experience at 5:3–5 or 6, first saying what God has said, next querying and investigating it, then confirming it.

5:10–19: the agent; foe ordered to devastate much of what remains:
 directions: destroy, lop off at 5:10;
 quote: people deny what is happening at 5:12–13;
 prophet role: the prophet is given God's words-as-fire into his mouth 5:14–19.

5:20–31: the foe takes up residence, is authorized to speak:
 directions: proclaim, announce 5:20;
 quote: people attempt faux repentance in 5:24;
 prophet role: there is no role for Jeremiah here, since God alleges that prophets are all liars, priests too, and people like it: 5:31.

6:1–15: though many have fled, some remain; siege begins:
 directions: some are told to flee, and some to sound the alarm 6:1; the agent is urged to make a final sweep to be sure that nothing remains 6:9;
 quote: the opponent talks at 6:4–5 and the people react in between those quotes;
 prophet role: the prophet at 6:11 is so angry he can hardly restrain himself and is encouraged to do his worst.

6:16–30: siege has expected result:
>   directions: the agent is told to take a stand by the roads and to look for—to find—the road to happiness: 6:16;
>   quote: God's people refuse it 6:16–17, though crying out their distress 6:24–25;
>   prophet role: The prophet commissioned to be an assayer and smelter 6:27–30.

Cumulatively: Though God remains the main speaker, a new masculine plural participant emerges even as God's people continue to be addressed and quoted.[11] The new actors, responsive to God rather than partisan to people, are bidden by God to engage: announce, proclaim, warn, advise, assist, survey, finish up, assess (4:5, 16; 5:1, 10, 20; 6:1, 4–5, 16–17).[12] The plot progression is clear: warning of enemy approach, urging preparations for coping with them, announcing the foe's arrival, describing the onslaught, calling out the emptying of the region with a rechecking for stragglers, suggesting siege, noting consequences, hinting aftermath. God's ongoing commentary, while first claiming that time remains to avoid catastrophe, moves quickly to insist that disaster is inevitable, continuing to blame and self-exculpate.[13] In the divine commentary God addresses and quotes Lady Zion and the men of Judah,[14] much as in section A: She laments, describes, emotes, sees what is happening. They lie and offer other false speech, deny, accuse. Both character sets withhold what YHWH desires to hear: repentance.

Jeremiah, emerging from his narrator and witness role, now participates—both speaks and is spoken to (at 4:10–11, 4:23–26, 5:3–6, 5:14–19, 6:11, 6:27). His process is crucial to note: Beginning by questioning and even denying that God has been fair with the people—having promised good things but sent bad—he moves to witness and interpret what he sees, incredulous and undertaking to investigate. But then, charged with fire-words, the prophet becomes angry almost beyond control and is assigned his smelter's role. We witness the education of the prophet, his coming to understand God's viewpoint existentially. The questions in play are once again overwhelmingly God's, with only one assigned to the woman's voice (4:21).[15] If the previous section featured the microphone "hogged" by the divine speaker though attributing obdurate language to other participants, here the prophet talks back.

Subsection C, 7:1–8:3, anomalous member of the overture, seems to offer a stand-alone moment of decision, where the book's narrator takes back the first level of narration from the prophet. The genre shift (from poetry to prose, from dialogic and imaginative exhortation closer to harangue) seems deliberately jolting, as though those under the duress just described in section B are summoned into another room and made a fresh offer, as may happen when litigants become more willing to settle a case once an actual jury has been impaneled. But in my effort to make sense of the unit as it appears in the structure I am defending, it is a sort of sidebar, where the people under pressure are challenged—proleptically but definitively—by deity and prophet to understand the reality they are facing. What is strange is that the unit evokes no reaction without evincing awareness that silence greets it.

The structure of the piece, for present purposes, is threefold, with a similar set of elements loosely constellated and progression accompanied by reinforcement and repetition. The subunits are 7:1–15, 7:16–26, and 7:27–8:3, each including an address of deity to prophet regarding his speech, met by silence of the prophet; the deity then charges worship violations, describes and ramifies them, both addressing the people (all masculine plurals except one address to the feminine singular entity [7:29]) and quoting males (7:4, 10); finally in each instance, the deity resolves on a plan, an outcome: exile, unquenchable fire, death, and nonburial.

First, God orders the prophet to position himself at the temple gate and offer—under God's own signature—an escape hatch from the scenes of invasion just made imaginable. The offer as rehearsed is extensive and complex: <Mend your ways and I'll let you dwell here; don't trust illusions or say <<temple, temple, temple>>; rather, execute justice; do not oppress the marginalized, shed blood here or worship other deities—and I'll let you remain in your heritage land as planned; but you are trusting illusions, stealing, murdering, committing adultery, swearing falsely, worshiping alien deities; and then you stand here and claim <<We are safe !>> <<Safe, here, in this place?>>>: YHWH reintonates the safety quote and asseverates its inverse, posing incredulous questions to the erstwhile speaker, buttressed by the claim of watching: <Do you think this house a den of thieves? I've seen!> (7:1–11). The deity changes tack slightly, offering a dis/incentive: <Go to Shiloh, and see what became of what was once there, as the temple is now at Jerusalem.> And as if distracted from the offer being made by the mere mention of the name of the place, the deity winds up listing all the reasons the Shiloh demonstration makes the nascent Jerusalem offer moot: <You sowed what you reaped at Shiloh. Expect the same here, now> (7:12–15). Quotations of the people testify to their inability and refusal to heed. The offenses under consideration are worship oriented but include justice violations as well.

God next reinstructs the prophet: <Do not speak on behalf of such people> (vv. 16–17), since there's no point in God's listening, given the evidence. Worship violations are reiterated, specifically family collaboration in rites for the Queen of Heaven, cultic excesses that God finds unimaginable. As before, the basic issue is long refusal to heed God's word. God promises destruction (7:17–20), present and past mingling together in disobedience and infidelity. The address is almost consistently to males, reiterating that these are not new offenses but persistent, inbred inclinations. Past efforts to dissuade and persuade have been fruitless (vv. 21–26).

A third time the prophet is addressed and simultaneously enjoined from interceding to God (7:27). Recall we are still in the directions to the prophet part of this communication and will not get farther in this overture.[16] Jeremiah is bidden to preach though promised it will have no effect. He will then pronounce a "hopeless" verdict, even a death sentence accompanied by a mourning rite, involving the shearing and tossing away of hair (7:29). The passage ends as YHWH's roll of condemnation intensifies: Jerusalem to Shiloh to Tophet at Ben Hinnom. The only moment of hope is grim indeed, as YHWH envisions the end of infant sacrifice atrocities only when the land is filled to capacity and the animals feast on remains lying exposed. No marriages will be celebrated. Only bones will lie before those cosmic elements once presumed to enjoy worship. Those who are not dead will wish they were (7:32–8:3). Only four questions are posed by the deity (7:10, 11, 17, 19), and none is placed in the mouths of those addressed, who in any case are given speech only twice (7:4 and 10). This interlude offers a moment of choice, not well managed by those whose options are diminishing. But the deity actually short-circuits the process by foreclosing hope, concluding that warnings will not be heeded. As bidden or constrained by these directions, the prophet falls silent. As the section concludes, the microphone in the deity's hand has been shared by no one. The participant convinced by the rhetoric is the divine speaker himself.

In D, 8:4–9:25, decisions from section C that God backed into while assigning the prophet to offer an alternative are justified, ratified. In terms of our overture, we recognize repeating themes and motifs. The tension from the attack called out in section B has abated, since damage was not prevented but inflicted and barely survived. Though repentance remains a theoretical possibility, there is no whiff of it, yet, the option all but foreclosed. The structure is not obvious here, but I will assay four similar units, each raising for analysis by deity and prophet—their voices and perspectives nearly interchangeable—the situation at hand. So consider:

8:4–12:
opens with an observation by the deity: obduracy of Jerusalem (8:5–7);
proverbial language for assistance: questions about normal human behavior, about the capacity of animals to know what is needful (8:4–7);
quote to bring in another perspective: what people do not ask (8:6), what they falsely assert (8:8, 11);
a solution raised to be dashed—tradition is available—but to no good end: those who might have instructed are unable to help, themselves speak falsely (8:8–12);

[prophetic voices mislead 8:10];
outcome: they will stumble and fall to their doom (8:12).

8:13–23:
opens with an observation by the deity: the vineyard bare of grapes and leaves,
   the fig tree shorn of fruit; the heritage is vanished (8:13);
proverbial language for assistance: invasion of serpents not open to charm
   (8:17);
quote to bring in another perspective: the people resolve to take measures
   for their own safety, since what they expected from the deity has not
   materialized (8:14–16, 18, 19a, 20, 22a);
a solution raised to be dashed: Is God not present in Zion? How can this be
   happening—to no good end: God refuses to cohabit with images (8:19); is
   there not some healing to be had, some balm from somewhere for all this
   shattering? (8:22);
outcome: death and tears, too much of one and not enough of the other (8:23).

9:1–10:
opens with God's wish to escape the dishonesty of the people (9:1–2);
proverbial language for assistance: no one is trustworthy (9:3–4), <even your
   neighbors,> comments the deity;
quotes are implied as God comments on the peoples' language (9:2–7);
a solution raised—smelt and assay them?—only to be dashed: it's too late for
   anything disciplinary; only retribution (9:6–8);
outcome: desolation profound, depopulation, even animals gone (9:9–10).

9:11–25:
opens with an interrogative exclamation by the prophet: how to explain the
   reason for what has been experienced (9:11);
proverbial language for assistance: stock verbiage from the tradition,
   commenting on radical infidelity and the punishment for it (9:12–15);
quote to bring in another perspective: the people: they lament their destruction
   (9:18–20), though without taking responsibility for what is happening;
a solution raised: punishment to the point of annihilation (9:16), but it is not
   dashed this time; the prophet is to speak it (9:21);
outcome: death from war and exile is the outcome; but any surviving will
   glory not in their own achievement but in God's mercy, which becomes the
   alternative (9:21–25); circumcision but of heart is required.

Fuller comment on content: The unit opens (8:4–12) as the deity, incredulous,
queries the obduracy of Jerusalem's infidelity, with no change of course as sometimes attends other human endeavors: for example, the fallen rise, the left-veering

adjust rightward. God's concern is to explain how such intransigence is imaginable. Opening with two general questions about behavior, God then asks a third more specific, supplies quotes of the males to demonstrate that here, as before, they don't ask what they've done wrong, seem not to anticipate what might be an apt question. Animals (horse and three birds) can do better, but Judah men evince no awareness of their plight. Though we might ask whether they are ignorant or stubborn, cannot or will not see their fault, YHWH moves past those alternatives to assign blame to scribe and sage, to priest and prophet, suggesting that they have either failed to teach the needed or been fooled themselves, perhaps both. In any case—though situations differ—the outcome is the same: With such ineffectual teachers, the people know nothing, their heritage already trashed, squandered, alienated.

In the second subsection (8:13–23), males speak to defend themselves, blame God, take refuge—such as it is—to await their doom, with no thought to escape it. God testifies: the heritage languishes leafless, fruitless. The noise of invasion is registered: People are quoted claiming to have heard war horses, but God corrects to say no, serpents rather than steeds, unable to be deterred. YHWH quotes the people at vv. 19a and 20, threading his own discourse with theirs, to blame others and then speak a foolish calculus, as though deliverance were a seasonal arrival like early autumn rains: <late this year, too bad!> In this microdebate, the deity toggles between distress and irritation, taking up the possibility of a cure only to dismiss it. Though this is a famous moment for prophetic tears, I think the weeper is the deity.[17]

The third subsection opening (9:1)—as if God says, <not a flowing fountain but a desiccated encampment—and extending (to v. 10), is somewhat reminiscent of YHWH's first speech of this unit, where the incredible obduracy of the people evoked indignant reflection. But now, God *can* explain it, underlining in several reinforced accusations that this is not simply error but dishonest and culpable behavior. God accuses beyond stupid and shameless to charge evil and concludes by saying there is nothing to do but smelt them (so God takes on the task formerly assigned to the prophet), punish them, stop their mouths. The outcome will be distress on the part of all witnesses, not simply Jeremiah but also mountains, pastures, humans passing by—fewer witnesses than might have been imagined, however, since animals will be missing.

The fourth small piece of this unit D again involves dialogue between deity and prophet: I assign the question of 9:11 to Jeremiah, picking up, perhaps, what God decried in 8:8–11, where the teaching of the wisest has been so inadequate. So who *is* in the know, Jeremiah asks, who *can* have learned so as to be able to explain— if not for a deterrent, for an explanation. And the reply is God's, not so different from before. But I would stress that the *root* is named—refusal of Torah—leading

to the *branch*—idolatrous behaviors and then to the punishments—*leafy* consequences that are underway as attack. The section moves toward its conclusion as
YHWH again quotes, but the females rather than the males. God urges his agents
to line up those able to lead the dirge, with the passing of the quote now on to
what such mourners will cry (vv. 17–20), as the words and wails of mourners es-
calate. This quotation is not self-serving or other-accusing, though neither does
it take on responsibility, contenting itself with grieving over what has happened
or is underway. Now the deity turns again to the prophet (masculine singular imperative), telling him what to say: how the bodies will fall and remain unburied,
same point as made at the end of section C. In certain ways, this is the climax of
the overture, since God seems to decide, now, on extreme action and instruct the
prophet to put it into play. In a foretaste of what will be, God inspects for circumcision: It will lack literally among the nations and figuratively among those
who lack attentive hearts.

The questions in this unit, shared among males, deity, and prophet, are
noteworthy. The males continue to be shown in denial (8:6, 8, 11, 14). But prophet
and deity move toward a rhetoric of concern for options, with YHWH becoming
more settled and less scathing in discourse. Though beginning dramatic and accusatory (8:4, 5, 8), God becomes more frantic and insecure in 9:6, 8, 19, 22. There
is no shard of wisdom, strength, or resource left to provide satisfaction for the
wise, strong, or rich. Only one thing has been needful: to know God. Nothing else
avails.

If there was a sense that the fourth large subsection of this unit had sunk
somewhat into repetition of an earlier unit and that forward progress had stalled,
that impression is broken up in the final brief section, E: 10:1–25, as unique in its
way as were sections A and C.[18] Here God hurls neither barbed questions nor
unflattering quotations. The voices of the four character sets come together here
to share an insight and goal, which, granted, falls differently on each of them. I
suggest as structure two rounds of speech from each: God at 10:1–5 and 17–18; the
people (including both the female and the male) speaking at vv. 6–10 and 19–22;
the prophet's words come in 10:11–16 and 23–25.

This first subunit works best if seen imaginatively as a sort of split screen.
God—with one foot still in Jerusalem, where the action of this long piece has
been set—shifts to the other to inspect the situation of those dwelling among
the nations, already transplanted, as is the case by the end of the book whose
overture we are now concluding.[19] God's warnings center on dangers arising for
those dwelling among the nations, famous for their propensity to seek omens in
the sky and to construct idols with apparent skill. YHWH's people are warned in
stock prophetic language (10:4–5) not to be taken in by such sights as can be seen
around them. The language is ironic, since God's discourse has already suggested

that those being addressed are themselves highly susceptible to such practices. But the words are not sarcastic, as indeed, the mode of worship of YHWH is a complex thing to know.

And for the first time—or in a way different from before—the masculine plural voice responds, conforming to the divine wish, able to voice insight about its unnamed creator, with the quoting voice inviting no censure (10:6–10), saying what God seems to approve, eliciting no charge or hint of insincerity or flattery. We have heard no language like this from the Judeans, who have either denied or disregarded the cultic violations with which they were charged. I am construing that to dwell among the nations—imaginatively and in overture mode—has been transformative for them. This, in my view, is not simply caving into a relentless bully but a genuine insight that something previously resisted is somehow—counterintuitively—desirable. How it happened between God's resolution at the end of chap. 9 and the present moment the fuller "symphony" will need to detail.

Now (vv. 11–16) there comes prophetic address to the males—presumably to these putative exiles themselves—urging them to speak out, now able to say themselves what deity and prophet had long urged. In this overture we might even suspect that their current prophet is absent from their lives in exile while addressing them there.[20] The instruction basically reiterates what deity and people have just said, granted in a slightly different register—hence my decision to alternate the speaker.

The deity, having heard these words, shifts weight back to the foot anchored in Jerusalem, as it were, or toggles back to the "home screen." Advising Lady Zion, God announces a decision (vv. 17–18), threatened before but now appearing more salutary. Having imaginatively or proleptically seen what has happened to those in exile, God now commits the people to that experience with fresh resolve. <I will inflict distress, yes, but they will 'get it,' benefit.> In the overture this is the moment when God articulates that the removal of some people from the land is more than a punishment. Insight can come in no other way. It is as though God seems to conclude that, threats and punishment aside, resettlement among the nations is the only way to cure the wound the prophet spoke of in the previous section.

The exiled community speaks now—again—in her own voice (giving Lady Zion the words of 10:19–22, since she was just addressed), describing the fate, seeking neither to avoid it nor blame it on someone else. This docile Zion/Judah-identified character set remains almost invisible in the story we will be told, but its presence here will help us discern its faint trace later.

Finally, the discourse of 10:23–25 is best seen as Jeremiah's, perhaps as transition to his laments of the type that he will produce shortly. The whole unit of 2–10 as well as the final piece of it ends with a wisdom reflection by the prophet, with Jeremiah begging for modulation if not mercy, for God to spare him so that he can survive the worst, which will be very bad (10:23–25). Pointing out that the nations are more to blame than Jacob, granted the infidelity of some of the clans, the prophet intercedes, briefly.

Summary of Discourse

The overture, having escalated from exodus to exile, winds down and circles back now, as a small flock is scattered. The dialogue, such as it is, between deity and people, having begun with an outraged deity berating the people with irate quotations demonstrating their inadequacy and with indignant questions showcasing his own righteousness, has shifted. In place of early and long-running words comes a spare pair of utterances, where the men of Judah and Lady Zion speak well and on their own. The deity has moved from high dudgeon and barrages of attributed quotations to something simpler and gentler, though resolute. As though he has listened to himself and heard his own voice through the anger of accusation, YHWH has decided and announced that not total annihilation but early removal holds remedy for the malady of his people. Lady Zion and the Judah men have also, concomitantly, been authored to break off talk of denial and manipulation, of rebelliousness and rudeness, to voice grief, even obeisance, and especially insight, wisdom. The male characters have spoken words of which YHWH can approve, and the female voice agrees. This happens once only, but once is good. The overture ends with Jerusalem, Judah, and Jeremiah's fate overlapped and surely grievous. A dread fate has been selected, since alternatives have proven untenable. But since it has already demonstrated fruit, though difficult, it is also hopeful. With the completion of the overture, the symphony proper will soon begin, its outcome already rehearsed.

The prophet's role is particularly key, since our eye is on him in this book. In A (2:1–4:4) the prophet's character zone is "simply" to be a conduit for God's words (however that is to be understood)—so a narrator—and a witness to God's long speech, with its many attributed quotations and accusatory questions (2:1; 3:1, 6, 11). In these instances the prophet is initially addressed, but the subsequent uttered speech is to the female singular and the male plurals, not to the masculine singular prophet. Section B (4:5–6:30) shows Jeremiah continuing those two roles—narrator and witness—still addressed more as the sort of ally to whom we nod in a speech, one who understands and receives sympathetically our point though without being asked to actually respond. But now, finally, he speaks as his own person. He questions and even accuses God (4:10), undertakes his own investigation and reports and interprets what he's discovered (4:23–26), shocking to him (5:3–6). He is given fire-words at 5:14–19, expresses his anger at 6:10–11, and is made smelter at 6:27–30. In section C (7:1–8:3) Jeremiah (for the first time since his call in chapter 1) becomes a character at the direction of the book narrator (who takes over at 7:1), and we see him given directions and handed words to utter. But he is simultaneously enjoined from speaking, crying out, or interceding to the deity, who will not listen (7:16–17); and he is told to speak while at the same time being informed that his words will be without effect on his human hearers (7:27), though he is given those words (7:28). Jeremiah makes no reply in this section, though he will activate these directions later, once we are past the overture. In D (8:4–9:23) he resumes his roles as intradiegetic narrator and as witness, but once again he wades into the God-people relationship—note, please, for just the second time. A comment or question posed at 9:11 receives a reply from God, and Jeremiah seems ordered to speak at 9:21. The question—Jeremiah's first of the overture—if not the reply, which seems more expected, may set up the basic issue that will have to be explained in the fuller performance of the book: How *will* the word be preached such that it can be heard fruitfully? Finally in the last section, E (10:1–25), the prophet responds to what is a notable transformation of the characters Lady Zion and the men of Judah, as they appear, at least to me, to have accepted the viewpoint that the deity has also come to understand and articulate with fresh clarity (10:23–25). If that turn seems sudden, the fuller prophetic narrative will have the responsibility to adumbrate it for us.

Role of Metaphor

Having heard the richness of the voices, we need to consider another aspect of this distinctive block of Jeremiah material: its metaphoric quality and capacity. I will establish some claims about cognitive metaphor, bring forward the work of Job Jindo on such metaphor in Jeremiah, and then conclude with the implications for the unit under consideration here.[21]

Metaphor is "a mode of expression whereby one thing (A) is understood and described in terms of another (B). . . . The relationship between the two things (A and B) is that they belong to different frames of conceptual domains."[22] Metaphors are not simply ornamental but are cognitively useful, helping us think and see new things. Resemblance or similarity is not the base of cognitive metaphor, though likeness has a job to do. The challenge is to talk about one domain in terms of another and claim—establish—similarity. Metaphors are crucial to our human processes, not optional. Criteria can help us ascertain whether we are dealing with metaphor: an assertion is a candidate for metaphor if it is not literally true; if it is not simply an adjectival description; if mapping works (see below); if we have the sense of hitting a speed bump when we meet it. We can establish some basic terminology: A *target domain*—more abstract and less easy to know—names the field we are most interested to investigate; a *source domain*—better known and easier to talk about—helps us in some ways to explore the target. A process of *mapping* the source onto the target (attempting a fit between them) prompts us to infer—construct—conclusions about the target from information available within the source domain. In cognitive linguistics, the equations go as follows: TARGET is SOURCE; and SOURCE maps to [——>] TARGET.[23]

Jindo has fruitfully married cognitive metaphor theory to close work on ancient Near Eastern texts and specifically to Jeremiah. He shows how Jeremiah's metaphors come from the rich stew of ancient Near Eastern culture, with imagery both distinctive and also cross-cultural. Jindo urges us to explore some of these the common tropes and mine them, clarify their metaphoric functions explicitly, not simply leave them implicit, lest we miss them. We must read imagery holistically rather than atomizing individual tropes, highlighting pathways among figures rather than isolating them.[24]

Jindo claims that the root metaphor for Jeremiah 1–24 rises from a figure common in ancient Near Eastern culture and literature, the experience of and response to the destruction of an ancient, beloved, and respected city.[25] Drawing on the work of various scholars working in the field of city laments, he sketches the metaphor's components as follows:[26] The gods are responsible for cosmic harmony, with diverse deities having responsibility for various regions and peoples, inviting them to dwell in the divine garden. But consequent on the radically inadequate behavior of the human guests—specifically the royal delegate appointed by the divine patron to maintain order and justice in the land—destruction of the heritage land has been ordered by the divine council. The outraged and grieving patron deity is plaintiff, bringing lawsuit against the humans, specifying causes of the violation. The divine plaintiff serves also as judge, eventually as lamenter. The prophet takes roles of both messenger of the news and intercessor for the city. Called on to carry out the sentence is the foe from the north, making use of a variety of weapons suited to that purpose. Agents are also delegated by the deity to inspect the work of destruction, a task the prophet seems to share. Lamentation over the destruction of the beloved heritage is shared by deity, prophet and people, the latter pictured as mother or daughter city. The contentious dialogue and particularly the efforts of the divine plaintiff to convince self and others that the course envisioned must be taken becomes meaningful in this root metaphor. Jindo maintains that Israel/Judah is distinctive if not substantially unique in knowing what it is that the deity wants, and also in envisioning that the intercession can be made by humans, not simply by deities.[27]

Jindo's formulation for Jeremiah's base or root metaphor works as follows in cognitive linguistic terms: THE COSMOS IS A STATE, transposes to YHWH'S ROYAL

GARDEN is ISRAEL/JUDAH, or JUDAH maps to ——> YHWH's ROYAL GARDEN. This basic metaphor has constellating component parts (submetaphors) and plays them out variously, though within the basic assertion. Jindo's quest is to follow the metaphor through chapters 1–24 of Jeremiah, and he makes a compelling and detailed case for the material.[28]

Granting that he has established his claims, I want to shift the metaphor slightly, making it less cosmic and more historical, ground it slightly more firmly in the social, economic, political and religious data of the late seventh and early sixth centuries, though without contesting its mythic roots. The sociologically more specific image remains rooted in the cosmic. I will also limit my scrutiny to chapters 2–10, again without doubting that the figure ranges more broadly, both in Jeremiah and elsewhere. My claim may be articulated as follows: YHWH's HERITAGE is JUDAH/ISRAEL, or, ISRAEL/JUDAH maps to ——> YHWH's HERITAGE/ THE >FAMILY FARM' WAY OF LIFE (target maps to source: to analyze what is happening more tangibly provides insight into what is less obvious but needs to be known). Having stipulated that Jindo has basically demonstrated the global fit for his root metaphor (of which mine is a nuance), I want to argue for significance before naming the component submetaphors. In other words I want to show why we benefit from recognizing how the root metaphor controls the discourse, ramifies it to substantial cognitive gain. Jindo says the following: "The drama of the book of Jeremiah revolves around the confrontation between his contemporaries, who adamantly believe in the inviolability of Jerusalem, and Jeremiah, who uncompromisingly proclaims total destruction and exile. The present study suggests that this disagreement stems from a discrepancy between the *general cognitive paradigms* through which the people and Jeremiah conceive the events unfolding in the world."[29] And: "Jeremiah's task is to re-orient the perception of the people so that they themselves can perceive world events as a cosmic lawsuit drama, and his extensive use of imagery is the very means of achieving this goal. . . . In order for Jeremiah's contemporaries to accept his orientation, they must make a radical leap of cognition. Such a leap, however, can be achieved only when they begin to notice irreconcilable discrepancies between reality and their own cognitive paradigm, which is only during, or after, the destruction and exile."[30]

I would qualify his claims in two ways: First, I think the basic discrepancy in viewpoints roots in a clash of understanding of what living in the heritage entails. A tenet like Zion's inviolability may be part of it, but I think the point of dispute is more complex. And second, the value of the vast and substantial focus of the book on events prior to 587 becomes clearer, if its challenge for later readers— ourselves included—is to become oriented to both the true and the false claims Jeremiah presents and contests. The issue is not simply historical, as though once the year 587 were past, it's best simply to push on. Rather the root metaphor and its "tree" embodies a wisdom larger than the particular historical circumstances, though it appears garbed in them.

To adumbrate a bit: What is under dispute, whether understood explicitly or not by all participants, is what it means to live as YHWH's people on the land YHWH loves and has shared with a particular people (as distinct from others): how to live responsibly and suitably in the divine garden into which their deity has invited Israel/Judah. Several misapprehensions were abroad: The nations (notably for Jeremiah, Babylon and Egypt, but others as well, as we know from the OANs) supposed, in their imperial way, that the small patch of conveniently located territory was theirs for the taking, to be milked in all the ways that empires did and continue to do to this day. Whether the heritage was conquered and burned, dominated and annexed, or simply pillaged for its produce, all participants needed to be shown another reality.[31] For the leaders of God's people, notably kings but the other elites as well, the error seems to have been to suppose that they were in charge and could negotiate freely and safely with one powerful overlord or another while, hoping to avoid or delay something unpleasant, certainly planning to maintain their own privileged positions. We may suppose that the sages, scribes, priests, and prophets were tempted to contribute their particular skills to that mistaken and myopic royal belief. Kings and their surrogates would have to learn a different way, for everyone's sake.

The mass of ordinary people, represented here by Lady Zion and the men of Judah, are constructed as dominated by the false assumption that the heritage had come without strings, that is, that people could inhabit it as they pleased without consequence. But some practices destroy the garden and threaten its inhabitants. I suggest that the multiple charges of "false worship" stand in for—represent metaphorically—the false notion that YHWH did *not* have clear expectations about and limits regarding worship. I am not, here, maintaining that these divine tenets are clear and verifiable now but rather that they seemed adequately clear to Jeremiah and his adherents in this book. Some expectations were worship-specific and some were more ethical, relating to treatment of the poor, with those two realms, of course, related. To live appropriately was to farm and herd locally, to worship and exchange goods in such a way that YHWH's ways were respected, so the land would be passed on in good condition to heirs. When adjacent empires threatened, such living was much more difficult, perhaps *we* might say impossible. But the viewpoint of Jeremiah and the Deuteronomic ideology/theology he and others expound is that YHWH's people must attempt to live in responsiveness to YHWH's ways. The danger was to refuse to see that to live on the heritage and violate these norms was deeply offensive to God—at least the deity as constructed by Jeremiah and others. The heritage was not an entitlement but a gift. God's people in general would need to understand, more broadly, what is entailed in dwelling in the garden of the gods. The challenge was not and is not a matter of facts but of viewpoint, attitude. The heritage claim was not and is not susceptible to proof, remaining a matter of faith and commitment. It matters existentially where humans see ourselves living—on commodity real estate or in the cosmic garden—and it will affect our behavior. Jeremiah's role was to find the best ways to reorient the view of his mistaken people. If Jindo is correct to assert that YHWH's people were distinctive in being privy to what divine expectations were, the matter is more serious than if they cannot be supposed to know.

So the next challenge, now, is to see how this root metaphor and its constellating parts operate in Jeremiah 2–10. The five sections each make the same basic point—that the heritage dwellers have forfeited their right to divine hospitality—but the primary image varies. The voices make excellent sense in terms of submetaphors specifying a common root, in that Jindo's claim that a lawsuit is involved here, with the deity as both plaintiff and judge. The defendants speak, granted in the judge's own language; we hear them in the discourse that the divine judge/plaintiff understands them to be arguing. They cannot and will not win the case. And yet they have a messenger and even sometime-advocate to inspect their side of the case, although he will not be able to corroborate their claims over against the deity's.

Specifically: In A, as is almost more than adequately discussed, the prominent facet is the husband-wife relationship, where the divine speaker as aggrieved plaintiff enumerates ways in which the close spousal bond has been violated. Other less intense images, related to the land but not directly to the marriage, make the same basic point: Reliance on rivers and cisterns in place of spring water, the spoiling of noble vine stock, behavior of irresponsible shepherds, the risk of destructive fire all speak to neglect of the garden. The metaphor centering on the couple's relationship is enhanced by other figures drawn from the breakdown of their life together "on the farm." In subsection B the crisis is explored metaphorically in terms of war, as an enemy, first dreaded and then experienced, wreaks havoc. Sounds and sights of devastation and ensuing suffering are stressed. Those whose heritage is invaded are powerless to resist, and many flee. Wind, storm, marauding animals, and hunt imagery also contribute to the destruction—minor metaphors reinforcing how the heritage land is radically vulnerable to attack.

In subsection C the central metaphor brought into play is violation of worship relationships and specifically cultic spaces, whether Jerusalem's temple, Shiloh's shrine ruins, or a site like Tophet, more notorious even than Shiloh, with submetaphors here exploring the effects of flawed worship on worshipers and worship space alike. The heritage becomes the gravesite for both dead shrines and their former worshipers, the land spreading out a feast of corpses for the animals that have survived the carnage. In section D war again presses powerfully, with imagery extending beyond agriculture and nature. At risk, we suddenly see, is not simply the beloved city/garden land of the gods but the cosmos itself. We are metaphorically reminded that humans must dwell wisely in the land they find themselves to inhabit. Finally as the overture comes to an end in the short section E, the metaphor speaks removal from the land, testifying that a decision has been reached by the plaintiff/judge. In a strangely atemporal twist, first the experience of exile is envisioned, consequences of the community's removal from the divine garden to survive outside, perhaps anticipate return. The land itself has been forfeited, the journey into exile commenced, and the danger is to learn of the ways of others while living in their midst. The root image celebrates the glory of the creator, in present circumstances, the owner of the heritage that must and will be abandoned for life elsewhere. And yet this remedy is not wholly punitive but somehow formative.

Conclusions

Having explored the unit of Jeremiah 2–10, focusing on its structure and momentum, its discourse—notably quotations and questions—and its root and subsidiary metaphors, we may draw some fresh conclusions. First, the material spans the whole relationship of YHWH and people—from freed from Egypt to removed from the land of promise—enclosing what comes between those moments. The unit thus functions as an overture to the longer book of Jeremiah, raising its key moments and themes. Second, the ancient Near Eastern root metaphor of deity bringing lawsuit against the people to expel them from the garden organizes the metaphors and also makes excellent sense of the discourse. The divine plaintiff, who is also the eventual judge, addresses, alleges, and accuses the people of gross and willful violations of their relationship. The defendants, split here into two (a single female and plural males), rejoin feebly and lamely, their self-excusing, reality-denying and hopefully placating words serving only to add fuel to the already kindled deity. The multiple smaller metaphors pick up aspects of "life in the divine garden" and the struggle to maintain the ancestral heritage, demonstrating that the survival of God's people in God's garden is indeed what is at stake. Third, the prophet is not transparently partisan as the unit begins. He briefly takes up an advocacy role for the accused, in fact charges that the deity has violated the relationship. But when Jeremiah has undertaken and completed his investigation, he becomes witness for and ally with the divine plaintiff/judge and will collaborate on that side of the lawsuit. But by the end of the overture, though assisting God, he speaks empathically for the people.

Fourth, as YHWH and Jeremiah continue with their task of threatening and punishing so as to induce a change of behavior, they gradually arrive at the conclusion that such a project is hopeless. No partial measures will suffice to accomplish the change of heart they know is crucial for the restoration and flourishing of the particular relations of YHWH and Judah. Only the very extreme experience of removal—suffering relocation—from the garden/heritage/land/beloved city, with its attendant hope of return, will enable the people to know and say who God is, who they are. Transplanting offers the best hope of at least some people coming to understand what the garden/heritage is and what living there entails. The only way back in is first to go out. This decision is not a matter of jubilation for prophet or deity. Indeed, the deity shrinks back and breaks off triumphant and self-promoting language, and the prophet voices grief and solidarity with the people.

Fifth, the central learning has to do with the issue of responsibility: whose for what, and why. Deity and prophet charge leaders (kings, elites, prophets, priests, sages) who have thrown their weight poorly and to the wrong side and, *mutatis mutandis*, the general set of people who has been led and allowed itself to go astray. And the nations are at fault as well, of course, though rather minimally here. In the prophets, and surely in Jeremiah, there is no case made that the family farm did not ask to be invaded by powerful others who would make survival impossible. But Jeremiah's analysis is not merely political and military but religious, and he chooses the worship aspect—cosmic garden/family farm religion, we might say—to highlight that reality. The fundamental sin or error was to forget, misunderstand, or deny what was due the deity in worship. This is metonymic, I think: That is, worship was not literally the worst thing, but it stands in for the most crucial facet of illness. The claim is both new and old, is newer than the multiple and embodied ways of worship of the neighborhood time out of mind, and yet not a fresh idea in the late seventh and early sixth century as we hear it. As the overture ends, we anticipate a reconsideration of its basic themes and motifs, turning to the laments of prophet and deity hurled against the silence of the people.

3

RESISTANCE—DEITY AND PROPHET AS PARTNERS AND ADVERSARIES

Chapters 11–20

> The book of Jeremiah provides an opportunity to test the potential of . . . a holistic, systemic approach to the Bible . . . with the dual challenges of paying proper attention to its undeniable complexity and of coming, nevertheless, to some understanding of the whole.
>
> Mark Biddle, *Polyphony and Symphony*

As we proceed with our reading of the book of Jeremiah and deepen our acquaintance with its named character, we continue to monitor the key issues of his world: how his people handle worship of YHWH and how they all understand the agency of God in the political events of their time. How will deity and prophet address the sense of betrayal of relationship by the people of Judah and Jerusalem, made so prominent in the overture? And how will the events of the late-seventh- and early-sixth-century Levant be adequate—even fruitful—for deeper insight about survival for God's Judah project? How will God and prophet help the people to manage the catastrophe swamping them, so that at least some can survive and thrive?

We have witnessed an overture arcing from accusatory and squabbling character voices using rhetoric of shame and blame, caricature and alibi but reaching eventually something more consensual for YHWH, Jeremiah, Lady Zion, and the men of Judah. We followed the prophet as he traversed flashes of insight into and intimations about his role: accusing the deity, scolding the people; searching hopefully for innocent citizens, railing at the hopelessly guilty; imploring God first for and then against the people. We heard him given a series of commands about his prophet role that were simultaneously thwarted, insuring his inadequacy and even failure. But we also saw him arrive with God and people at a moment and place of compassionate resolution. The key question for God and prophet, characters and readers, is what creates that moment and how is it constructed, such that it can continue to be mined for insight? Where is a healed relationship and a fresh life together to be found for God and God's people? How will all players learn of it and help each other? Some, it appears, need to—be able to and agree to—leave the heritage land for exile and will learn to experience there an insight available nowhere else. The question for us as we move forward is how that process happens. We will watch that learning for the rest of the time of this present book.

We will approach chaps. 11–20 of the biblical book in two moments, cued by the two macrogenres employed in the material.[1] We will look first at twelve collaborative "ministerial" moments in the relationship of prophet and deity, united in efforts to change hearts of posited hearers. These scenes seem designed to share with us, reading, the process by which Jeremiah must first learn and eventually communicate and make persuasive what God shows him. These pericopes are primarily prose. Interspersed with these more collaborative scenes are poetic lament soliloquies, six from the prophet and eight by the deity. In these moments, less mutual and more private, we will listen to these two main characters react, each in himself and occasionally together, to their experience with the people. Though recognizing the prose/poetry distinction as complex and sometimes artificial, I will make the distinction significant, even decisive.

The purpose of this present chapter, then, is to deal primarily with the collaborative prose teaching efforts, leaving the detail of the soliloquies to the next chapter. But since the two genres are in fact intertwined, we must note how the ministry efforts trip off the soliloquies, just as we will in the next chapter—while focusing on the soliloquies—name what seems to have given rise to them, what situations mutually experienced YHWH and Jeremiah are struggling to resolve. Hence these chapters 3 and 4 are related, inversely. Though modern scholars remain in disarray over the arrangement of what seems a scramble of elements, I have preferred to take advantage of and to exploit this alternating genre arrangement rather than to override it.

A bit more about the prose material as a whole before turning to the individual scenes. Ostensibly, their common purpose is for deity and prophet to instruct Judean addressees as to what behaviors would be better than their current ones. These are all narratives of such scenes from ministry, or more accurately, rehearsals of possible scenes, where the audience is implied or imaginable, though not actually present—not so very different from what we saw in section C (7:1–8:3) of the overture. In that scene, beginning with instructions for a prophetic performance designed to be persuasive but not for the moment enacted, God arranged the setting and gave the directions but became so wroth that the carrying out of the directions was aborted (until chap. 26). In these units featuring YHWH and Jeremiah engaged with people, the spotlight is on deity and prophet, present and engaged with each other, at least until the final scene, when other characters step forward. Here the initiative typically is YHWH's, instructing or programming the prophet for a deed of preaching or prophesying, using some pedagogy that uses symbolic action. The prophet appears to or presumably will go along with the instructions, but most oddly and not well explored in commentary material, these remain "dry runs," or if enacted, generate virtually no reply until the end of the whole sequence. Hence my claim that they are ministerial may be misplaced, except insofar as the point is to suggest that virtually no recipient of these efforts reacts at all except those most intensely involved—prophet and deity, who ruminate. It seems best to see their purpose as educative and formative of the prophet—also of deity, a process shared with hearer/readers. In this section, Jeremiah is given a more active role than he had when called or when shaping the OANs, and he is more consistently engaged than in Jeremiah 2–10, where he was more an observer and a witness, with small though significant voice and action. That the genres for action vary may be less important by far than that no one pays any attention, as these scenes are narrated. Or perhaps it is useful to say that no matter the approach of deity and prophet, reaction is minimal. That lack of audience or audience response becomes the most important point, plausibly setting off the soliloquizing of the two main protagonists. But as is often the case, the ministers or teachers may learn even when the recipients of their efforts do not appear to do so.

These twelve scenes share a common general shape though with prominent distinctive features, for example, several with some kind of symbolic element, in that something is used to help generate a point and some insight. They do not simply draw on verbal imagery but often utilize props. Some scholars feel sure these were preformed, but as we have these twelve I am dealing with, that is not so clear.[2] Though presumably conceived and aimed to be persuasive, they generate exactly nothing by way of response, until the final scene, where they trigger repression of the prophet that catalyzes him to burst forth with fresh prophecy. This "ten-chapter moment" of effort to reach the common people will not be continued in this same way in the next sections of the book of Jeremiah, where interest in and address to leaders will take over. These scenes, undated, give the appearance of belonging to a time when danger was not pressing so clearly as it will and options remain open. But time seems not to help in this "heartland" ministry of the prophet. When finally someone responds—Pashhur ben Immer—his reaction is perverse in two senses: It aims to shut off the information but rather accomplishes the opposite effect, generating more of what he didn't want to hear.

So what are these twelve units, and how do they function? The point I want to explore and establish is that over the length of these, God helps Jeremiah inch closer to the possibility that only quasi-willing removal from the land is viable, feasible, and that this untimely going will not include him. Most hearers remain unpersuaded, and we are to conclude that they missed an offered opportunity. We must wait a while before being shown the group that does hear and heed, and we will have so little information about them so as to be reading in negative space, as it were, inferring the alternative to what we are about to witness here.

Twelve Moments of Collaborative Ministry

The whole set of these, 11:1 to 20:18, is framed by the book narrator, who has spoken only at these two places (previously at 1:1 and at 7:1, though the narrator will speak four more times in this long unit, at 14:1 and 18:1, to introduce soliloquies, and in 19:14 and in 20, to narrate action). My point here is to name these twelve pieces distinctively, to characterize their genres, to note the presence of interlaced and responsorial soliloquies, though leaving discussion of them to the next chapter (see Chart of the Book of Jeremiah Assumed, at the beginning of this book).

a: **unappreciated past, 11:2–14,** is a covenant speech:[3] This lead-off unit begins at 11:2 with a series of "envelopes" indicating YHWH's speech to Jeremiah and destined for the ultimate addressees: man/men of Judah, dwellers in Jerusalem.[4] The males addressed are to hear and heed, and Jeremiah is to speak out the words of the covenant.[5] As the actual words addressed begin: <Cursed are those who do not heed the words addressed to your ancestors when they were brought up from Egypt, the iron furnace: <<Obey my voice, do what I have commanded, so that we will be God and people to each other as I swore to undertake, including to give the land flowing with milk and honey, where we now are.>>>[6] The claim voiced is that the pact remains mutual: If one party reneges or falls into arrears, the other will necessarily be in violation as well. Thus there is cause for anxiety on both parts, though it is God's mind and mood we are presently learning.

Jeremiah, interjecting at v. 5, replies with an "Amen, YHWH." The first and very general statement of the case God brings has been made. The charge is clear though general, serious, perennial. It is a fitting summary of what is lacking, wanting, sanctioned. Prophet and deity concur.

The speech resumes in vv. 6–8, with another directive from YHWH making the same basic points: <Call out the words in the same two venues: Hear and do.> The reason is again included: <I put your ancestors on notice when I brought them up from Egypt and do so to this very day: Heed my voice! But they did not do that but did something else,> still referenced very generally as following the evil of their own hearts. So, relates the deity, <I carried out the covenant terms, since they had not done what they needed to do.> Still an accusation generally clear, grievous, long running. We detect an apologetic tone (in the technical sense of the word, explaining and justifying a matter in need of defense): <I had to follow through on the agreement, had no choice.>

Jeremiah, again speaking at v. 9, introduces God's words addressed to him: <A conspiracy exists/can be found among men of Judah and Jerusalem: They have gone back to the practices of their refusing ancestors, done the same, have gone after other gods to worship them, broken the covenant I swore to their ancestors. So I will bring on them evil they cannot escape. They will cry out, but *I* won't hear. They will cry out to the other gods, but nor will *they* (be able to) help them at their time of evil.> Then at v. 13, addressing people rather than prophet, an explanatory note about these other gods: <So many towns, that many gods; so many town squares, that many altars of shame for sacrificing to the Lie.> Only here near its end does the speech begin its detail about the target: multiplicity of site and sacrifice, many rather than the one, with the implication that this is not a new problem.

And, still with this unit, v. 14 swivels back more directly to Jeremiah, making an *inclusio* with vv. 11–12: <As for you, neither pray for this people nor raise a cry on their behalf, since I will not listen to them when they call out from their evil (or to you either).> This aspect of Jeremiah's ministry we have heard before.

The key word has been "hear": Most refuse it, and so God will refuse to hear when they do call. Deity, prophet, ancestors, current people of Judah and Jerusalem: united in contagious hearing loss. Rather than attributing speech to others as was so prominent in chaps. 2–10, God here quotes Godself, stating the complex dilemma that has resulted from these reciprocal refusals to hear. Breach of ancient promise, a most serious thing. <No choice,> God insists, three times: <Not my fault. Had to be done. It's decided.> This is an apt opener, going back to the early days of relationship while standing in the present, naming the root refusal of relationship and its cognate consequences, promising that neither true not false divinity will be responsive to pleas, and rendering the prophet both obligated to speak and advised not to do so. Left unexplored is the basis for the refusal, the reasons for the breach of bond. How can such a conspiracy be operative and from so far back? This short prose piece reiterates much of the material presented in the overture: the perennial problem.

This first moment of ministry sets off four soliloquies, the divine two framing and enclosing the human pair:

YHWH: #1: fire and the green olive (11:15–17);
Jeremiah: #1: the trusting lamb (11:18–23);
Jeremiah: #2: sheep for the slaughter (12:1–6);
YHWH: #2: heritage destructive and destroyed (12:7–13).

Leaving the detail of these poetic utterances for our next chapter, we can simply observe that God, though deeply grieved, seems resolved on the most negative outcome, and that Jeremiah seems frustrated at what is happening to himself at the hands of opponents. We may sense that the prophet's ready "Amen" (11:5) may show both unity and discrepancy of angle here: not simply the people clueless but the prophet not attending to the depth of what is being said. The only straining participant here is the divine speaker. The prophet is as deaf to tone as are the people to content.

b: **uprootings, 12:14–17,** is a YHWH resolution, with oracular language, playing on keywords: This unit, introduced by Jeremiah, is clearly presented as an utterance of YHWH against wicked neighbors who have encroached the heritage reserved for YHWH's people: <Watch me uprooting these troublesome neighbors from that land, uprooting Judah from amidst that group; but after such uprooting, I will return mercifully each and both to the appropriate place.> The oracle raises the likelihood of removal, of enforced exile and makes return and replanting contingent on a reversal of teacher/learner status: If the erstwhile encroachers can become learners of the good instead of teachers of the bad—learn from YHWH's people to take oaths in YHWH's name—as YHWH lives—instead of swearing by the Baal name and prevailing on God's people to do the same—then they will all be built up in the midst of God's people. But if they—any, presumably—do not heed, God promises to uproot and destroy them.

This language is clearly linked to the ministry of Jeremiah, since one of his signature jobs is to uproot, with building included as well.[7] It recalls as well language in the OANs, with negative consequences potentially reversible. The language catches the final measures of the overture (10:1–25): how Judah/Israel can learn the lesson only when living in the midst of strangers, though to live there is itself a painful outcome to undergo, and here we see, a dangerous one. Without naming the early days of deliverance from Egypt, the resolution catches their whiff: living off of heritage land is at base, by default, an undesirable thing. Whether this is a hopeful teaching is also not clear, since the teachability of the nations is not obvious and the capacity of Judah to override their influence is small as well. We are left, as before, with the question of how removal can possibly work. It may, but how? We saw it rehearsed in the overture, but we are also shown that, should it fail to work, the destruction will be compounded instead of reversed. The stakes are high, the outcome open.

c: **parable of the loincloth, 13:1–11,** is a sign-act, functioning as an analogy: Narrated by the prophet, it comprises three sets of directions, each commanded (vv. 1, 4, 6) and then obeyed (vv. 2, 5, 7), with minor commentary: <So buy a loincloth, wear it, do not expose it to water; go away, remove, hide the loincloth; return to it later and dig it up.> In the third lap of the story, the prophet confirms that the linen garment acquired, worn, removed, buried, left, and recovered was ultimately ruined, had become useless. Then, introduced at v. 8 and speaking directly at vv.9–11, YHWH interprets and expatiates the analogy: <So will I ruin the pride of Judah and the pride of Jerusalem—the great, this evil people that refuses to hear my word but goes in the stubbornness of their heart, goes after other gods to serve them and bow down before them—such people will become like this loincloth that is useless for anything, including the basic function for which it was designed and that it once did successfully: clinging to the loins of its owner.> We hear God more deeply: Consider the objects first: people as pride of the land Judah and of the city Jerusalem and a man's intimate garment, both once related and functional, now sundered and ruined, useless. Then ponder the process: As the loincloth ought to, is made to cling to the loins of its owner, so I fashioned a people (house of Israel, house of Judah) to cling to me, to be my people for honor, praise, glory; but they refused, became useless, redundant.

The sign-act is interesting from two points. First, the general analogy of intimate relationship, to be likened to an undergarment sounds odd, at least to the modern ear. As a metaphor, however, it is vivid. The discrepancy in roles of wearer and worn works well, as does the contrast between what is functional and what is ruined. The angles of time and space are similarly productive in terms of insight: Two locations, two conditions: In the land, the garment worn and untouched by water; outside the land—at the Euphrates—the garment removed and lost to its owner, disintegrating.[8] So this is not simply geographical but relational. The loincloth runs into trouble when it is both at the Euphrates and removed from the wearer. The Euphrates itself is not the problem but the sundering of the clinging that happens there, the dangers of the watery climate to which the loincloth has not been made accustomed. The conundrum and challenge seem similar to those in the previous piece, where uprooting is inevitable but fruitful replanting is an open choice. Analogies, symbols, metaphors, and dramatic actions can be pushed too far, can be pressed to offer meaning too literally. But I think the details of this simple trope can carry the load asked of it here. The narrated action, meant to provoke thought, does not open directly the question of why "the loincloth" was carried off and stashed in a damp place, what "it" had done to deserve such a thing, how it got separated from its wearer, whether such a journey and sojourn could be helpful. Those details cannot be pressed from what we have. The issue at point is about clinging, and in that action, the garment fails. Again, the prophet makes no rejoinder, nor, of course, does anyone else. The deity seems resolute and clear here, not conflicted or grieved, not defensive or apologetic, certainly not optimistic.

d: parable of the wine jugs, 13:12–14, is a proverb, presented and then twisted to surprise:[9] Neither apparently related to what has preceded nor contextualized at all, this fourth prose piece shows YHWH instructing and informing Jeremiah: <Tell them a proverb from me: <<Every wineskin is (to be) filled with

wine.>> And when they say to you, <<Duh, don't we know every wineskin is filled with wine?>> then twist it: <<I'll fill full—all the dwellers of this land and all kings seated on the throne of David, all priests and prophets and inhabitants of Jerusalem—with wine too much/drunkenness, and I will smash them, one against another, fathers and sons together: I will have no mercy or pity, there's no stopping me.>>>

This scene works on the complacency of those who think they understand the utterance sent, know better what the proverb means than does its sender. But the speaker, twisting it, compounds its possibilities and confounds the hearers, who are left speechless, their "duh" changed to a slack-jawed "huh?" The saying also plays on the theme of the cup filled and overflowing with wine forced on drinkers, more than they want or can enjoy until they are made ill and powerless, a complex theme met in both the OANs and elsewhere, rehearsing the inevitability of the cup, offered to and in fact forced on the guilty and the innocent alike.[10] Bleak. If the deity began this set of twelve scenes with undertones of conflictedness, they have given way to something more determined; except insofar as the deed is not yet done, there may be hope. Are there more proverbs that might work more effectively? Or does the default complacency of the hearers render such language powerless?

These three prose teachings generate two soliloquies from YHWH:

#3: the flock-whisperer (13:15–27);
#4: wandering feet (14:1–10).

In both of these, tremendous poignancy at refusal returns to the deity's language, prompting us to reconsider what we are hearing from God here. We also ponder the silence of the prophet, who seems to have resumed his role of witness and medium so far in this section of material.

e: on intercession, 14:11–16, is a reported dialogue:[11] The deity-prophet encounters become, now, more analytical, as the prophet speaks up, talks back. YHWH's words to Jeremiah, who reports it (v. 11): <Do not pray for them, their good; when they fast I will not be listening to their cry, and when they offer holocausts, I will not look favorably on them. But by sword, by famine, by pestilence I will finish them off.>[12] Jeremiah rejoins at v. 12, thereby doing what he has been forbidden to do several times, and just now: "But I said, 'Alas, my Lord God! See, their prophets are saying to them, "you will not see sword nor will there be famine for you, but reliable peace I will give you in this place.""' The prophet, re-enacting the role we saw from him in section B of the overture (4:4–6:25) brings into this moment of his prophetic preaching a key theme: When prophets speak falsely, people are not to be blamed. The false language here alluded to (v. 13) is the illusion that things can go on as they have been, without need for radical change. No need to anticipate alternatives to those choices already in hand: Stay as at present or attempt negotiation with the power planning Judah's defeat. The alternative, as previously noted, is to choose a third way. But God's reply withers that prophetic cavil: <Not my prophets, not my words. Expect death.> The theme of bodies not only dead but unburiable, since only the dead remain, is a chilling image. Like the four collaborative units preceding this one, little hope can be conjured, except the security of knowing what is not possible.

God's response to Jeremiah's intervention is not agreement or even sympathetic understanding, since the ignorance Jeremiah would excuse is moot. The prophet relates YHWH's response to him: <Their false speech will cost both its speakers and hearers. Death in the land for liars and lied to, for self-deceivers and those who collude in it.> The very things those "false hearers" are assured they will escape will get them in the end. Two points: Jeremiah's intervention is declared pointless. And the presence of false prophets renders ineffective the mediating office itself. Once prophecy is corrupted, there is not good served by any mediator.[13] This is a signal moment.

This report generates YHWH soliloquy #5, tears amid drought (14:17–22). Sustained commentary in our next chapter will help us construe this dialogical plaint, but a question to ponder here is whether the speech ascribed to the people in 14:19–22 is sincere or specious. In reply to God's and Jeremiah's frustration with false speech, insincerity would suit well.

f: also on intercession, 15:1–4 is a pronouncement, a sort of ukase fending off what is *not* to happen: As though picking up on their previous exchange, Jeremiah reports another utterance of God to him concerning prophecy: <Even if Moses stood before me—and Samuel [implicitly, any other intercessor[14]]—there is nothing in me for this people. Send (them) from my presence, and they will go. If they say to you, <<Go where?>> tell them, thus says YHWH: <If to death, then death; if to sword, sword; if to famine, then famine; if to captivity, then to captivity. I will enact on them four means of punishment: sword to slay, dogs to drag, birds and wild animals to devour and destroy. Consequence? I will make them a horror to all the kingdoms of the earth, the result of Manasseh ben Hezekiah and what he did in Jerusalem.>>[15]

With no effective intercession, absent all competent mediators, there is only one thing that can happen. People will go to the places they are pining for: death, sword, famine, captivity, destroyed by sword and three wild animals. Again we see that the interdiction on Jeremiah as intercessor is part of a larger matter, with the position of intercessor and intercession itself brushed aside. The most God's present prophetic interlocutor can do is direct people to their final grim destination when they ask where they should go. The decisions have been made and will be visited on those who are destined for them—a prophet assisting that process. This seems the job of both failed and false prophets: to enable the peoples' desire for self-destruction and to lead and direct them to it. Jeremiah falls silent, has nothing intercessory to say, prompting us to wonder what his role can be, if as we have already suggested, some are to select the alternative that can lead to their survival. How will Jeremiah assist that group, and where are those ears as we watch the present set of encounters?

This pronouncement sets off two soliloquies:

YHWH #6: grieving women, whining sons (15:5–14);
Jeremiah #3: tasty words (15:15–21).

The deity rehearses a wider set of options, and the prophet complains about his speaking role, a self-pitying point God does not indulge.

In **#g: prophetic identity, 16:1–13,** we hear directions for a set of sign-acts, interpreted and then explicated as to cause when they will, hypothetically, be queried, then finished off by a shifted proverb.[16] The first of these units runs from 16:1–13, comprising three sets of directions and explanations from deity to prophet, splitting at v. 10, when the people who are to witness the sign-acts and perhaps hear explanations, imaginatively ask the cause. That is, though they haven't asked, since we are in the directions phase, God anticipates that they will ask or ought to ask and thus explains to Jeremiah how he might reply, using language similar to what we saw in chap. 11. In the first nine verses, three things are forbidden Jeremiah—his odd behaviors meant to provoke query from others: First, he is not to marry or beget in this place (v.2), with God at once explaining why: Sons and daughters and their mothers and fathers will die gruesome deaths here, neither mourned nor buried, but left lying like dung on the earth, to be finished off by sword and famine, their corpses eaten by birds of heaven and beasts of earth (vv. 3–4). This set of outcomes piles together a number of events prophesied previously, compounding their already grim impact. Second, Jeremiah is told not to enter the lamentation house, nor to mourn or gash himself for any of the dead (v. 5a), with, again, explanation following fast: God pronounces that he has withdrawn his well-being, favor, and mercy from this people, with the result that they will die—great to small—and not be buried or mourned, not gashed-for or tonsured-for. None will break bread of mourning nor offer consolation, no one will take the cup of consolation over the death of father or mother (vv. 5b-7). Again, mourning is utterly obsolete and futile, perhaps impossible, since only the dead remain and in large quantities. And third, Jeremiah is not to go to the banquet house, to sit, eat, or drink with any celebrating (v. 8), because, God explains again without being asked, <Just see me making cease from this place, before

your eye and in your days, the sound of sweetness and joy, of bridegroom and bride (v. 9).> Begetting and burying, feasting and mourning—a pair of merisms for human existence—will be ended, Jeremiah's behavior is to signal. First told not to intercede, the prophet is forbidden also to perform actions that anyone might do for comrades, since circumstances will have become so deranged. Jeremiah seems to have no questions, no reply.

But, God continues, when you tell them all this (both prohibitions and their interpretations, presumably) and (should) they ask you why has God spoken all these great evils and how they can have been prompted (v. 10), then you will say: <Because your ancestors abandoned me and went after other gods, served them and bowed down to them; me they abandoned and my instruction they did not guard. And you, you have done more evil than your ancestors, and there you are, going each in the stubbornness of his evil heart, refusing to heed instruction (vv. 10–11). Consequence: I will hurl you from this place to the land that neither you nor your ancestors have known, and you will serve there the other gods, day and night. For I will not give you any pity> (v. 13). God expects the question, whether a feint or a sincere query, though as before, it matters not which it is. Though these situations are future and hypothetical, it is already too late to understand and avert them. The unit is presented with great rhetorical balance: Three interdictions, three explanations. Two questions, one about the people and one about God. Two sets of answers: one about what the deeds of the ancestors, one about those of the addressees, in both cases what they did and ceased to do. Consequences will arrive. Though it is possible to see these next five verses as the conclusion of the unit just examined, I prefer to let them stand on their own so that the change can be registered.

For in **h: worse fate: 16:14–18**, an oracle shaped around a proverb, we have a whiplash, reversal of sorts:[17] This is the most unexpected moment we have seen to date in this section of collaborative ministry, and perhaps the most confusing. The deity speaks, presumably from the angle just instanced: But a time is coming when the saying, "brought out of Egypt," will be replaced with one, "brought back from the North." The reason: <I'll bring them back to their land I gave their ancestors.> But the tone at once goes negative: <I'll send fishermen to haul them in, hunters to search them out, whether from mountains and hills, clefts of the rocks. I'm watching and seeing, nothing is hidden, and they'll pay double for what they've done, defilement of my land, filling it with corpses of abominations.> Whether the object of this rumination is the captors or the captive is not clear, and a shift from exiles to their hosts is one way to make sense of the utterance. The other possibility is that we are shown the deity, still trying to grapple with the possibility that removal from the land can be anything but negative, continuing to grasp the glimmer of awareness that exile will be helpful—a point we saw established in chap. 10 of the overture, where dwelling off the land came to be seen by all as necessary and salutary. Whoever is the object of fishing and hunting has not done well, though neither have their opponents. But the topic of removal is on the horizon, occasioning a new measure: The time in Babylon will become newly focal, eclipsing the time in Egypt.[18]

This pair of prose units prompts two units:

YHWH soliloquy #7: hearts indelible, irrevocable, gone off (16:19–17:13);
Jeremiah soliloquy #4: reluctant shepherd (17:14–18).

In the divine rumination, God broods on alternatives, good and bad choices, rooted in the profound mystery of human perversity. Even God is stumped at the dark mysteries of human hearts going bad. But the soliloquy also raises the possibility that some can do well, with the tree securely (trans)planted serving as the base metaphor. Without our quite hearing why some trees respond better, we learn that they do and see them thrive and prosper in relationship. Jeremiah's lament focuses on his role of service to the ungrateful and the nasty, and he turns retaliatory against them, begging that he be vindicated over against the people to whom he is sent. Of the various places where the prophet names or shows his relationship with his people, this is perhaps a low spot, understandable but not sustainable for him.

#i: In teachings regarding Sabbath, 17:19–27, we hear a dictated preaching on gate options.[19] YHWH next speaks to Jeremiah, who reports it with careful envelopes indicating level of discourse.[20] The directions indicate a straightforward covenant speech, unified by topic and catchword.[21] Jeremiah is positioned at a gate so as to address what his hearers must cease to do—carrying items in violation of Sabbath practice—what they must begin to do—honor Sabbath law. But the deity, instructing, notes that the prognosis is not good, since ancestral practice has been poor (vv. 19–23). But the future remains open nonetheless: <If *you* can obey and not violate Sabbath practice, ingress and egress of the usual persons can continue here, Davidic kings with officers and dwellers of Jerusalem, the city inhabited for a long time to come, people coming in from the towns of Judah, from the environs of Jerusalem, the land of Benjamin, from the Shephelah, the hill country, and the Negev, all bringing whole offerings and sacrifices and incense offerings and bringing thanks offerings to the house of God> (vv. 24–26).[22] As we expect by now, there is no reply.

The content, all focused on Jerusalem's gates, is meristic and comprehensive, as these divine speeches tend to be: What to avoid and what to do, bringing out and bringing in, house and city, ancient forebears and Jeremiah's contemporaries, kings and commoners, peoples near and far. The Sabbath command is, perhaps, emblematic or metonymic for all worship or all of the Torah. Additionally, we catch reference to Jerusalem ingress and egress, a matter deeply on God's and our minds by now. How to keep the traffic flowing, juxtaposed with the affirmation that it has not worked well in the past. We can pull forward from the end of the overture the image of Lady Zion, bidden to gather her bundle and move out of the city, toward the exile that is her only hope of survival (10:17). That choice is not rehearsed here. Rather, the options are the two dispreferred by deity and prophet: things can be counted on to remain as they are, else destruction. The first, though emerging as a theoretical possibility, is at once rendered dubious (vv. 24–26), thus making the second inevitable—rehearsed in grim detail: fire in those very gates, consuming the treasuries of Jerusalem and not able to be extinguished (v. 27). In this profusion of persons, gates, and burdens, what we miss, so far, is the "middle way:" how Sabbath observers, leaving the city and land, can survive.

The piece we are calling **#j, parable of potter, 18:1–12**, is a demonstration of process, in fact the narrative of a sign-act: This unit follows right after what has preceded, with no soliloquy intervening, and somewhat atypically, it is introduced by the general book narrator (v. 1): God told the prophet, "Go down to the potter's house and I'll tell you my words when you get there" (v.2). Jeremiah then takes over narration: "I went down to the potters's house"; and then indicates what he found: the potter at the wheel, remaking with his hand pots that went spoiled, whatever seemed valuable in his eyes (vv. 3–4). At v. 6 YHWH (introduced in v. 5) takes over to interpret for Jeremiah the words addressed to the house of Israel: "Can I not deal with you as the potter does with the clay?" It seems a genuine "rhetorical question," to which response is neither given nor expected. But as is often the case with such queries and with metaphors for the divine-human relationship, the trope does not quite conceal its negative or absurd pole. Can God, does God deal with people as a potter does with clay?

But God rushes on: "Like clay in his hand, so are you in mine." Again two sets of options that include the extreme edges of the possibilities: <I may say of a people, <<uproot, pull down, destroy,>> but if it turns back from wickedness, I change my mind regarding what I had planned to do; or I may say of a people, <<build, plant,>> but if they disobey, I change my mind about the good I had planned to do> (18:6–10).[23] The visual at hand underscores the point: A pot may be going badly and then be shaped well, or it may seem off to a good start but then have some flaw that calls for its demolition. The future is open. But the divine speaker breaks off and commissions Jeremiah to communicate that, in fact, the option that is already determined (v. 11): "You tell the men of Judah and dwellers of Jerusalem." Thus says YHWH, "Here I am even now shaping you an evil, planning for you some schemes. Turn back, each from his wicked way, improve your ways and your deeds." But, God concludes (v. 12), <they will say, <<It's no use, for after our own plans we will go, each in the determination of his wicked heart we will go.>>> The pot has made up its mind to go bad, odd though such a phrasing is—language familiar to us from the long overture, where God was prone to this type of quote and so the potter "has no choice" but to smash it down on the wheel.[24] Is there a good pot that can persevere and be brought to a happy completion? We do not hear of it, though it may be implied in the extremes. The demonstration suggests that the prophet's ministry is pointless, as God already knows, a point offered several times before. Perhaps the very team ministry we are witnessing is the clearest referent for the scene described. No demonstration and no prior knowledge seems useful for the scene's participants. The people addressed are learning nothing, while the prophet is being shown that options are narrowing. We watching, consider both, God's choices as well. Education, formation of a prophet to accept the inevitable. This unit, though like that of the loincloth, ends badly.

This pair of prose teachings invites:

YHWH soliloquy #8: anomalies (18:13–17);
Jeremiah soliloquy #5: the pits (18:18–23).

God's last soliloquy about anomalous disappearances is vitally important, and the prophet is nearing an extreme position as well.

We arrive at **#k: parable of potsherd, 19:1–13**, a denunciation with an illustrative prop, followed by **#l: 9:14–20:6**, the a response of one prophesied to, a pushing back on his part, to whom Jeremiah pushes back as well.[25] It is related to a sign-act, but with some special features. It is thematically related to the potter demonstration as well, though even more ominous than was that language. Jeremiah is addressed by God and told to acquire an object (a potter's jug), to invite a special audience (some elders and priests), and to convene all at a particular site (at a city gate giving access to the valley of Beth Hinnom, one whose name either is or puns on potsherd).[26] Further directions are promised once the stage is set (vv. 1–2). Those words, coming next with no intervening narrative of the prophet's compliance, begin once again with the careful clarification of God as authorizing them. The words spoken (vv. 3–9) offer no options or choices but simply announce a negative decision already made. "Say to them, <Hear the word of YHWH, kings of Judah, dwellers of Jerusalem; thus says YHWH: <<I am bringing on this place such evil that the ears that hear it will ring.>> Why? they do not ask. <<Because they, like their ancestors, have abandoned me and made this place [contiguous to Jerusalem, though lying outside the gate] foreign to

me, sacrificing in it to other gods whom neither they nor their ancestors, kings of Judah, had known.>> So the sins of the present have been innovative as well as long running. The present generation has surpassed its forebears. Specifically, <They have filled this place with innocent blood; they have built shrines to Baal, and their sons they put through the fire as whole offerings to Baal, such as I never ordered and had never entered my mind> (vv. 3–5).

Next: a re-naming: <The days are coming, when this place will not any longer be called the Tophet or the Valley of Ben Hinnom but Valley of Slaughter. And I will frustrate the plans of Judah and Jerusalem in this place, I will fell them by the sword of the foe seeking their life,> giving bodies to become bird-of-heaven and beast-of-earth food, making the city an object of hissing and horror to everyone passing by it. God promises to make its citizens eat each other, such the desperation (vv. 6–9). The future looms worse than the past. Blood illicitly and immorally shed will thus attract new and more blood, the blood of the shedders of others' blood. The ones with plans of sacrifice will become themselves offerings for the hungry animals. And worse: they will become food for each other. This language surpasses in brutality anything we have heard to date, apex and nadir of violence. It is difficult to conceive an end more dreadful than this one, or to imagine how a site will recover from all the carnage piled up. The valley, implying both nearness to Jerusalem and distance from it, seems to include in its sweep the whole nation, the whole project. And yet there is more.

At v. 10 God orders the jar to be smashed, as all assembled watch and hear pronounced to them: <Thus says YHWH: <<So I will smash this people and this city as a potter smashes a pot, which is not able to be mended again.>>>This is no lump of clay, able to be recast. Time has moved on. In Tophet—the site is called by its new name—they will bury until there are no more places, and presumably the rest of the corpses will lie unburied, will be devoured by animals. The city Jerusalem and the Tophet will be the same, filled with unspeakable carnage. A final comment to compound the horror: <I will make the houses of Jerusalem and the houses of the kings of Judah become unclean of it like Tophet, all the houses from whose roofs offerings were made to the host of heaven and libations poured to other gods> (10–13). As blood draws blood, so bad worship sites will draw uncleanness. No reply emerges from those assembled.

The twelfth moment of prophet-deity collaboration hooks right on, but the break is suggested by the intrusion of the book narrator at 19:14, similar to 11:1 and in 18:1.[27] This unit, serving as transition, is the first of the set of 11–20, where God does not initiate so persistently and Jeremiah seems to interact in a more spontaneous way. It also brings the first reaction from narrated participants. The prophet's action seems placed as he returns to the city and in fact to the temple from the valley outside the "Potsherd Gate." Jeremiah addresses those at the temple courtyard: <Thus says YHWH-of-hosts, God of Israel: <<Here I am bringing to this city and to all its towns the bad thing I have spoken over it, for they stiffened their necks so that they would not hear my words (19:15).>>> A brief summary follows of what will happen and why. But when the priest Pashhur (credentials given in 20:1) hears it, he strikes or flogs Jeremiah and puts him in stocks (or in a cell) at the Upper Benjamin Gate in the temple area, releasing him in the morning. Before the priest can speak, Jeremiah—on his own in a way we have not witnessed previously—addresses him and interprets the scene for him (20:1–2): "Not Pashhur, but YHWH has named your name Terror on Every Side." Then the prophet explains: "For thus says YHWH, 'I am giving you to terror—you and all you love—and they will fall by the sword of their enemies in your sight. I will deliver all Judah into the hand of the king of Babylon and he will exile them to Babylon or put them to the sword. And I will give all wealth, all riches, all prized possessions of this city, and all the treasure of the kings of Judah into the hands of their enemies. He will take them and plunder them and take them off to Babylon.'" Jeremiah, hurling language that sounds like God but that we have not specifically heard him instructed to say, enters a new phase, a role he will expand in chaps. 21–38. It is language that we will see come true after other choices have timed out.

This is detail like nothing we have heard since the end of the overture in chap. 10, where exile became not only necessary and inevitable but salutary. Though the deity has been educating and forming the prophet for ten chapters, now, Jeremiah here, without being nudged, adds the column and says that exile to Babylon is what is going to happen. And more: "And you, Pashhur, and all who live in your house will go into captivity. You will come to Babylon and there you will die and be buried: you and all your friends to whom you prophesied falsely." Exile will not be salutary for some. Perhaps in Jeremiah's view, not (yet) for any. But a corner has been turned.

This scene opens to Jeremiah's soliloquy #6: enticing deity (20:7 to either 13 or 18). It will need to serve as transition to Jeremiah's more independent ministry, aimed more specifically at leaders and somehow effective with a small group of Babylon-bound journeyers, who will, unexpectedly, thrive. They are still largely invisible, except for implications from hopeless alternatives.

Conclusions

In twelve prose units where YHWH and Jeremiah have functioned as partners, we have witnessed pertinent relationship realities under negotiation among deity, prophet, and people: a relentless beat of what sounds inevitable amid the variety of options pondered and sorted. Without repeating the detail of what we have etched or anticipating the richness about to be added by the soliloquizing of YHWH and Jeremiah, a preliminary summary is in order. As we review the edges of what we have been shown—the first and last encounters of the ministry team with the people (units #a and #l)—we heard God summarize the case for a divine reneging on the project. God reviewed what had been offered, what was asked, and the basis for each obligation. The implications of persistent and eventually outrageous refusal were detailed, the trajectory of the troubled relationship tending from negative to disastrous. At the end of our ten-chapter unit we watch Jeremiah, apparently adequately instructed and formed, step out into his first "live encounter" with the people, specifically with the priest Pashhur. Prophet addresses priest in line with what we have witnessed, though now without specific prompt. Jeremiah's human partner moves as well, beyond silence, denial, and threatening words to punitive deeds, flogging and imprisoning Jeremiah, if briefly. Jeremiah, God, and we ourselves can see that there has been no learning, no openness to instruction. Jeremiah reiterates the outcome of such refusal: death, whether in or outside the land. Pashhur, in turn, shows Jeremiah something of the prophet's own role, which will be largely that of enacting to Judah and Jerusalem their trapped and doomed situation.

Between these edges are the ten other prose units we rehearsed possible fates—choices—presented to the people, which we can group into three. The easiest, possibly dominant choice is to hold fast, remain without change, hoping that the threatened things will not come to pass or that it won't happen soon (units d, e, f, i, j, k). We have seen that "hope" dashed to bits like a jar, smashed like a pot. We have, second, seen defeat and forced captivity described as a negative uprooting with little good coming from it, seen it accompanied by a refusal to cling faithfully, to end irresolutely, without relationship (c, g). Captivity is to be the lot of some, but it will not be fruitful but mostly destructive. The third option went by so fleetingly that it is easily missed: the transplant eventually brought back home (b, h). Perhaps we glimpsed a pot thrown by the potter—possibly with a flawed start but somehow gathering a healthy shape under the hand of a competent artisan—with the result that good can happen (j).

Insofar as the team ministry has proven largely ineffective, we also witness its disintegration, as Jeremiah is forbidden effective prayer, intercession, marriage and procreating, mourning, and rejoicing (e, f, g); he devolves largely to directing condemned people to their fates (f). The prophet speaks back to the deity once (14:13), to protest, as in the overture (4:10), that God has been unfair to expect apt choices from those whose prophets have betrayed their calling. But that cavil does not persuade the deity. As the prophet steps forward with greater initiative, it cannot be with much hope. The deity, largely thwarted in efforts to conduce a change of heart, has to be wondering how to proceed, how the future can be different from the past and present. How can the options so persistently resisted be made more palatable, the single viable option adumbrated be offered so that it becomes thinkable, if not attractive? To these ruminations we will now follow our main protagonists.

4

DEEP LEARNING—EXPERIENCING THE HEART OF GOD

Chapters 11–20

> A variety of characters play the role of lamenter. Israel's God, the primary
> lamenter, bemoans his role in the destruction of his beloved estate.
>
> Job Y. Jindo, *Biblical Metaphor Reconsidered*

The purpose of this chapter is twofold: First, to examine the poetry in chaps.
11–20 and demonstrate how the pieces can—in terms of genre and rhetoric—be
seen productively and reasonably as soliloquy laments of prophet and deity,
where each main speaker responds to impinging realities—notably those we have
just seen unfold. The second task is to suggest how each group of poetic outbursts
works as a set and with its partner set—that is, what each soliloquizer learns on
his own and what we can see listening to both. If, as this book centrally claims,
what the prophet must come to know and trust is that a quasi-voluntary journey
to Babylon is necessary for the survival of God's people—an insight so counterintuitive and abhorrent that he will struggle toward it only with great difficulty
and present it with little apparent success—then the soliloquies of this partnership of YHWH and Jeremiah will evidence the struggle to grasp and appropriate
this truth to share with any who will listen. The unthinkable must be rehearsed,
refused, ruminated, resolved. Implicated here is the question of whether the best
means toward the insight is threat, punishment, and retaliatory violence, or if
profound learning arrives by another route.

We will proceed in three steps. First, I will discuss briefly the six prophetic
soliloquies, often called "confessions," which have been comprehensively treated
in the literature. Second, I will spend more time on the divine soliloquies, not so
readily recognized or read in the literature. And finally, I will suggest the key
learnings of both sets, ask now they intersect each other, and make an additional
proposal about their relation to the prose units in these chapters.

Prophetic Soliloquies

The prophetic soliloquies or so-called confessions of Jeremiah are generally agreed to and can be seen for what they are, some six laments of the prophet.[1] They are here identified as follows:

11:18–23: trusting lamb;
12:1–6: sheep for slaughter;
15:15–21: tasty words;
17:14–18: reluctant shepherd;
18:18–23: the pits;
20:7–13 (or –18): enticing deity.

Scholars ask a variety of questions about them and consequently offer a wealth of insights, generally tending to see the lament or confession form as composed of miscellaneous elements. I suggest that this soliloquy genre is distinctive and constellates the following features: address to deity inviting and occasionally prompting the ascription of divine response; consistently recurring metaphors for deity, prophet, opponents; prophetic quoting of opponent and deity; asseveration of prophetic innocence; call for a retaliatory response or for some envisioned outcome.[2] Other rhetorical features less consistently present include questions and proverbs. These prophetic soliloquies thematize most prominently what we may call the turning of tables: Jeremiah's experience and feelings prompting him to invoke God to visit on his opponents the things he claims they wish for him. Let me here both demonstrate genre consistency and establish crucial content for each.

First prophetic soliloquy: 11:18–23: trusting lamb:[3] The prophet opens his self-talk, speaking both of and to God. Characterizing himself metaphorically as a trusting lamb on the way to slaughter and as a tree whose extirpation is under discussion by others, he names his main concern: the plotting of his foes bent already for some time on the obliteration of his language, ministry, existence, and memory. Now, finally, aware of the danger—thanks be to the knower of hearts and deeds who has informed him and saved him for the moment—Jeremiah invokes God as smelter and judge to sort fairly who deserves what and to recompense Jeremiah's opponents suitably. God is reported to reply affirmatively to that expressed hope, condemning and quoting those who have tried to silence and then sentence to death their prophet kinsman, visiting on them what they had hoped for Jeremiah: destruction of stock. They and their offspring will die, whether by sword or by famine. None will survive.

Second prophetic soliloquy: 12:1–6: sheep for slaughter: Jeremiah speaks here to God, prefacing his question with the admission that he knows he will not win an argument with a just God who is able to rebut any charge Jeremiah might bring, such as divine responsibility for the prospering of the wicked and the concomitant suffering of the good. Implied is the metaphor of God as judge and prophet as defendant with the power differential between arbiter and accused, whether exercised fairly or not. In raising the matter as he does, Jeremiah-plaintiff concedes that God-judge knows better than the prophet can argue, but the very pressing of the case implies that his view may have merit, accomplish something. The question posed is general and metaphoric: why the wicked, planted by God, blossom and thrive, however evil they may actually be, appearing to be healthy when it is not the case. But Jeremiah moves away from that deep and pertinent question to claim his own innocence as grounded in God's knowledge, to beg God to treat these diseased trees like sheep for the slaughter—as in the first lament they had been assessing him in that same image pair. Jeremiah moves on to develop the inverse of his initial theme, claiming that, whatever seems to be the case, the land is *not* thriving but languishing, bereft of bird and beast, due to the presence of the wicked who foul the habitat shared with other creatures. The prophet quotes such people to say that God is blind, sees poorly (perhaps cannot discern good from bad, healthy from sick). This claim as well is brought forward from the first prophetic soliloquy, where Jeremiah claimed—hoped?—that God discerns well.

The rejoinder, which I will take as Jeremiah's "invited divine language," is proverbial, offering us access to what God has observed: <If your own kin have dealt badly with you though they speak smoothly to your face, what when you have serious enemies who do worse?> These soliloquies leave prophet and attentive audience to ponder what has been said: <Get ready for worse, but count on the heart that you asked me to know and test.> Implied as well, I think, is that Jeremiah has learned not to believe his kin when they lie, is gathering resources to withstand any false words from more skillful dissimulators as well. Jeremiah has asked for an assay or diagnosis, and God assures him it is underway but not to expect it to be more pleasant than it has already been. Those who see badly are not to have the last word, whether they are talking about themselves or about deity or prophet. The prophet's initial question is refuted, or deepened. Appearances are not reality.

Third prophetic soliloquy: 15:15–21: tasty words: Jeremiah continues to speak of his opponents, begging God to preserve *him* and destroy *them*, reminding any listening that his own suffering is due to his relationship with God and implying (or leaving us to infer) that his opponents' capacity to inflict suffering rises from their nonrelationship with God. The prophet next explains that God's words, found and devoured, became a joy and a delight to *him,* deepening his identity as "overwhelmingly God's man."[4] He then asserts, almost as though rebutting a false accusation, that he has *not* celebrated and has in fact sat alone, filled with indignation due to his relationship with God, with God's words. Jeremiah moves on to name his indignation metaphorically as the pain of a wound incurable and refusing healing, and he names God—proverbially—as a wadi, unreliable, misleading, disappointing, dangerous.

God replies with bracing advice, urging and commanding the prophet to return and be accepted back, to speak well rather than worthlessly and be strengthened as promised in his call: a fortified wall. It is not quite clear to what the deity's speech is referring, some misstep by the prophet—like claiming his wound as incurable or God as unreliable, the sort of thing the prophet's opponents say? In any case, the prophet's self-justifying words are countered by the deity. The prophet, calling God an transient water source, is challenged to mind his own consistence. Lacking such moves, it seems he cannot expect what God promises in this lament: survival, deliverance, bailing out.

Fourth prophetic soliloquy: 17:14–18: reluctant shepherd: In this lament the prophet pictures himself now as shepherd rather than as clueless sheep, calls out to God for goods recently sought: healing from a wound incurable, rescue from suffering—because YHWH is his praise. Jeremiah quotes his adversaries as sounding unintimidated by the prophet's presence, mocking the word of God such as the prophet might hurl at them: <God's threatening word? Bring it on!> they seem to jeer, suggesting another aspect of incapacity of the prophet to proclaim effectively and reversing their earlier interdiction of such prophetic speech. Reminding God, again, of his own dedication and loyalty, Jeremiah claims he has not abandoned his shepherd's job—difficult though it may be—has not desired the fatal day, perhaps the moment of reckoning that the opponents so insolently called for. The question here may be the one generally familiar from the 'day of the Lord' threats: good news and bad news, but to whom? Jeremiah reminds God consistently in these laments that God knows what the prophet has said, begs God not to become a terror to *him,* the sort of threat Jeremiah will shortly make to Pashhur (20:3), renaming him "terror." Jeremiah calls down on his opponents what they wish for him, urging "disaster and double destruction on those" who have wished it on him. Terror will come, but for whom? Jeremiah begs, <Not me, please.> God's nonreply is prominent, since in each previous lament, we have heard something by way of response.

Fifth prophetic soliloquy:18:18–23: the pits: Here Jeremiah opens by characterizing his opponents: plotting against him, and describing him as expendable, redundant, irrelevant, refuting his words and countering them with their own. Whose words will prevail? Jeremiah implores God for a fair judgment, to rule in his favor and not for his adversaries, perhaps the most consistent petition of these utterances. The proverb is prominently at issue, familiar from where Jeremiah quizzed God about trees and fruit: Does good produce, deserve, and invite evil? But *how* does the proverb address present circumstances, sort reality? Jeremiah points to good deeds not deserving evil as envisioned by those he claims dug a pit for him while he was preaching God's word, or even as interceding for opponents in the face of God's anger, until warned to be silent. But now he urges the opposite, begging that God give *them* over to famine and sword, wiping out mothers and fathers and children, until cries of mourning ring from their houses (consider in light of the silence from his own, given his wifeless, childless, and mourning-less condition). Jeremiah, turning to hunting and trapping language, begs that those who laid snares for his feet be tripped up themselves. Whose words will God heed? Whose words will endure? No reply from God enters this lament, despite the prophet's apparent effort to provoke it. Jeremiah, interceding now in one way, now in another: heeded by God, or not? Heeded on what occasion and when not?

Sixth prophetic soliloquy: 20:7–13–18: enticing deity: This last outburst features the prophet accusing God of having misled and overwhelmed him, while he himself allowed it to happen, with the result that he has become a laughing-stock to his peers. Jeremiah seems to have lost confidence that God hears and will answer in his favor, a point reinforced by the fact that divine response has lacked since the third lament, reassurance since the first prayer. Jeremiah first quotes himself, his words—presumably from God—shouting "terror round about," language not welcome in the ears of those who hear it. Jeremiah names his dilemma—that he now feels, rather than joy and delight (as in his third lament), reproach and derision—and then goes on to share his resolve to remain silent, as previously urged on him by both opponents and deity. But he fails, as God's words *will* emerge from the prophet: a fire in the bones, he says. We are back, it seems, to the complaint that opened this unit, or have drilled into it more deeply: <I am caught in a vortex I can't swim out of.>[5] This complaint, more complex and perhaps more desperate than any preceding, shows Jeremiah overwhelmed by divine words, turning and turned against him by his opponents and perhaps by God as well. Jeremiah hears the words of others quoting his own—God's—words against him: "Terror round about," they are saying as he has said and will again, invitation to denounce him, though he just prayed that the terror indeed on the way not be aimed at him (17:17). His peers, prominent in these prophetic prayers, watch for a stumble or even actively rehearse ways in which they can trick him and deal with him as they feel he deserves (vv. 9–10), taking on the character of the deity who enticed and overpowered.

But suddenly at v. 11, the prophet rebuts that possibility, begging God to look on his heart and assay it (as before), to trip up the feet of those eyeing the prophet's own feet while hoping for a slip. If he has previously wavered, Jeremiah now asseverates that he is God's man and God will deliver him. A quick verse of praise to God is followed at once by another cry, that of the day he was born, a quotation from Job or Job's of him, where he begs for nonexistence.[6]

To add the prophetic lament column, incipiently: What is the prophet learning and thus teaching? Five points: First, the factors of the prophetic laments (address to God, a few standard metaphors—notably the figure of the two trees as signifying human hearts, quotations, asseverations of innocence, calls for retaliation) compose the soliloquy genre consistently. The most elusive facet is divine response, which seems to fall outside the genre in the first lament, to occur within in the second and third as an invited voice, but then ceasing, with effect uncertain. That is, the deity begins as reassuring, then offering a challenge, then a critique, finally falling silent. Insofar as response is expected, we miss it when absent. Second, Jeremiah's laments all center on his opponents' treatment of him, which he feels and claims he does not deserve. Five of these sets of opponents are his human peers, but in the sixth soliloquy, God is accused directly, thus adumbrating earlier stealth reproaches. The prophet consistently asserts his own innocence, though his pattern of turning on others what he hates when they do it to him undercuts his claim somewhat. His begging for his opponents to suffer what they want for him makes him resemble them. The issue of "deserve" is made more complex, as all involved may need to go beyond such simplistic justice. Third, metaphoric terms are strikingly and provocatively shared between prophet and opponents, reinforcing the blur between accuser and accused: sheep due for slaughter; tree whose health and fate are more dire than they appear; trapped and trappers, hunted and hunter changing places; enticers found among humans and deity; the wifeless, childless survivor; the speaker of God's word; terror; wounded participants. Besides noting slippage between accuser and accused, we see some reversals: prophet as lamb and then as reluctant shepherd; prophet as plotted against and then as inveighing against those plotters; prophet claiming to intercede well for his opponents but now to plead for their downfall. The movement seems to be that what began clear—clear edges between himself and them, a precise expectation that God must be on his side and not theirs—becomes messy. He is not so different from them, at least in terms of language. Jeremiah will need to come to see that his fate is more bound up with his adversaries than he would wish it to be.

Fourth, we can hear a set of three questions posed, consistently: Who will survive, and who will be extirpated? Do the deserving get what they presumably deserve—to be blotted out—and will some nondeservers survive? How are such things decided? Things are not what they appear to be, at least as they appear to some. Though God is charged with some responsibility for the apparent unfairness of things, there is no doubt more to be said. Insofar as Jeremiah is caught on the branch of the calculus of who deserves to survive and how God can effect it, the prophet will be an unlikely catalyst for his role in the process. A fifth point follows: Is God a reliable partner to the prophet, or is Jeremiah a reliable partner for the deity? What is apt responsibility? What is the project on which they are working together, that reliability is key? To whom does God listen, and who listens well to God? Can interconnections between God and prophet be subverted? Who experiences God's word, and how? Who "works it" viably, and how so? Jeremiah claims a share, but his opponents take divine language and use it against him. Jeremiah claims to savor God's word, but it also goes bitter for him. He shouts it out and would choke it off, but he is unable to stop himself from uttering. It seems difficult to trust Jeremiah's speech unproblematically. God is not so unfailingly preferential to Jeremiah's view. If Jeremiah is to become effective in his role as persuader of what is radically unthinkable, it will not be by sheer opposition. Jeremiah will not persuade by battering either deity or humans. If the name of the game is retaliation, with people getting what they deserve, there is no way forward for any. If the survival path is to wind fruitfully, it will have to be on some other basis. As Jeremiah's laments conclude, he seems to have conceded, even owned such an insight. Whether he can make use of it productively remains to be seen.

Divine Soliloquies

With considerable work in both standard and evolving form and genre study, I have "guesstimated" a genre of deity discourse, characterized by a set of stable elements, where God speaks with rhetorical and thematic coherence, to be explored here in eight substantial units. These need more attention than do the prophet's laments, since they have not been studied so intensively or as a set and are far more complex than the prophet's laments. My claim is that these eight units work convincingly as stable sense units rather than being simply disorderly piles of formal fragments, as is the usual claim. The hallmarks of the genre are ten, as follows:

Firm or defensible *edges* and a coherent *structure* that works effectively;
Deity as main and *orchestrating speaker,* adequately identified by tag/activity;
Soliloquy/self-talk genre: *purpose* to ponder, resolve, justify, learn;
Other *voices invited* to participate in multiple, complex ways, rarely to their
    credit;

Abundant and skillful use of *rhetorical questions;*

Significant use of *aphoristic or epigramic language* as pivot for decision-making;

A basic, *hosting image sustained* through the unit and contributing significantly
    to meaning and making use of repetition and rhetorically provocative
    language;

Issue under discussion is always *responsibility for crisis:* whose fault?

Divine soliloquizer tends to resolve the problem to the negative;

Attention to the *roles of the prophet* as speaker/writer/character and to our
    reading.

Let us give some attention to how these work, selecting for emphasis the weight-bearing image, the interplay of voices, the logic or rhetorical plan, and the apparent effect. Though I am calling this genre divine soliloquy, it is, of course, prophetic poetic language, catalyzing deity, prophet and audiences to understand what needs learning. If it is the case that Jeremiah's laments show him grappling with a key learning about the bond between himself and God's people, the deity will be ruminating something crucial as well.

    First divine soliloquy: fire and the green olive: 11:15–17:[7] The basic metaphor is the people-in-right-relationship as a leafy and fruitful olive tree but seen now mainly in the breach, almost savored in a fiery destruction. The oil-laden tree suggests both the paneled house of worship and illicit cult, collecting the community at worship: first properly, next falsely, and then—vaporized—not at all. The base image also hosts the range from proper sacrificial fire to false fire, finally on to destructive fire. Those who burn illicitly will be consumed in a larger fire. Harsh and heartbreaking contrasts emerge: What had once been moist, leafy, and olive-laden is quickly reduced to ash; appropriate liturgical sound, overtaken by some sort of criticized exulting, gives way to crackling of broken branches as they burn—implicitly, imaginatively blending with cries of those suffering. Agents become objects, then go out of existence or are recycled to something more basic than once they were.

    The voices are simpler than we will see in some other spots but complex enough. Jostling each other with little grammatical consistency are the divine main speaker, speaking in the first person: "my beloved . . . my house" (v. 15) The address is first to "you" (feminine singular) and then of "her/them," as though over the head of the addressee in appeal to reliable witnesses. Such addressive inconsistency is common in Jeremiah and vintage to this genre, where the soliloquizer shifts person constantly for rhetorical effect, confronting, speaking against, ruminating about, rebutting as needed. We also see a familiar shifting in self-designation, where YHWH uses both first and third person for self-reference, no matter any potential confusion. No one replies verbally here, but the alleged cries and then crackling of the people–as–olive tree are shocking, poignant. Though the divine speaker will typically invite others into these units of self-talk to take roles strategically necessary for the speaker's point to emerge, the only need sounded in this small unit is the crackling of branches being reduced to ash. The speaker interprets plainly as the unit closes (v. 17): The one who planted you has destroyed you, or rather, your provocations in false life and liturgy brought on your own selves the fire that annihilated you. Burning to the Nothing leads to being burned down to nothing.

The logic of the unit, a rhetorical plan, is discernible: Assertion through the clash of intolerable blends, the conflagration ignited eventually by unsustainable incompatibles, jarring mixtures. The false worshipers seem unaware, a point reinforced by their lack of discourse. The sounds they emit while burning come too late. The divine voice is intensely conscious of what is wrong and both accuses directly and also comments as though to some silent but sympathetic witness. The speaker appears to have reached the end of patience, and so the beloved and once-valuable olive with its leaves and fruit is suddenly fired, quickly consumed. The growing outrage of one party overwhelms the clueless habits of the other. At issue is how the people did not grasp the offense of their deeds, weigh the gain of their destructive works. There is only one rhetorical question here (perhaps two implied by the parallelism), starting the unit: "What about my beloved in my house, her doing violence?" Perhaps we do well to feel a sarcastic question or thrust offered at the end of v. 15: "Will you rejoice then?"/< That will make you happy!> The proverbial expression, which in most of these units will function as turning point for the speaker, the wisdom by which the deliberator comes to a decision, are also spare here: I would suggest that such language comes in v. 17: either the image of the leafy olive tree for Israel or the descriptor as the community bearing God's name. The mere presence of what is so painfully absent precipitates the decision to light the fire.

The issue under construction is agency, responsibility for the violence of these reversals, with recognition that the fire is of YHWH but also the counter-charge that the beloved kindled it herself. Fire as anger is alleged metaphorically, also as offering, in war. Who consumes and is consumed, why and how? There is a contrast between the tree as planted and fruit bearing and those same branches snapping as fire kindled destroys them, flames fed by their oil. It is impossible to sort clean responsibility out of so complex an image. What is produced and inversely thwarted: why fruit, why sacrifice? The sacrificers are sacrificed and the worship site immolated, to whose gain, divinity included? The olive tree self-destructs, despite having been named by YHWH. The exultation ironically and accusingly anticipated is presumably snuffed out in the fiery destruction. The short image is characteristic of the YHWH-speech that asserts intense anomalies as if to express deep feeling, to provoke radical insight, to conduce decision. Time is relevant as well, delaying resolution. The rhetorical strategy: to shock into a response? The conflagration of the temple has to have been nearly unthinkable, until it happened. Can this be productive? Can the soliloquy to strengthen the will of the deity, educate the prophet?

Second divine soliloquy: heritage destructive and destroyed: 12:7–13:[8] The host image set is the heritage—comprising what we may call land, people, and implied way of life—both destructive and destroyed. This second divine soliloquy extends the imagery of the first one and sustains the same subject/object ambiguity, melding abandoner and abandoned, victim and victimizer, handing over what has already been frittered away by those evincing little regret. Quickly images tumble from the deity's grief at having forsaken and abandoned his beloved (v.7) to fierce anger at his beloved's treating him as an opponent—a lion in the forest (v. 8). Images toggle so quickly that they are difficult to register, with the ultimate effect being breakdown of clear expectations. Smaller member metaphors contribute to the texture of the heritage. Four animal sets—once in apparent solidarity with the beloved of YHWH—make the deity their foe (vv. 8–9): The lion in the forest roars at YHWH (who is more often lion [for example, 25:30, 38] than "lioned at," as here); a predator threatens the heritage; birds of prey are already present, with additional wild animals now invited to the destruction of the heritage, beckoned by the one who both abandons it and simultaneously decries its bereft condition.[9] These wild animals are, in some sense, not part of the heritage but serve as opponents, though in a deeper sense, they clearly belong to the land but have been "in remission" until defenses are breached. The snarl of owning, sharing, abandoning, and forsaking makes the implied responsibility complex.

The main voice is consistent, its identity not so contestable as sometimes: first-person subjects, pronouns and adjectives testify that the speaker is YHWH. More ambiguous and interesting is the rhetorical question and the command (v. 9), with addressee unspecified. As before, the "guest" in this rumination is God's people, who have no direct discourse but only alleged and inarticulate speech (vv. 8, 11). Here, with persistent ambivalence, the heritage calls out to its owner in threat, in grief. We have in a few verses come full circle: the beloved grieves for the heritage he abandoned, and the destructive land cries out to its angry patron in distress. Predators are part of this scene as well, circling, hovering, and trampling mutely. A shift to third-person reference at v. 10 moves the engagement of deity with heritage to language about leaders (v. 10) and then invaders (v. 12), with the singular subject of v. 11 uncertain: Who has preserved her a desolation?[10]

So the rhetorical strategy leads from the assertion (vv. 7–8) that the heritage and its owner have both acted destructively with a state of hatred ensuing, at least from the perspective of the owner. If v. 9 hides a rhetorical question, its focus suggests something like: <Is it possible that things have come to this, my heritage turned on me like a predator, and I on it?> Then assertions of devastation continue, pile up, intensify: insider-shepherds wrecking the vineyard, trampling it to a horror, making it a desolation (vv. 10–12) that now cries out to God. That heritage shepherds have ruined the place while it cries out, reminding us that humans account for only part of God's garden. Yet no one takes it to heart, the speaker claims, refuting the assertion while making it. More destroyers, these from outside, a third layer, as it were: the heritage, the shepherds, the invaders, but the speaker says he participates as well; all peace is gone. The proverbial language threading all these soliloquies emerges clearly by v. 13: sowing wheat and reaping thorns, spending for what brings no gain. If, as is my claim throughout, the proverbial language provides the "spring" of the unit, the rhetorical means by which the soliloquizer comes to a firm decision, then here we have the deity-prophet contention of agency, responsibility (as in 12:1–6). Since the basic question under rumination is whose responsibility is this catastrophe—shared—and how advanced it is—reversal seems ruled out—the agency of the heritage is clear: outcomes that frustrate the gains of the producers, effort in pursuit of a pointless and fruitless goal. Gnomic language reflects once again on both process—fruitless effort—and outcome—shame at YHWH's anger.

The soliloquy does not neatly assign fault, as the common weal is savaged by all parties. If fault is the word, everyone shares. Plenty of collaborative destruction to go around. The images are drawn from war and defeat, from agricultural and economic collapse. Effect accumulates, compounds, until ruin is advanced. Speakers do not shift, but perspective does. What is happening and why? How to analyze? What to do? Will the heritage survive this destruction? Is destruction the only alternative? Feeling runs deep.

Third divine soliloquy: the flock-whisperer: 13:15–27: This longer divine soliloquy seems a viable unit, set between a pair of prose teaching parables and another poetic divine rumination introduced by a superscription.[11] The immediate challenge is to argue for the unified divine voice: The speaker self-identifies at v. 15b as YHWH, and the identity is reasserted by v. 24., though it is not obvious that God is the speaker throughout. Nor are the marks of a divine soliloquy so clear as in other cases. Commentators call this unit by various names (for example, oracle that starts oddly) and in fact mostly see it as split into three or four pieces.[12] The test for its effectiveness in my genre project requires first, to establish it as a plausible unity, then to urge that the speaker is YHWH throughout, finally to label it as a divine soliloquy by other marks.[13]

The best argument for rhetorical unity is from the root image: shepherding. The plight of the flock opens the unit (v. 15), and that of the shepherd-leaders concludes it (v.27). The thirteen verses making up this piece are held together by various tensions—primary the image of people as sheep in trouble and of leaders as shepherds who have done poorly by the flock. Each set is unable or unwilling to change their ways, to admit trouble. Both sheep and shepherds are presented with choices of space and time, the urgency of diminishing options compounded by self-delusion. Time is running out: dark descending (v. 16), space closing off, foes approaching from the north, the neighborhood undergoing siege and exile (vv. 20–22). At the start, though choices are shrinking, the flock may still be able to choose well, and even the shepherds are issued an invitation. But by the end, no hope remains—a perennial feature of these divine soliloquies, which tend to resolve to dire outcome. A feeling of too-lateness comes to dominate, pushing the hope of change aside first as undesirable, then unlikely, finally impossible.

If the unit is held together by sheep and shepherds pressed by time and space diminishing chances of their survival—worsened by their refusal to be galvanized by their plight—and if they are unified by lack of response that seals their shared though distinct fates, then we ask who is trying to whisper them to safety? It is not strange in these soliloquies for the deity to speak of self in the third person, and so we need not posit a change of speaker on the grounds of toggling reference. The question is whether the unit works well if the deity is seen as speaker throughout. I take seriously the signature of a divine address in the first two verses (vv. 15–16) aiming to persuade the people imaged as sheep stalled in the hills to a safer footing. The speaker bids them to hear and heed, to refrain from being high/going high(er). These addressees are urged as well to give due glory to God, before time runs out. With light diminishing—however desirable daylight might be—with feet stumbling on hilly paths, only disaster can be expected. There *is* no more daylight. The speaker adds as further incentive (v. 17): his tears running down, his eyes weeping in secret places as they contemplate the flock's stranded situation on the heights. Granted, this is a famous place in criticism for Jeremiah's own tears; still, cannot the deity weep when his flock is endangered, doomed, and resistant to entreaty?[14] This is a moment of failure for all concerned. The flock does not respond to the whisperer's cajoling.

With such nonresponse from the sheep, the speaker turns attention to the shepherd-leaders (vv. 18–19): king and his lady (queen or queen mother). Now (via someone's address) *they* are bidden to come lower as well, to take off their crown and settle, to hand over their glory also, presumably to the speaker who has asked it as well from the sheep.[15] Temporal and spatial options are also closing off for them: The Negev is shut down, "all Judah" already gone into exile.[16] The enemy approaches, visible from the north. Where, the speaker asks (v. 20), is the flock given to the king and queen, their glory? <Why be a stubborn shepherd when the sheep are lost?> There is no immediate reply from these addressed, though we know the answer to the question: The flock stumbles unattended—except for the flock-whisperer—on the mountains. The speaker's urging intensifies (v. 21): <What will you say when "it" comes on you—when those you had trained to be master-shepherds (allies, partners) are over you?> This question matches the urgency facing the sheep (v. 16). Like pangs overtaking a woman—expected eventually but still a shock when they actually arrive—so this outcome is inevitable though deniable right up to its onset. The speaker presses the silent addressees to speak, attributing words for these invited royal shepherds (here, the woman) to speak: "Why is this happening to me?" (v. 22). God's answer to this "what will you say" question pried from the queen is returned quickly, even triumphantly: "For the multitude of your iniquity your skirt will be stripped off and your legs laid bare."[17] The speaker is not, I argue, inevitably threatening rape but exposure, the removal of divine clothing from the one who clings to her own crown.

Next (v. 23) the divine speaker turns to proverbial language to make his decision: "Can a Cushite change skin color, a leopard spots?" Clearly not, so the speaker does not have to answer his own questions but add a third member: <Can a steeped wicked one repent?> "You also, can you do good, formed in wickedness?" Another negative, in fact, an impossibility. Change not only *will not* but *cannot* happen. Royal shepherds will not, cannot mend their ways, agree to resign their royal status. The incentive for these addressees is not divine pathos as was felt for the sheep but indignation, though with similar result: freeze, stalemate. So the soliloquizer's resolve is announced in a double image with himself as agent (v. 24–25): <You cannot act? So I will.> The plan already underway moves forward rather than reversing or delaying. The speaker resolves first to scatter the holdout group like chaff before the desert wind, a violent image though not so disturbing as what comes next, maintaining its stress on clothing (vv. 25–26): <This is your lot, the measure of your cloth from me: Since you have forgotten me while trusting in the lie, I myself will be the one to strip off your skirt over your face and your ignominy will be seen, become apparent.> And then, finally and in the last verse of the soliloquy (v. 27), the speaker bursts into a sort of boilerplate of sexual imagery, blunt and accusatory: adultery as idolatry, humans behaving like animals, in the fields and on the hills, violence as uncleanness: How long?

To recap: one speaker, attributing speech to a guest in his own rumination, drawing from her what she should say; one comprehensible unit, tied together by a three circles of powerfully interlocked imagery (sheep-shepherd, time/space diminishing, voluntary/enforced removal). Collaborating factors characteristic of the genre I am arguing for: besides attributed speech, rhetorical questions, proverbial language, resolution to a dread possibility. The logic of the unit can be clarified by additional brief reconsideration of the fruitless appeals, the attributed speech, the rhetorical questions, the proverbial language and their cumulative effect. Attributed speech more prominent in other divine soliloquies is conspicuous by its minimal and grudging character—though, of course, no less revealing. The sheep speak not at all, and the royal woman is a reluctant speaker at best. Urging her to articulate her plight, the divine speaker first prompts her ineffectually and then forces from her the damning and futile "why is this happening to me?" speech, half in her mouth and half in God's. And that is the high point of dialogue, suggesting a determined reluctance to engage, as though the royals have learned that when they enter into speech in God's self-talk, their words will be only turned against them. That, of course, is what happens in self-talk; it is hardly an impartial forum!

But if dialogue is spare, questions abound: where is the flock? (v. 20); what will you say? will not pains overtake you? (v. 21); why is this happening to me? (v. 22). There are two, maybe three questions in the proverbial language: can a Cushite . . . , can a leopard . . . , can you. . . ? (v. 24); and a final one, how long? (v. 27). Similarly, the queen's avoidance of the invitation to anticipate her reactions to what is inevitable, followed by her irritating or poignant "why me?" testify to the root problem exposed in the soliloquy: self-delusion, self-destruction. The question finally wrung from her shows—either or both—refusal to admit or actual failure to see the link between action and reaction, behavior and consequence. And that, I think, is a support beam in this soliloquy: To invest in "the Lie" is to become taken in by it. Since the proverbial speech is also cast in question form, we can catch it here as well. The divine speaker comes to a decision via proverbs. The pair about skin and pelt have two aspects. A creature cannot alter its own hide, nor can any change what grows from the inside. The proverbial sayings are extended or resolved by the third member: That royal shepherds steeped in evil cannot change themselves or even suffer change assists the speaker to know that any action will be his, likely without basically altering those who suffer it. The deity resolves to do what the addressees clearly cannot do, but with no gain for them—for any soliloquy participant. This is truly a negative moment in the unit. The sheep-whisperer turns into a shepherd-shouter, or worse. We may sense the deity's own self-deception here, pretending to discern a decision that in fact has already been made and requires now simply justification, though we, of course, must be privy to it.

The effect of all this on participants within the narrative is nil, even negative. But the deity comes to a decision, is in fact catapulted into the language of hurled insult by the end of the piece. The pattern may not, unfortunately, be difficult to relate to: As indignant speakers get started verbally and receive a dispreferred response, it is all too easy to pile on invective just as the deity does in the final verse here, pointlessly and to the detriment of all. The extratextual impact can also be suggested in two points here. First, I hear powerfully a portrait of self-delusion, the danger of consorting with and investing in the Lie. The issue is not simply recalcitrance or bad will but those comingled with a genuine incapacity, a condition learned in the constant presence of the Lie. To choose to keep company with the Lie is harmful to health. And second: the book of Jeremiah, along with its Hebrew Bible prophet peers, is heavily invested in receiving and perceiving, shaping and speaking forth disapproving, minatory, and even abusive language in God's name. Over time, and within Scripture, it becomes literalized so that God's default silhouette is as drawn here: angry, regretful, determined, justified, retaliatory, and ultimately harsh. Is there a way to preserve the valuable insight while disabling the abusive divine portrait?

Fourth divine soliloquy: wandering feet: 14:1–10: This unit begins with the book narrator's identification of it as God's word to Jeremiah and concludes with the divine speaker's own direct judgment speech.[18] In between those two tags come the testimony of the divine witness (vv. 2–6), the invited participation of other speakers (vv. 7–9), with their pleas trumped and refused (v. 10). In this soliloquy the deity shares a rumination with the prophet, bringing other voices to bear against the vision God describes and contemplates doing. Their words are ultimately unpersuasive, even counterpersuasive. By the end of the unit God, having decided a matter previously uncertain, declares a judgment. The prophet says nothing, charged simply to report the soliloquy.

The base image is surely drought. The first verses (2–6) describe the drought in its various effects: on Jerusalem's gates and passing citizens; on nobles and the servants they send for water; on farmers; on earth that cracks in response to dryness; on animals: the birthing doe and her newborn fawn, the panting wild asses. But an image intersecting is wandering feet, of which we have several instances: servants in search of water, animals desperate for moisture, the deity said to pass heedlessly through instead of stopping to help, and people charged with loving to wander and never thinking to restrain their feet. These potentially unrelated images now join tightly to create the root imagery of the soliloquy, even to suggest a brief plot: Feet wander due to drought, and drought has happened due to wandering feet—causes and effects both religious and sociopolitical. Thickening the texture of this piece is the specific reaction of those suffering drought. Prominent and perhaps unexpected is shame. That the servants of nobles are unable to find water, causing them to cover their faces in shame, invites speculation. Why *shamed* is the question. Implied is moral responsibility, suggested even before the deity says it bluntly at the end of the piece. The humans in the soliloquy confirm emotionally and by gesture what they will shortly deny verbally: responsibility. The animals are shown not so much shamed as acting uncharacteristically: abandoning offspring, going blind from lack of needed nutrients, panting atypically. The earth reacts as though conscious, aware. The drought pushes all creatures to extreme and unaccustomed behaviors—in fact, to death.

As before, smaller images and tropes shape and contribute texture to these main ones: Personification and *abusio:* City gates slump on their foundations, unbalanced by the desiccating and shifting earth on which they rely, testifying to neglect at the hands of those who would normally care for them. Buckets return empty from water searches. Vegetation and herbage are notable only *in absentia.* Earth is described as not only bereft of water where it would be expected to pool but also cracked and dry from a more serious and prolonged drought. Corresponding to earth is heaven, having withheld rain. Merisms abound: gates sagging and voices rising; fruitless action and despairing inaction; silent gates and crying humans; exposed earth, covered heads. The imagery of drought and the wandering and fruitless feet that have caused and respond to it make a lattice of imagery in the speech of this eloquent witness. Key words and catchwords reinforce and link key ideas and themes.[19] Present as well is *accumulatio:* Jeremiah's propensity to speak in triads.[20]

The blend of voices is typical for the divine self-talk: Initially the deity testifies, both to describe and to interpret the mute players' actions.[21] But, as we may recognize from our own self-talk and have seen previously in the prophetic book, "invited guests"—others with language ascribed to them—speak as necessary to assist with the rumination without their words escaping the main ruminator's control. When these voices—of those suffering drought—speak, they utter in the first person plural; address the deity by name, title, and characteristic; offer praise, concessions, requests, questions, and demands (vv. 7–9). Their attributed speech has two parts: First, they bring to their lips some standard contrition, matched by petitions and praise: <Yes, our guilt accuses us, our apostasies and sins. Having admitted that, we expect action, O God whose name we bear, O hope of Israel, O saver> (vv. 7, 9b). They twice address God with titles (or traditional affirmations of confidence): <hope of Israel, savior in trouble-times.> They accuse, as is typical of invited discourse in these soliloquies, with rhetorical questions: <Why should you be like a sojourner passing through, a stranger just spending the night? Why act like a man unable, like a warrior weak?> (vv. 8, 9a). Each rhetorical question accuses, underlines in synthetic parallelism the sense of outrage at God's transience, lack of effective concern, thus highlighting the issue. Both questions and all four images imply lack commitment and effective action, push responsibility toward the deity rather than onto selves: perfunctory contrition, entitled praise, outrage at God rather than compunction for themselves.

But their words are ineffectual, and the deity responds, signing his speech formally, referring to self in the third person, countering what has been urged and drawing a conclusion. The verdict is given not to the "guest speakers" but over their heads, rendering their speech irrelevant though necessary to bring the speaker to a decision. Cued by the divine response it generates, I hear the attributed speech as perfunctory and grudging, as anted up by those feeling they have to say the right things to get the results they want. The admissions of guilt are impersonal and spare. But then picking up on God's report of their own faithless feet seeking water, the quoted speakers counteraccuse divine feet of wandering—God's poor choice. So their speech both compliments and asks while also reproaching the object of their make-nice words. My case is buttressed by the reaction of the orchestrator of voices. Does God ever spurn true repentance? In all the divine soliloquies, the people given speech by God refuse responsibility, thus tipping God into action.

God moves to a verbal counterattack of the peoples' own wandering feet, pronounces that *they* have loved their wandering, have not restrained *their* feet. God finds those feet the basis for deciding not to intervene to help, as has just been asked. The deity does not rebut the peoples' charge but simply brushes past it: <*My* feet unstable and unable? You are the ones who have not slowed *your* traitorous feet, and you've enjoyed every minute of it! And for that reason, for the blend: accusing me of what is your own sin, I will not have pity>.[22] Before moving on, it is important to underline a particular rhetorical feature attending all the divine soliloquies under consideration here, their dependence on the logic of aphorisms. In the eight units I am proposing, the divine soliloquizer typically solves his conundrum with the aid of gnomic utterances, as though selecting from common lore what is needed and customizing it for definitive resolution of a present problem. Here the factor that God selects as rhetorically useful is wandering feet, the image serving up the picture the speaker turns into slogan.[23] How, if the peoples' own wandering feet are the problem, is anything gained when God is accused of the same trait? The language helps the deity decide.

The logic of this exchange: Whatever problem is being pondered by the divine ruminator, presented by him for his own reflection, requires the participation of others, who play roles the divine speaker assigns them, whether we judge it to be what he hoped for or dreaded, to be sincere or insincere, desperate or perfunctory.[24] We, reading, must diagnose the logic, the gain from the soliloquizer's introducing the words of others. I suggest we see these speakers as saying the right thing inadequately and then the wrong thing too forcefully—bad combination. A final comment here, with the whole unit in view: This soliloquy—my reading of it—aims to show how the drought being suffered is both caused by wandering feet and causing them as well. In sociological terms, shame is socially constructed and ascribed rather than simply personal and internal, best described as having both valences: social and moral. A "natural" drought becomes moral as it evokes shame and inexplicable behavior and redirects participants to consider the origin or cause of such effects. The drought and the feet attending it occur as a basic metaphor for the moral ecosphere, an image easy enough for us to grasp, aware of many ways our ethical behavior registers in "nature." As the soliloquy develops, that specific point is stressed by being contested among speaking voices. The shame sensed and expressed wordlessly at one moment and refused verbally at another, is in fact projected onto another. The drought is a pervasive image of human wandering, and the invited voices raise and debate the question of responsibility. Earlier (2:13, 18) Jeremiah develops the negative image of abandoning local springs—artesian water bubbling up—to go abroad for water, specifically to the Nile and the two great eastern rivers. The matter may be linked to worship as well, but effectively the language characterizes the royal quest for Egyptian and Babylonian alliances as problematic.[25] The choice is rendered stark: Either Judah's kings seek to broker some sort of deal where they feel they will maintain some semblance of the way of life they have had, or, as the deity and prophet prefer, they abandon any sense of being brokers and choose to go to Babylon with a modicum of autonomy—granted, not much. These are the very alternatives that God must aim to point beyond.

Finally the effect of this rhetorical piece: Do droughts change hearts? Can chastened and chagrined feet wander their way toward good water? Does scolding conduce to reform? Not tangibly so. This divine soliloquy has no immediate effect on the characters we are given to meet, with the possible exception of the deity himself, who at the end of this unit addresses the prophet with one of the interdictions on Jeremiah's intercession (7:16, 11:14, 14:11, 16:5–9). <Don't even think about begging me to relent.> This language, too, is intensely rhetorical, is aimed in a complex way.[26] God warns Jeremiah not to do what might in fact dissuade God from the purpose just announced. Though Jeremiah had not opened his mouth (and does not do so in God's soliloquies), God tells him to close it, simultaneously admitting that for the prophet to speak is not only possible but to be urgently forbidden. No need to interdict what is not likely to happen, and no need do mount guard against actions easy to ignore. So rhetorically God demonstrates, just on the other side of this soliloquy, a divine fragility combined with a firm resolve to hold fast. The divine character continues to show complexity here, ambivalence and vulnerability. If the rumination is a search or assay for viable options, some seem excluded, but perhaps not all.

Fifth divine soliloquy: tears amid drought: 14:17–22: This short piece, introduced as words of YHWH, handed to the prophet to pass on directly to his hearers, is called by commentators a prophetic lament (vv. 17–19) followed by a communal lament (vv. 19–22).[27] I, rather, construe it as a rumination God shares with invited speakers, uttered with intended effect, though provoking a reply other than ideally desirable. But as a scenario to be proclaimed, it is effective.

There is no marked change of speaker though the shift is evident, with the part-ner speech in this utterance as ascribed, not uncharacteristic of the genre I am aiming to discern.

The basic imagery is moisture and its inversions: tears that will not cease, on-going drought as an implicit larger matrix, grief and eventually anger expressed at aridity and sterility. Related to weeping eyes is discourse of looking, investigat-ing, testifying as to result of the search: active eyes, sights surveyed and reported, some well and others poorly. Seen here, as in the previous divine soliloquy, are destruction and devastation, ignorance and impotence. The drought and tears both persisting show the havoc unending and pervasive. At odds with the natu-ral and social events and their effects witnessed is the sense of God's throne and covenant, which are to be sought, though not simply verbally. As with peace, so with healing: to be approached appropriately.

The voices, less confusing than sometimes, still present challenge. The divine speaker initiates (v. 17), beginning with the outcome of the search: "Let my eyes stream with tears . . . and not cease," followed by the reason for the tears, overt this time rather than hidden as before: <Why should I weep, you ask?> "Because my dear people . . . a great blow . . . a grievous wound" (v.17). And then additional explanation, ramifying both the tears and the assault situation: <Wherever I look, field to city, I see signs of it: sword to famine—effect of drought.> In addition <those whose charge is protection and defense are powerless, plying their trade but without knowledge and without effect> (v. 18). Naming the cause of the tears ends YHWH's first-person speech.

The response, invited or prompted—desired and hoped for—from those for whom the divine speaker is concerned begins at v. 19, continuing to the end of the unit. YHWH quotes them to rejoin (v. 19): <Why have you struck us down with no healing?>[28] Thus is the first part of the divine testimony partly corrobo-rated but also contested: A blow has been landed—major and debilitating—with divine agency charged. <Is this a result of your hating us, that you have struck us beyond healing? Why have you rejected . . . do you loathe . . . have you struck with no healing in sight?> Though the condition is granted, the cause is not. The speakers then move on to concede some responsibility for themselves and their ancestors: <our wickedness . . . the guilt of our ancestors . . . sinners all> (v. 20). In other words, <Yes, this is partly our fault, but, don't get carried away or let us get carried away.> The community here asks God to do what they themselves need to do: <Remember to act for the sake of God's glory and God's throne, and for God's covenant,> in other words, for the sake of the long relation between them and in recognition of mutual obligations. The voice argues that the opponent is YHWH, and implicitly the deity's tears are thus contested. In effect, <Why weep over your own deed?> The people imply their own investigation, running parallel with that of the inspecting deity, turning the responsibility back toward God: "We look for peace . . . healing and find nothing good . . . terror" (their question of v. 19 matching God's implication at v. 17). And the plea: <Do not spurn us, for your name's sake . . . or dishonor your own throne; do not breach your own covenant with us> (v. 21). Those are common enough pleas, that God should act for God's own sake if for no other reason. Will such motivation suffice? The final verse contains the question and the proverbial speech that we have seen before, as though such language would help the interlocutors find the way out of an impasse: <Do the gods of the nations bring the rain, or the heavens themselves? Is it not you, O Lord? In you we hope, for you have done all this> (v. 22). The object of the plaint, here, is the drought. Rain is needed, and who can be asked for it reliably? The drought must end, and those petitioning for it use any means at hand that might be effective.

That the soliloquy breaks off here seems unsatisfactory, but perhaps that is the point: a standoff once again. The deity, grieved, has testified, and the people have been handed inadequate and in fact counterproductive language, have been drawn to reveal that their issue is only peripherally their sin and more urgently their dried-out condition. Only perfunctorily do they own their heritage of guilt while urging that the remedy is with the deity. This language reveals what is wrong, and so there is no reply from the soliloquizer, hearing nothing new. But if we compare this engagement to the nonverbal noise of the first two divine ruminations, or to the faulty language of the third and fourth, is there some progress, some faint hope for growth in insight? What is contested between speakers is basic responsibility. Who will change whose ways, and on the basis of what? Forbidden worship and wrong alliances are the issue—false reliance—and though the people's response names the possibility of their deed, they also undercut it: <Others' gods are not the source of rain.>

The logic is that God testifies to the completeness of the damage without accepting responsibility for it—in fact, the reverse: God is devastated by the devastation. God's testimony at first seems to leave open the question of responsibility. Implied if unasked: <How, why has this happened?> But the guests invited to the soliloquy reply, missing the point. They refuse to entertain any but peripheral responsibility but counteraccuse God, if incredulously, of rejecting, loathing, striking. We may note that on other occasions, YHWH has employed such language, though so far more as a threat than a reality. Now such words may be believed, but not appropriately. "Why have *you* . . . ?" But the solution reached for is not repentance but that God should stay faithful to commitments already undertaken. The onus is placed right back onto God. God is asked to solve the problems. At an impasse, God falls silent, letting the words of the people stand. Threats have not helped, and perhaps they have hindered.

Parallel phrases raise questions, making clear as well what is on the people's mind: <Who else can do rain but you? Whom are we expecting to assist but you, the creator?> Though the drought is moral, as has been suggested previously, water is not the base of what is deficient in the situation the deity has just reported on. And yet to end the drought is what the people think this is about. So the language of aphorisms, though in the mouths of the people, firms up the nonresponse to their pleas by God. <This is not just about drought!> God might well have said. But speech breaks off, and we may assume the tears of the deity do not cease. Effect: human righteousness and defensiveness, divine suffering and failure.

Sixth divine soliloquy: grieving women, whining sons: 15:5–14: This divine soliloquy, even so-called such by some commentators, offers stable edges.[29] The more challenging question is whether it is one continuous piece or isolated fragments. I suggest it is a long divine soliloquy, laced with an unusual number of questions.

In other divine soliloquies, a prominent metaphor and sustained imagery can provide a firm place to ground unity. But here the base metaphor is not immediately clear. Mothers/widows are prominent in a few verses, as are sons in others. But threading through the unit is allusion to something untimely gone or taken: Jerusalem is alone since she departed from her lover, and YHWH seals that choice (vv. 5–6); people are winnowed like wheat but scattered to the winds (v. 7); sons die, and childless women increase (vv. 7–9); goods are given as booty (v. 13); people are exiled (v. 14). So unexpected alienation, the inability to endure and survive as rooted, seems most basic, with mothers and sons being instances of it. The metaphor reads "sudden inability to hold firm" and is shown by "a city abandoning and abandoned—even pushed away" (vv. 5–6); "inability to hold firm" is illumined by winnowing but then scattering of harvest (v. 7a); by wives/mothers bereft of children unexpectedly (vv. 7b-9); by daylight disappeared by noon (v. 9); by people handed to their enemy (v. 9), treasure and booty given away to no gain (v. 13). What any expect to count on is taken or goes from them and they from it. The image may seem less clear in vv. 10b–12, compounded by translation challenges. But the speaker is complaining that he cannot hold onto what he thought was his due.[30] Granted the apparently negative valence of what vanishes untimely, the metaphor sustains the possibility of a group removed from Judah, a fate apparently painful and catastrophic, but possibly salutary, depending on the group's response. This is a piece we have been expecting since the end of the overture, glimpsed in collaborative ministry units b and h.

The voices: The deity is clearly the speaker in vv. 5–9 (tagged in v. 6) addressing first a partner (vv. 5–6) and then a third-person listener (vv. 7–9);

God is named as speaker in vv. 11–12 and implied in vv. 13–14. Though Jerusalem is ostensibly silent in vv. 5–9, the deity prods her to speak, comments on what she is silently or ought to be asking, her voice discernibly implicit in the divine words, spoken *almost* as if from her point of view. The speaker's strategy is to compel her—actually others listening in—to a viewpoint she has resisted so far. The difficulty comes in discerning the speakers in vv. 10–12. Commentators want to assign v. 10 to the prophet, who talks in similar ways elsewhere. But I suggest that the speaker is an untimely taken son, bidden to speak in the divine rumination as his mother Zion was urged previously. This voice laments his existence somewhat classically and uses aphoristic language to support his complaint (v. 10): <Woe is me to have lived! They are all against me and curse me, though I don't deserve it, being neither a lender nor a borrower.> In v. 11 the deity is quoted by the whining son to address a masculine singular person. The son says: <YHWH claims: <<Have I not set you free? Am I not on your side no matter the hard times?>>> My best call here is that the whining and disappeared son has misunderstood God's act, whether deliberately or inadvertently.[31] The son raises incipiently and without insight what may be the case: assistance, liberation, or more specifically, that removal from the land as salutary. The closest match for this utterance occurred in 4:10, where one of Jeremiah's first addresses to God was to say God had in some way misled the people into thinking something bad was good: <This is working well for you!> The presence of it here, again, underlines its significance, as in God's soliloquy, the son is scripted to miss the point that "going off untimely" might be good. Hearing such talk—ventriloquizing and appraising it—the deity reclaims control of the soliloquy discourse, makes a firm resolve with the help of the aphoristic thinking introduced by the son—both his own whining and his "misquote" of God—and demonstrates that the viewpoint of the son is wrong—incorrect and egregious.[32] God's threats conclude this soliloquy harshly, as members of this genre almost inevitably do. Those who cannot take an early resettling will perish in their refusal.

So this soliloquy is just that, the self-talk of the deity who ponders what bereft mother Jerusalem and her exiled son should and should not be saying, faulting and rebutting both their silence and their attributed speech. The invited voice—here, the intrusive voice of the son—is disclaiming his own responsibility and counteraccusing the deity, two constants in this genre, part of the self-talk strategy. And as is again typical, the inadequate language provokes divine correction. The most obvious purpose of self-talk is self-vindication, but it may also conduce to self-knowledge on the part of participant-listeners—those listening as Jeremiah's God proclaims this piece of revelation. The change of address from feminine to masculine fits the participants and is not anomalous. The shift from second person to language about parties not present makes sense as well, since in a soliloquy, the others are in fact not actually present and the speaker can justify self or explain as though to a sympathetic witness.

In order to appreciate the logic of this piece, we need now to scrutinize the questions asked in the unit and to understand the aphoristic language crossing both imagery and voices. There are arguably six questions in this unit.[33] The first three (v. 5) are effective though not difficult. The deity, speaking, asks Jerusalem in three ways who will meet her need for kindness, with the clear implication that no one will do so—with blame not to absent condolers but to the uncondoled. The questions drip reproach and blame without quite losing the undertone of pathos as well. The threefold question underlines the fault, intensifies the shame.[34] The speaker next moves from these questions to justification for the shocking actions he admits to, with the result that the blame is Jerusalem's not the deity's, even to the point of hosting his <I got tired of relenting> comment.[35]

The next two questions (v. 11) are more difficult in several respects. Crucial is to identify who is speaking and who addressed.[36] In my construction, where the speaker is a recalcitrant son indignantly misunderstanding the deity, the issue is how to translate and then make sense of the questions. They are parallel to each other, and ask (assert) something like <Have I not liberated you//have I not met/stood by you in tough times?> I take them to refer not to God's dealing with Jeremiah but to son Judah's reproach of what God *seems* not to have done but claims to have done. <You, God, said, <<Didn't I do my part for you?>>> To which the son says <No!> The issue at dispute, then is whether God's action of untimely removal was a help or not. As suggested previously, this is the crucial learning of this section, perhaps of the whole book: How can God resolve, Jeremiah understand, support, and proclaim effectively that an early and somewhat orderly departure is helpful, salvific? Here it is clear that not every son "gone off untimely" has yet understood or made useful his fate nor will he inevitably do so.

The last question (v. 12), also proverbial, offers its share of challenges to interpreters. I hear it also in the mouth of the prematurely disappeared son of Jerusalem but attributed to the deity as though he were reproaching the human speaker. Being proverbial, it has no stable meaning but elucidates a particular situation. Abstract proverbial language seems obvious, even trite, but its power lies in the context, assumptions, and rhetorical strategies of the user. In these divine soliloquies, aphoristic language helps the soliloquizer come to decisions. Here not the translation but the referent is the problem: "Can iron from the north break iron and bronze?" Is the proverb to be answered with a yes or a no, and by whom, thinking what? If iron from the north is "the foe," and if iron and bronze are Judah (specifically the son here who is whining about his undeserved fate),then—in the deity's "original" mouth the answer should be yes, the foe is stronger than Judah; once the quote emerges from the mouth of the son, the tone will shift to suggest that though God had promised help, it did not come through as anticipated.[37] Again the contentious issue is whose responsibility are these deeds and their redress, and new is whether "gone off untimely" is a help or a hindrance. The proverb may sort the issue of whether removal might be helpful. The other aphorism is uttered by the complainer in v. 10, who says that though he is involved in neither lending nor borrowing—activities generally understood as causing social friction—he is under attack of some kind. It is a meristic claim of innocence, at least insofar as the suffering being experienced. <I've done nothing to deserve *that*.> If one lent money, then the borrowers might have cause to resent him; or if he were himself a debtor, those whom he owed might come after him. But by the totalizing logic of merisms, this speaker cannot seem to find any fault in himself at all!

The deity, as is typical in the eight instances of this genre, comes to a firm decision guided by questions and gnomic language. Resolution: The punishment will not abate but intensify. The speaker has recited a string of terrible things— winnowing, bereaving, killing—which did not change behaviors. Consequently, more episodes ensued, with God tiring of relenting and son Judah showing no sign of repenting. Jerusalem, invited to explain herself in v. 5 says nothing, but son Judah, blurting out a rather cosmic claim of innocence in v. 10 and then compounding it by accusing the deity wrongly, is what brings God to the boil in vv. 13–14, where the depredation of goods and people will continue until they are both removed to a strange land with no gain accruing, no benefit from any of the brokering: fruitless exile. God likens the process to a fire that once kindled, feeds on the fuel until there is nothing left to be consumed. In a classic metaphor for anger, God owns a rage insatiable and unstoppable. The deity and humans are interlocked, collaborating for destruction. There is no gain here, nothing helpful when it is only resisted.

To converge the impact of this divine soliloquy: The topic for the deity's pondering is the unexpected bereavement of mother Jerusalem and disappearance of Judah/sons taken off against expectation. The topic is not rare in the book of Jeremiah: Why is the catastrophe happening, and whose fault is it understood to be? Is "taken off" inevitably a catastrophe? How might it not be wholly negative? What emerges here is the consistent issue of responsibility: The divine soliloquies are designed to allow the deity, helped by speech of invited guests, to enact the refusal of Jerusalem and sons to take responsibility for their own misdeeds or to reach out in any way to the one who might help them. The soliloquy guests leave YHWH "no alternative" but to move ahead with the divine plans. The prophet, as just instructed, does not intercede. Those who cannot understand their best and only true option are consigned to the pair that will not be useful: death in the land or eventual removal by force to exile. The middle choice remains unsaid.

Seventh divine soliloquy: hearts indelible, irrevocable, gone off 16:19–17:13: This poetic unit nestling between the eighth prose teaching and a fourth prophetic lament/confession is split by virtually all commentators, who assign it to various speakers.[38] So to claim it as a unit of divine soliloquy—with just two invited quotations at its edges—is far from obvious. There are also grave textual difficulties. My challenge is to see how it works as a unit of divine self-talk—sibling to seven other such units, and to claim it as God's prime moment of insight.

The firmest place to stake my genre claim is rhetorical structure, offered here as follows:

- A. *introduction 16:19–21: a pair of "invited quotes" and then a divine comment on them:*

o 1. One pair of claims addressed to the deity: 16:19:

- three asseverations of a speaker: YHWH my strength, my stronghold, my refuge on a day of distress; v. 19a;
- two claims by the same speaker about nations: they will come to YHWH from the ends of the earth with a confession, quoted: surely a lie our fathers inherited, wind; no gain in them. v. 19b;

o 2. Rumination by deity in response: 16:20–21:

- question/aphorism: Does a human make itself gods? [No!] So they aren't gods! v. 20;
- decision: I will "learn them" three things: my hand, my power, my name: YHWH. v. 21;

- B. *Central section of three more extensive divine ruminations: 17:1–11:*

o 1. Claim regarding the condition of Judah, consequences, condition of YHWH: 17:1–4

- sin of Judah is etched: how—with two tools; where—on tablets of heart, on horns of altars; //When her children remember: what—altars and asherahs; where—trees, high hills, mountains of fields;
- consequence: your security and wealth//treasures I will give as plunder, your high places [I will give] for your sons in all your borders;

- The numbers spelled out refer to the blended sets.
- ■ The prose narratives of deity/prophet partnership are represented by the # lowercase letter used above.
- o 'God's prophetic soliloquies by number.
- Jeremiah's prophetic soliloquies by number.

- consequence: you shall let drop for yourself your heritage that I gave you, I will make you serve your foe in a land you don't know;
- collaboration: My anger is a fire you have kindled in my anger/nose, forever burning;

o 2. Alternative trees: 17:5–8:

- cursed the one who trusts in mortals//who makes flesh a strength//who turns the heart from YHWH:
  s/he will become a juniper in the arabah//he will not see good if it comes,
  s/he dwells in wilderness, salt waste, uninhabited;
- Blessed the one who trusts in YHWH//YHWH becomes his/her trust:
  s/he is like a tree transplanted by a stream, sending out its roots//not fearing if heat comes;[39] it will make luxuriant leaves, not worry even in drought, not stop bearing fruit;

o 3. The human heart: 17:9–11:

- Assertion: twisted the heart . . . more than all . . . desperately sick, v. 9a;[40]
- Question, answer, purpose/outcome : Who can know it? I YHWH probe heart/test kidneys v. 10, to give all according to their ways//. . . to the fruit of their deeds;
- Assertion: . . . [someone] nests but does not hatch//one makes riches but not with justice; in half of a span s/he leaves it, ends a fool vv. 11–12;

- C. Conclusion: a pair of "invited quotes" and a rejoining comment: vv. 12–13:

o 1. Three quoted asseverations addressed to deity and commented on: vv. 12–13a:

- throne of glory, high up from the first; place of our holiness; hope of Israel:
- YHWH, all abandoning you will be shamed;

o 2. Response/concurrence/decision of deity: v. 13b:

- result: All turning aside from me will be written in the earth;[41]
- reason: For they abandoned the fountain of living waters // YHWH.

In the face of vast scholarly opinion seeing virtually no unity here (beyond catch-words), let me make a few modest claims. The introduction and conclusion (A, C) match in general structure: alternate views expressed, with a nondivine speaker addressing praise and opinion to the deity, who responds with a plan. But the first divine plan ("I will make them know") is somewhat undercut by the second (in effect, some will refuse my knowledge). God comes to learn something, resolve some matter. In the first trope there is an unexpected turning to God, but by the end the all too familiar turning from God. The central section (B) has two units (1, 3) surrounding its center (2, the pair of trees). The first of the ruminations, though negative, stresses the interrelationship between what humans do and God does; the third set of language relies less on God's role but stresses the incorrigibility of the human players named. God has shifted viewpoints while soliloquizing. The two trees, central to the whole section, show that same thing: The first tree is on its own and beyond help, while the second is able to collaborate with Life even in difficult times. Central issues: agency, responsibility.

Assigning most of the section's speech to the deity does not seem difficult except for the opening and closing lines, which are clearly enough not the same speaker.[42] God does not make such statements of self-praise, even if sometimes talking of self in the third person. There are several specific markers of God-talk (16:21, 17:5, 10) and of actions that the deity is the obvious one to perform (17:3, 4). God speaks, typically in this ruminative genre, both *about* Judah (16:21, 17:1–2) and *to* Judah (17:3–4); God uses first-person pronouns (17:3) but other times third-person (17:5, 7, 13). The divine speaker also throws out a question as to a sympathetic listener (perhaps most obviously the prophet).[43] The only speaker invited into this rumination is the voice at the edges of it, which I will call unrepentant or baffled Judah, speaking, as it were, to set God off on the soliloquy. So the first invited speech is not "friendly," since God contradicts the sentiments. Hence I mark that speech as flawed in some way, needing to be argued with, as again we all know happens in our own self-talk. The closing words do not evoke correction and so may be better. That is, though these comments of 16:19 and 17:12 would sound inoffensive if we met them in another rhetorical situation, here they may not be so benign, since God contests at least the first of them. The final words may be what has been learned, though we have to ask how so. The deity, struggling, is moving toward insight and decision, Jeremiah tells us.

The divine rumination does not lack questions and aphorisms, which need comment before we move on to consider the imagery. Probing questions: God asks one at 16:20 and another at 17:9: "Does a human make his own gods?" And "Who can understand the human heart, in all its sickness?" The questions are in each case answered by the asker, who ramifies each, drawing inferences. The first answer: <No, since humans do not make Gods for themselves, what they have made is not a God.> God resolves to be the "maker," to do the work needed to make humans know who God truly is. The second answer: <God alone knows the heart, not humans themselves; and moreover, it is God's job to recompense hearts accordingly.> Both questions and responding claims single out work that is peculiar to the deity but that others might arrogate to themselves. Humans cannot make God, and though God has in some sense made humans, there is a limit to what more can be accomplished. God is learning limits.

Aphoristic language: As before, questions and aphorisms help the divine ponderer, and possibly here the invited speakers. There is no shortage of aphoristic language.[44] The two pieces I will deal with are the quotations opening and concluding the piece, where God is praised for divine qualities to which the speaker pledges allegiance. Three praises and two claims at the opening: God as the speaker's strength, stronghold, and refuge, and YHWH as the goal of the nations who own that their former heritage is a useless lie. And a matched utterance at the end: God as the speaker's glory, holiness, and hope, so to turn away from such a one is shaming. To hear those words spoken spurs the deity to comment. Why? As noted previously, it is not the words themselves but the way they bounce in context that signifies, that makes a problem: who says them, and why. Without knowing precisely the particulars of those matters, I infer fault from God's judgment of inadequacy, offense. God rejoins the first by making an observation about false claims about God and then with a resolution that this time, *this time* God will make the knowledge of who he is stick. But the final outburst from God is an admission that such "sticky knowledge" is not possible for all and that those who resist it will have their names written in earth because of their basic choice: exchanging the source of life for death, refusing the source of water. The middle part of the soliloquy helps us know how God decides that all the "informing" in the world will not lead to the hearts of all being "informed." Hearts go off.

Having disassembled the pieces for closer examination, how do we read the soliloquy when it is reassembled? I suggest: God imaginatively presents a Judahite glibly reciting certain standard claims about who YHWH is, then following these up with a description of the nations themselves owning that YHWH is their deity while forsaking the commitments of their ancestors as false and futile. The words are potentially, theoretically good, but God takes offense and says humans do not come to such words on their own—not Judah and certainly not the nations. But God resolves to help—even make—them learn this vital information: <This time they *will* learn and I *will* teach them so that they *do* know effectively.> But by the end of this whole unit, when the Judah voice offers another triad of praise of YHWH and repudiates those who stray, God sweeps past the glib praise to agree with the final outcome: God now confirms that all will *not* be taught about YHWH but some will turn away, without God's being able to prevent it. And, concludes the deity, their names will be inscribed in earth and the nature of their sin pronounced: mistaking for fresh and natural springs the opposite.

In between those matched units, how does God ponder, decide, soliloquize his conundrum to practical gain, and what other clue are we given? Three moments. In the first rumination, God reflects on the engraved nature of Judah's sinful heart, scored so deeply that Judah and offspring persist in false allegiances, with the consequence that YHWH and Judah together throw away the gifts Judah had been given. Judah kindles and YHWH burns unquenchably. There is nothing hopeful, no alternative to the deep sin that leads to more sin. Destructive agency is shared, collaborative. The middle portion of divine reflection, the center of the whole soliloquy, is a beautifully balanced reflection on human ways, seen as the mysteriously contrasting trees. Again agency, responsibility. Neither tree escapes challenge, but the tree trusting in itself is blind to what good comes its way and so compounds its choices until, languishing in the desert, it dries out. The other tree, trusting differently, is met differently and produces differently, not seeing or fearing when bad comes, but stretching toward water to make leaves and fruit with the crucial moisture. One tree refuses water/life while the other—transplanted—revels in it, collaborates with what moisture there is. Finally the section of rumination comments on the first two: <What about those human hearts?> God asks, remarks, pronounces: <Pretty tough, the most challenging of all cardial specimens.> All God can do—and only God can do it—is discern them, sort them, recompense what they have already invested in. God appears to have given up on "informing them," seems content to go to the sites where hearts are not utterly closed off, to be available there for collaboration. The comment on that divine job description reinforces what has just been said: A creature who broods without hatching, one who piles up unjustly, will get precisely the apt return on the investment: notably no offspring and false riches, ultimately the label of "fool." God makes no move to intervene. By the end there is not even the collaborative image of one igniting and the other burning. God speaks alone and says the most that will happen is that the false claim will be laid bare, will be named. The concluding comment replays the imagery of the middle of the rumination: the refusal of water by the "thirstless heart." God seems to be drawing back, to have learned some limits when dealing with human hearts that are incorrigible, which is not all of them.

Finally a quick comment on the basic imagery that tends to pervade and unify these divine ruminations: the deciding and decided heart (alluded to in 16:19–21 and named explicitly in 17:1–2, 5, 7–10), the heart perhaps rewritable but ultimately made up and committed irrevocably. God's reflection begins with the possibility of changing hearts but drifts toward discerning and classifying them, compounding their choices. The unit bristles with imagery about the making up of hearts: They are made to know (16:21), written, engraved with permanent marks, analogous to the way altars are (apparently) inscribed and thus drawing the children of worshipers into false worship (17:1). Some hearts may claim to be reprogrammed while others are not. Bad-heart parents produce bad-heart children. Hearts remember. The imprinting of hearts from one generation to the next leads to the loss of the heritage goods, sold off to no gain for any (vv. 3–4), not ransom so much as plunder, heritage let go to no purpose, perhaps unavoidably, surely pointlessly. Hearts go off, often of their own accord, without hope of rescue. Two kinds of hearts are contrasted as trees: those that rely on humans and those that trust in God. Each tree is stuck in a hot, dry, and challenging place (vv. 5–8). One of the trees cannot see good, much less respond. But the other does better, is transplanted near enough to water as to stretch toward it. This second tree does not lose focus when heat and even drought come, as may happen. It sends its roots to water and retains leaves, even bears fruit. The heart is summed up in v. 9–10, inscrutable to all but YHWH, who alone can assay it and will do so. This soliloquy, like the others, is about responsibility, with the deity learning that aside from some gentle collaboration, humans will mostly go their own way. God learns here the limits of divine power. The responsibility for the looming catastrophe is the human heart, little for God to do but point out, label, recompense—or transplant.

Eighth divine soliloquy: provocative anomalies: 18:13–17: This final and brief divine soliloquy is clearly a speech of YHWH, urging an action, asking a pair of metaphoric questions, responding to those queries first with one reading of the image but followed up with another metaphor of departure that details some consequences. So we have a rumination of YHWH, addressing first an unidentified plural, perhaps the nations themselves or, more likely, those on site among the nations to seek information. In any case the witnesses are envisioned as understanding and agreeing with the speaker, once a suitable inquiry has been accomplished (though we do not hear them report back). The addressees are clearly the partner in the soliloquy, contrasted with another group spoken about rather than to. We saw a similar thing as the overture ended in Jeremiah 10.

The basic metaphor source domain comprises factors that—anomalously, unthinkably—get out of their proper place, including the nations as a place where valuable information might be sought. Natural elements like water—snow on high peaks, water streams in high mountain areas, cold flowing streams (v. 14)—leave their place, go inexplicably astray. Part of what is provocative is the possibility of reading the snow and water as either subjects or objects: That is, the Hebrew allows both for the snow and water to abandon their accustomed places, or for one to abandon them. As most clearly exploited by the divine speaker, the inexplicable abandonment is people of deity, the path long known for something trivial and foolish: agency, responsibility. With this reading, the metaphor targets worship offered and worshipers either offering to what is empty or offering in vain, without effect, badly, pointlessly, harmfully. Such worshipers will be blown away before an enemy, scattered as if by wind, end up on the wrong side of the deity: back rather than face (v. 17), as God pictures self turning away after helping scatter the people, walking away from them as they languish out of place.

But if the source elements of the image are objects, then we can rethink the source and target: a primordial site, with its erstwhile reliable snow and fresh water, will be abandoned; those long accustomed to ancient paths will be led on byways strange to them, leaving behind them a land that will become desolate in their absence. As before, one way to intensify a basic image is to describe others' reactions as well as a main group's experience, and so heads of witnesses shaking and their mouths hissing testify to the anomaly under discussion: the group abandoning their deity and the group being led from its accustomed heritage. The hissing of wind-as-breath testifies to the shock of this complex image.

The voices are easier than sometimes: The deity speaks, to someone and of someone. The objects of discussion do not speak, and invited witnesses (or witness-interrogators) make no report, yet. Others on site emote without language but by gesture, sound. Proverbial language emerges in v. 14 and serves as warrant for the plan—plans?—of the deity. God's questions highlight the logic of the soliloquy, intensifying the metaphor: Imagine melting mountain snow—impossible! Imagine false worship: Hardly possible! But why is empty worship so unthinkable at this point? It may be offensive, but unthinkable seems odd. Perhaps the present issues around "climate change" and melting frozen water help us here: This behavior is not puzzling so much as ominous, terminal, signaling a danger long courted that will indeed arrive: Wrong-place worship will lead to wrong-place living. But imagine as well the unthinkable notion that the deity would lead a people into the heartland of the opponent, that something good might come of that. But inquire, and let us see, the voice urges. Ask those among the nations, in the know. So the soliloquy with its use of proverbs to help the "ponderer" come to a justifiable plan of action is not so much gleaned from new behavior but from watershed behavior: snow melting is not so easily reversed. A decision to blow the false or vain worshipers away is justified on the basis of irreversibility. And the others? Can anything good come from such an experience? We have yet to hear. But to this place have we been led, again, and primarily by God, almost not at all by the prophet as character.

To add this column of information, as we did with Jeremiah's prayers: What are the trends in these divine soliloquies? Three points by way of summary: First, what has been performed here works as a genre, looser than a form, constellating a stable set of elements in ever-fresh but coherent ways, allowing discernible change as well as consistency. These eight divine soliloquies meet the requirements claimed for them at the start of the unit. Rumination—by metaphor, invited dialogue, question, and proverb—has indeed proceeded, brooding and repeating but moving toward possible resolution to the impacted central issue of the book: How God's project with Judah can thrive. If, as argued, these soliloquies rehearse God moving toward a decision the prophet and hearers need to accept, resolution emerges toward the end, though incipiently: untimely removal of some who can collaborate in the transplanting—an insight we did not hear in the Jeremiah laments, where though expressing resolve to hang in with God, the language is primarily of retaliation. If Jeremiah has a role in the breakthrough, he does not know it yet.

Second, as we look across the constituent soliloquy elements, we see metaphors beginning as extreme and irreversible: destructive fire, heritage trashed, darkness falling, time running out, trees doomed to drought, skin and pelt indelible, hearts incorrigible. But the last three units move to metaphors of things removed untimely, inexplicably, but possibly in certain cases for the good: a tree transplanted and thriving, local waters gone from accustomed heights, paths leading to new places. The voices can be construed in a similar way: The invited guest speakers—first silent or nonverbal, then emitting grudgingly, blaming and accusing their divine interlocutor, denying their own responsibility. But shortly before the last of God's laments, a whining son says what is true, though without himself registering or believing it, and in the seventh soliloquy, false praise, or pious words spoken insincerely give way to words of praise not reproached by God. Finally, those living among the nations are asked to give testimony about anomalies and seem able to do so. Mark Biddle summarizes that the voices can be sorted by attending to language: God pushed to the limits though not quite beyond; the people not able to see what they have done, why they are charged; the prophet as petulant.[45] I think that is generally accurate while disregarding the possibility of progression. God inches beyond stalemate and will draw a few others with him.

Third, the topic consistently under consideration for God has been that of agency and responsibility. For the divine speaker the question of responsibility is not difficult, at least at the surface: God—having consistently proffered relationship—finds the people as inveterately answerable for their persistent refusal of relationship. But running alongside and eventually overtaking that appraisal in God's ruminations is the sense that they cannot help themselves, are deeply and mysteriously incapable of doing much better. If change will come, it must be radically assisted. It will not, cannot be self-starting or self-sustaining. The more uncertain issue involves the remedy, which I think God works out with the speakers in his soliloquies—and notably, not yet with the persona of the prophet. The action will be primarily God's, possible in certain cases when the peoples' most egregious utterances die back. The change agent is the deity, and the recipients are those who go off untimely, are transplanted, traverse alien paths, end up among the nations. The open question is whether such a cure will be sufficient even for a few. So much is dug in, slated for destruction, about to be burned to ash, given over to foraging animals. This, I suggest, is the fate of Judah and those who remain there or are carted off from there after brutal defeat, a fate to be symbolized by Jeremiah himself. The unthinkable is the early rescue of a few, by removal to a place that seems almost wholly negative, punitive, bitter, enacted and enforced in divine anger—but not without a wisp of hope. *How* can this option happen? The question left open, it seems, possibly batted now to the prophet, is whether this can be salvific in any sense, or not. We reading have to recall that the quasi-voluntary exile of a small group seems obvious and safe to us now but will have been almost unimaginable at the time it becomes proposed. What will be the prophet's role in this rescue in which he will not be included?

Converging and Concluding

There remains, now, one last question to address to this set of material, ranging from chapter 11 to 20. How to follow the trajectory of the twelve prose collaborative ministry scenes, the six prophetic laments, and the eight divine soliloquies, as presently arranged in the book? That is, what emerges as the deity and prophet collaborate and then ruminate, in our presence? If I am right to be looking for some sort of progress, the intercalation of these units is the definitive place to show it, to see it. Let us consider seven steps and suggest some development:

- *One: Clear and Hopeless: 11:1-12:13:*

- #a: The basic charge is brought: a long, persistent pattern of divine offer refused; God resolves to move ahead with reprisals.
- o #1: The sentence is carried out: God's beloved but rebellious olive tree is consumed by fire, with nothing left over.
- #1: The prophet, endangered, wants revenge: Once threatened and unaware of what was happening, he now knows and wants help from God, who seems agreeable.
- #2: The prophet, still and additionally endangered, calls for reprisals; God warns him that there is harder terrain ahead.
- o #2: The sentence is carried out: The ancient heritage lies desolate—loss for all.

- *Two: Clear and Hopeless, with Alternatives Raised but Not Likely: 12:14-14:10:*

- #b: Uprooting is possible for some encroachers and encroached; if those who have learned poorly and taught badly in the past can do better, then good may come; but there is no inevitability, and it seems unlikely.
- #c: To cease clinging (people to deity) is the basic problem, whether it happens in Judah or at the Euphrates; survival is not simply about geography.
- #d: Jars are filled full with destructive liquid and smashed, with those theoretically witnessing the act careening from smug to clueless, from observers to implicated.

- The numbers spelled out refer to the blended sets.
- The prose narratives of deity/prophet partnership are represented by the # lowercase letter used above.
- o 'God's prophetic soliloquies by number.
- Jeremiah's prophetic soliloquies by number.

○ #3: Alternatives are urged but rejected: It may not be too late for the sheep and shepherds in Judah, but there is no sign that they can move from where they are stuck.

○ #4: Alternatives again urged and rejected: Feet in search of water fail, not least because they accuse God of what they themselves are doing.

● *Three: No Human Initiative (or Even Response) Is Likely: 14:11-22:*

■ #e: The prophet will not intercede nor God attend to intercession.

○ #5: YHWH, if at a point of insight, stiffens his resolve: Though seeing that the people of Judah are radically incapable of understanding their own predicament and persist in blaming God and feeling entitled to rescue, the deity resists helping.

● *Four: No Human Initiative, but One Inadvertent Possibility Named: 15:1-21:*

■ #f: Intercession is again forbidden, the role of effective intercessor removed from Jeremiah; intercession will not help the problem; rather, the prophet will direct various groups toward their assigned fates.

○ #6: The deity raises the possibility and implications of gone off untimely; some experiencing it complain that it is not helpful.

• #3: Words start one way and invert, transform: Jeremiah, still complaining of his treatment, reflects on how God's words feel now one way, now another; God recommissions him, urges him to maintain integrity in his call.

● *Five: Flailing Continues: 16:1-17:18:*

■ #g: The prophet learns how to fulfill his role by acting out what the whole group is experiencing, a demonstration in negative space, as it were.

■ h: Some may leave the land not to positive effect; return sounds punitive: fishers' hooks and hunters' snares will get the exiled back.

○ #7: YHWH decides hearts cannot help themselves but can be transplanted and survive. This is a major shift, as God seems to achieve clarity about what is not going to work, ever.

• #4: Jeremiah self-identifies as a reluctant player, hoping now to do no harm; he reflects on what is difficult for him, though he is faithful to it, as best he can do; he still wants help for himself and shame for his opponents.

● *Six: A Glimmer or Two: 17:19-18:23:*

■ #i: Gate options: The possibility of business as usual in Judah and Jerusalem is broached: Can life continue as it is? It could, God says, but with no indication that the people can do what is asked, remaining and thriving is not a viable option.

■ #j: Pottery: The demonstration at the pottery wheel shows bad pots getting thwacked down and fresh pots started. We may anticipate without having seen so that a few good pots may finish up well at the wheel.

○ #8: Waters inexplicably on the move: God contemplates how long-settled things may move, and though unwelcome, it may not be bad. God sees and says it, invites witnesses.

• #5: Feeling thwarted, wanting revenge, Jeremiah seems stuck in the same place, and we are sensing that his role will be worked out largely in negative space.

• *Seven: Distinctions Emerge: 19:1-20:18:*

▪ #k: Potsherds a disaster: There are no viable pots in Judah, only smashing to death.

▪ #l: Jeremiah now moves into his next step, enacting: Having coministered, lamented, and presumably witnessed God's soliloquies (though never with a role in them), Jeremiah finally now undertakes an action on his own: His preaching and prophesying result in his first incarceration; but when he has been freed, he uses his "stocks experience" to intensify what he has said: not even all who go out of the land will thrive. Removal in itself will not suffice.

• #6: Though feeling totally wretched, Jeremiah decides to trust God nonetheless: In this last lament, he feels no better in any discernible way (arguably worse), but he commits his cause to God nonetheless. This is his role.

So: What has been worked out is that there is no viable option of remaining in Judah, nor is removal in itself a hopeful promise. But things will not remain as they are, and no amelioration of the threatening factors is possible. To go off early and unexpectedly may be the best path, for those who can take it and find life. How Jeremiah will help communicate that remains unclear. And to that portion of his life as a prophet we will now turn.

5

WELL-BEING OR DISASTER— THE CASE ARGUED

Chapters 21–39

> The tragic plot of prophecy may be traced to the undermining of the false
> security of those ruling Israelites who unheedingly build their domains of
> power at the expense of community, only to see them come crashing down
> in military and political defeat. The tragedy of these leaders is sometimes
> viewed as "unknowing," but it is finally stigmatized as willful and culpable
> ignorance, a choosing not to know at one level what is known at another.
>
> Norman Gottwald, "Tragedy and Comedy"

As we have done with the complex material of Jeremiah 11–20—looking through
it twice so as to catch more detail and significance, so we will consider this long
section of Jeremiah 21–39 twice: first, to suggest an overall pattern into which
the material seems to fit—a nonsymmetrical chiasm; second, to offer a closer
examination of Jeremiah's interactions with King Zedekiah and eventually of his
relationship with the community already living in Babylon. As throughout, our
main focus is the characterization of the prophet and the nature of his contribution to God's project with Judah. As we concluded the previous unit, comprising
both prose material, where deity and prophet worked together with a nonrespon-
sive populace, and also poetry, where each soliloquized repeatedly, I suggested
God was heard concluding that any salvific moves to be made must be at divine
prompting, since the humans consistently showed themselves radically incapable
of healthy initiative. The material of chaps. 11–20, marking themes of the overture
of 2–10, made clear that certain options were not viable: to refuse acknowledging
the crisis, to resist responding to it, to remain in Judah hoping for some reprieve,
to be removed from the land though lapsing from relationship with YHWH. The
choice remaining appears to be a quasi-voluntary resettlement while maintaining
trust in YHWH, God's strange ways notwithstanding. The urgent question now is
whether and how the prophet will be involved in communicating and catalyzing

that choice effectively, if only for a few. Jeremiah's laments showed him forthright with God, angry and retaliatory toward his human opponents, but finally and somewhat inexplicably in deepening partnership with God so as to continue his mostly bleak ministry.

My claim in this chapter is that the prophet becomes more explicit in clarifying options to Judah and Jerusalem—leaders primarily but people as well—and that those various choices both ramify and atrophy as they are engaged. As Jeremiah becomes more insistent and clearer on the generally poor but uneven paths available, and as his addressees generally coalesce into those resolutely remaining in Judah and others finding themselves anomalously removed to Babylon, those two main paths grow more distinct from each other even as variations within each clarify. At base is the question of how Jeremiah will understand God's plans, can help his peers to do so as well, muster their collaboration. In this present chapter we will survey the whole set of material, leaving fuller consideration of the Jeremiah-Zedekiah relationship and the situation of those resettled in Babylon to the next two chapters.

In this long set of material we have a rough chiasm, where the pieces can be shown to correspond in content though not so closely in any other way. As is readily evident to any consulting scholarly opinion, there is no consensus about the arrangement of the material, implying that its plan is not obvious or amenable to questions asked of it so far. A sampling of views shows almost as many opinions as opiners. But consider the units here, sketched as A–F, with a center called G, complemented by a F' through A' match to their partner pieces:

A hinge: Jeremiah imprisoned: 20
  B warnings to kings and other leaders: 21–23
    C demonstrations of alternative outcomes: 24–26
      D prophetic words interpreted, contested: 27–28
        E timing and true liberation: 29
          F words of hope: 30–31
            G land deed needed: 32
          F' words of hope: 33
        E' timing and false liberation: 34
      D' prophetic words contested: 35–36
    C' liberation contested: 37–38
  B' the end of monarchic Judah: 39
A' hinge: Ebed-Melek released: 39.

For the most part, the second "half" is briefer than the first, though the enactments are clustered more prominently in the second structural portion with fewer in the first. Though there is no shortage of poetry, the action takes place in prose units to a degree not seen before. That is, prophet and deity make their verbal case more fully when time remains, shortening their discourse and moving to enactment once options have shrunk—or once the fresh and salutary though distasteful choice has been engaged. What follows, then, is an overview consideration of the units with a summary at the end. Those units not slated for additional discussion must be sufficiently clear, and those to be featured in subsequent chapters need adequate introduction.

Overview of the Chiastic Elements

A 20—Jeremiah Imprisoned

For this hinge episode (already considered in our previous chapter), comprising both a prose unit and a prophetic lament, we watch Jeremiah enter a new phase, where he enacts more tangibly options available to and chosen by his peers. This is the first narrated attack on him: He has by lament alleged such things before, but in a general way. The narrator's report of aggression against him lands differently from the prophet's own claims. Pashhur the priest imprisons Jeremiah the prophet briefly, while the prophet rejoins to curse the priest, rename him, hurling nonsurvival words at him (20:1–6) as he will do for various individuals in this long section of the book.[1] This is also the first named reference to Babylon, where Pashhur and those he loves will perish, driven there unwillingly when it's too late to choose. Jeremiah's final lament follows, articulating by internal emphatic rebuttal that God *is* a helper and insisting by its Job-like epilogue that the prophet *is* prepared to suffer in relationship with God. Pashhur the priest goes his way doomed, while Jeremiah's fate is mixed: imprisoned and then freed, he remains vulnerable. A similar ambivalence is seen in the matching unit A′, where Ebed-Melek is given his life and Jeremiah, though reprieved, remains at risk.

B 21–23—Warnings to Kings and Other Leaders

This stretch of material comprises some one hundred verses of alternating poetry and prose, indicting Judah's leaders—kings, prophets, priests—for dereliction of their duty and more: for corruption of their responsibilities as leaders. With brief addresses to people, to Zion, and with a short intervention from Jeremiah, the consistent target of God's reproach is leaders. God proceeds now with a minimum of attributed speech, charging that leaders have not simply *not led;* they have *mis*led, led *falsely, harmfully.* They can now expect apt response from God: a twisting and repudiating of the customary divine saving role. Beyond critic, God becomes opponent, destroyer. This material splits into two uneven piles: address to or about kings (21:1–23:8), to or about prophets (23:9–40).

The first piece (21:1–14) is set as a narrative scene, with King Zedekiah sending messengers to Jeremiah asking him to engage God's help in the matter of

Nebuchadnezzar's siege of Jerusalem, hoping for a mighty deed by which God distracts the Babylonian from Jerusalem (21:1–2).[2] The Judean king's naïveté is checked sharply by the withering nature of the response sent back via Jeremiah (vv. 3–4). In a word, God promises a reversal to Zedekiah's hopes: Not an *ally,* YHWH will become an *adversary* to Judah and a helper to the Babylonians. God will invert the very weapons the Judeans aim at their opponents, with the result that they themselves will be destroyed, holding their wilted weapons. Jerusalem's king is shown foolish and futile, his *wistful wish flattened,* rebuffed, reversed.

The address to the people (21:8–10) is angled slightly differently, offering them a blunt and unnuanced Hobson's choice: <Dig in and die, submit and survive.> There is time for Judeans—some of them—to leave the city, avoiding the triple fate of those remaining: sword, famine, pestilence. Survival in Judah is not to be imagined as viable, YHWH promises. To have one's life as booty is an unpalatable outcome, implying that bare survival is about all that can be expected. But it is better than the alternative: nonsurvival. No response is made to this offer, and as usual, no delivery is described.[3]

The next subunit, loosely connected, swivels back to address the palace, calling its inhabitants back to their primary task: execution of justice, described first in terms positive and then negative (21:11–14). The deity pictures himself as besieger—a virtual Nebuchadnezzar—sitting ready nearby, listening to those who announce that they are safe in their walled city: <Who could possibly get in here?> <Fire can,> is the deity's response, a consuming fire that will leave no structure standing. The alternatives for the palace are not so clear as those for people, but to name what can still be seized before fire is kindled implies a choice.

A new if perhaps *faux* narrative scene commences in chap. 22, as deity dispatches prophet to the king's house (compare the king's sending to the prophet); and here is a somewhat disjointed series of statements to be made. First (22:3–9) comes a general indictment of royal injustice and a call to reform, proffering as incentive the continuation of Davids seated on the throne and riding through the city portals, and as disincentive the ruin of that enterprise. In a poem (22:6–9) built around opposites of height/status and collapse/disgrace, the deity reminds the lofty city that Gilead's glory can become wasteland, habitation turn to desolation, cedars to ash. And God helps the addressee imagine what the others will say, speculating aloud on the cause of the reversal but knowing—as those addressed are refusing to acknowledge—that massive covenant abuse will not go unchecked.

The next relatively long subsection (22:10–30) of this reproach to leaders includes specific comment on the last four kings of Judah. *Josiah* is not to be mourned, though or since he is gone. More lamentable is his son and first heir, *Jehoahaz* (called Shallum), reigning briefly but removed to Egypt and not fated to return. His forced exile will bear no fruit, neither there nor back in the city of David (vv. 10–12). A unit starting at 22:13 is addressed first about and then to one who built for himself to the detriment of others—the king quoted as savoring his dwelling as luxurious and high, though built with injustice; hence it is susceptible to the fate of high places previously described, destined to collapse. God deftly reminds this king that it takes more than tall cedar to make a king, contrasting the just deeds of this man's father with his own neglect and abuse. Offering what are likely proverbial assists, the deity suggests that Josiah (or some other righteous king) managed to eat and drink while doing justice. The present incumbent, likely *Jehoiakim*—about to be named (v. 18)—is fixed only on his cut-by-violence, his gain from shedding in one way or another the blood of others. <Don't be anticipating yourself as mourned,> the deity says, taking up the earlier theme of unfortunate kings. With rich irony the deity recites four mourning cries that will *not* be called out over this Josiah son, told to expect the burial of a once-useful but now inconvenient and ungainly animal, its corpse dragged out of the way and thrown outside the city to endure whatever becomes of such bodies, whoever they may once have been.

A slight break comes, once again, as the female singular Lady Zion is addressed at 22:20–23. She is bidden to go up to Lebanon and let loose her cry of distress over the fate of her lovers (the male plurals that characterize Judah's elites) with whom she has been complicit in refusing proper relationship with the deity. Reminiscent of parts of the overture sampled in chaps. 2–4, her fate is tied in with theirs, though distinguishable. Pangs and anguish are anticipated to come on her as the end arrives and she has none to help her, no opportunity of survival. Warned as were Judah's sons, she pushes away those words as do they. Lady Zion's interlude here is simply an alternative way of picturing the destruction of Judah, how it appears to another participant.

The language reverts back to named kings in 22:24–30, weighing now the fate of Josiah's third heir and grandson *Jehoiachin* (here called Coniah). This unit is more ambiguous than what has preceded, since in narrative time (as distinct from what will have already occurred by this book's production time) the precise valence on the fate of this scion is not so clear.[4] The deity, again resorting to proverbial language, images and in fact addresses Coniah as a signet, presumably integral and needed, yet inexplicably torn off the master's finger and hurled away, accompanied into his distant place by his mother, fated to die there with others counting on return from Babylon. And then multiplying imagery for additional comparison, the deity asks others if Coniah is to be regarded as a broken pot or a mundane jar, catching the attention and gaining the favor of no one. Is this the way of it? the deity muses, challenges. Awaiting no answer except his own, God

invokes the land to witness and to mark the unfortunate Coniah as sterile, failing to prosper, leaving no heir for the throne.[5] Submerged here is the larger and
more positive footprint of exile, since as is well known, it involved not simply
the royal house and not merely the first generation of those who experienced its
bitterness.

Finally, the unit on the royal leaders shifts a bit in 23:1–8, picturing hope amid
all this ruin. New shepherds, God promises, while continuing to castigate the old
ones for their abuse of the flock: scattering instead of accounting for them. God
will undertake the shepherding, to the vast improvement for the flock, reversing
what the sheep formerly suffered. God, echoing language more like Isaiah than
Jeremiah, also anticipates a righteous shoot for David, a king willing to do justice,
prospering, able to save Judah and to provide security for Israel.[6] The short oracle
sounds a bit generic and lonely amid the many verses of royal critique where it
precariously perches. And yet the promise tantalizes: Can Coniah lead a surviving group? Indeed, as the unit closes, God indicates a new saying, where the
liberation valorized in language will not be that from southern Egypt but rather
from the lands of the north, a deed that God once before managed without kings.[7]
The promise of return from exile seems more prominent than the survival of the
royal house.

The second major unit of these three chapters (23:9–40), shorter than the
first, speaks of and to prophets, characterizing them, like kings, as misusing their
position. The section appears to start with a comment from Jeremiah, though it
is not introduced as such and may still be the main speaker, resorting to anthropomorphic language to signal divine distress as we have seen before. In any case,
the speaker characterizes his anguish in terms of broken heart, wobbly bones,
indeed the gait of a drunk man, overconsuming wine as he contemplates God's
word and the situation into which it is thrust. Abandoning that metaphor to re-
sume clear divine status (by v. 11), God images the leaders as adulterous and their
land as dried out—consequence of their abuse of power. Not simply the kings but
prophets and priests will find themselves plunged into treacherous terrain and
deep darkness, surely a bad combination (recalling the fate of the sheep lost on
God's mountain in 13:15–17).

The next few verses (23:18–32) describe leaders' behaviors, again somewhat
metaphorically, the common thread being their "misspeech." If kings neglected
justice, prophets have neglected truth. Their pollution will be forced back down
their own throats, God promises, warning people not to be deceived by words
emerging from lying mouths. The lie is specified as emerging not from collaboration with God but from the prophets' own contriving. Whether done deliberately—
as seems to be the charge—or in error— as we might suppose—these condemned

guides have spent no time in the divine council learning of the deity's plans, nor have they any familiarity with the storm God has already promised or threatened to unloose. God describes the prophets as running without being dispatched and as talking without having been addressed. The proof: They do not speak words that catalyze genuine return to God. Bursting again into language that ruminates by way of proverbial speech (v. 23), God asks whether he is a deity at hand or one far off. Commentators divide on what the expected response is.[8] It may be unanswerable, giving way in any case to a divine claim that the deity is, however, able to find those hiding even if they are unable to discern divine truth. God's own availability is more selective, as has been previously suggested, a matter of who has been a witness in God's council. Prophets are also charged as being too reliant on dreams, emerging as those do from liars' imaginations.[9] As before, God charges that the dreams are not simply specious but toxic, causing people to forget the truth, as though false dreams overwhelm truthful prophecy: like comparing grain to straw, the deity claims, again reaching for imagery to make the point stark. God aims a series of culminating rebukes at these leaders, for stealing the truth from those who might have heard it, for lying and perverting the path that needs to be taken, for initiating discourse that was not given them. <I did not send them or instruct them, and they are of no use,> God concludes, possibly a reference to those who claim access to God's nearness.

The last unit (23:33–40) ramifies the basic charge in a way yet more complex, drawing on the double meaning of the Hebrew root *ns'*, "lift up," and its cognate nouns, "oracle/ burden."[10] The false prophets and priests are ridiculed as asking (presumably) Jeremiah what an oracle of YHWH might be, to which query he is instructed to retort, <You are the "burden," and YHWH "lifts you up" to cast you off. Should these liars simply say the word "oracle/burden," I mark it as bad,> the deity claims. <And when you address such persons, Jeremiah, use the language of God's response of speech rather than "oracle/burden," since they ask each other about YHWH's speech or "oracle/burden," language to be construed as false and as referencing their own utterances. Should they bandy about the "oracle/burden word," condemn them for persisting in something they have been instructed to avoid.> God's final pun: those who persist in the *ns'* "lift up/oracle/burden" language will be "lifted right out" of God's presence and removed from Jerusalem, stigmatized by eternal reproach and disgrace.

The match to this long piece on failed and condemned leaders shrinks to the single image of Zedekiah, trying to escape the breached Jerusalem. Unable to choose until it is too late and he finds himself fleeing toward a nonviable option, he exemplifies precisely what deity and prophet are trying to persuade leader addressees to avoid.

C 24–26—Demonstrations of Alternative Outcomes

The material that makes up these chapters coheres generally well. By overview: Chapter 24 poses more starkly and unmistakably than before the value of early or "voluntary-exile figs" over indigenous dug-in-dwellers. Chapter 25 both counters and intensifies that insight by making it manifest that though the Babylonians may appear ascendant and omnipotent, the cup of divine anger will be served round and all—even Babylon—forced to drink. God's position as lord of the dreadful banquet is underscored in a variety of ways, first in prose and then in poetry. And finally in chap. 26 options for those remaining in Judah are reviewed—in fact enacted, with the impact of God's word through the prophet as focal and as catalyzing action. This scene, like the fig unit, clarifies options and hardens the lines of decision: submit to Babylon as somehow—mysteriously and counter-intuitively—compatible with God's plan, or refuse to acknowledge that what God forewarns through Jeremiah is going to take place. Positions are clung to, most notably by the Jerusalem palace population and, of course, by those already in exile, with one swing group suggested.

A closer look: The teaching about early and late figs (chap. 24) is the most vivid image yet offered of the early resettlement, picking up as it does the quick scene concluding the overture (chap. 10), the collaborative teaching of prophet and deity who talk though harshly of return (12:14–17; 16:14–18), and the resolve of the deity to take the initiative to remove some long-settled participants to strange new places (18:13–17). The prophet narrates, thoughtfully linking the event to the departure of Jehoiachin and his companions for Babylon in the year 597 (24:1). The historical circumstances of that event are little detailed in the Bible, an omission intriguing to speculate about. But it seems clear that the departure was in some sense voluntary, at least compared to what will happen ten years later. One king, a royal household, and part of a community goes to Babylon while leaving the Davidic dynasty, central city, and hinterland to go on as before. Jeremiah, prompted by his divine interlocutor, is able to identify the positioned figs and assess them: early ripe figs to reach for and rotten inedible ones to refuse as well past eating. God interprets that the good figs analogize the resettlers and the bad those remaining elsewhere—Judah or Egypt. And, God explains, the group in Babylon will *benefit* by being watched over, returned, *built up,* and *planted,* not *overthrown* or *uprooted*—these four distinctive words from Jeremiah's call signaling that this group is part of his responsibility. They will be given hearts recognizing and responsive to YHWH and they will accomplish their return to being God's people. The others, characterized as king and his elites, remaining in Judah or seeking refuge in some other place—notably Egypt—are likened to a series of unfortunate conditions that Jeremiah likes to name in rhetorical *accumulatio:* a fright, a calamity, a reproach, a byword, a taunt, a curse as they suffer sword, famine, and pestilence and are consumed from the heritage that was once theirs (v. 9). The figs' fates are thus starkly opposed.

What is not and cannot be fully adumbrated is why or how either group makes its choice. To discern that journeying to Babylon is salvific and that to be stranded anywhere else is destructive.[11] Location is what counts, not—at least so far—how the location was selected or the qualities of those selecting: location and timing. As with fruit, early is good, with time not on the side of the choosers. Brueggemann is useful in pointing out first, that fig fates also come to represent competing ideologies that will console and enrage; and second, that at least at the moment of the first exile, such a fate will not have appeared to be the more desirable.[12] The unit ends, as we have come to expect from similar past scenes, with no response from either prophet or audiences.

The second subunit is also narrated as an experience of Jeremiah, though the book narrator introduces it before handing it over to the prophet for his construction. Chronology is clearly not the determining key here, for we are given a setting well before the first exiles depart, though at a time of Babylonian triumph, the accession of Nebuchadnezzar after a victory over Egypt (25:1). Jeremiah declaims that he has persistently delivered God's word for some twenty-three years, to little apparent effect on those within earshot. The prophet quotes the deity's sense of the charge—persistent refusal of relationship—and then the verdict—devastation and destruction—though with a promise of the reversal of Babylonian hegemony after some length of time (25:2–14). The point to ponder may be that a long-term (seventy-year) choice involving Babylon may work out better than a short-term effort, and the dischronology allows us, reading, to view the matter from two angles: first in setting order, that is, before any exile occurs; second in discourse time, where we have been given, proleptically, the information about the figs: picked early is best.

That transition serves as context for the next section (25:15–29), when the prophet describes himself as taking the cup of wrathful wine from the hand of the deity and offering it to—indeed forcing it on—the nations, one by one, beginning with Jerusalem and Judah and culminating with Babylon (called Sheshak here, v. 26).[13] From the humiliation first of Judah but eventually of Babylon can be inferred the bare possibility of eventual good news for exile, though it remains implicit here. The question we may construct is *how* Judean cup drinkers can survive until the Babylonians are served, with the implication (or inference) being: by going into voluntary exile there before being exported by force. Following on the prose narrative come some poetic lines, successively changing register to stress the depth of the travail when the sheepfolds and pastures are ravaged by the divine destroyer or his agents. The deity remains the focal character in these verses (25:30–38), and though the sheep are the clearest victims, the suffering made audible and most imaginable is that of the shepherds, whose grief—or frustration—is not envisioned with pity. The passages stress divine omnipotence and the collective powerlessness of virtually every other player. The whole chapter rehearses the inevitability of what is described, with reprieves and survivals not made explicit but imaginable, once we have studied the figs.[14]

The last material in this "clarifying and hardening of positions" section revisits material begun in Jeremiah 7, where the deity, instructing the prophet in a warning to be uttered about how to construe temple reliability, became so caught up in the hopelessness of the matter that the options all curled back on themselves.[15] Now the scene resumes to advance action, with the book narrator managing (as was the case in Jeremiah 7) so that Jeremiah is finally allowed to deliver the words addressed previously. The usual careful distinction between directions and enactment blurs, and indeed there is finally on this occasion a reaction by those to whom the words are addressed.[16] The divine address is briefer here than in chap. 7, with detail spent rather on the bounce of what Jeremiah declares to priest, prophet, and people (starting at v. 7). The narrator draws the scene to show hearers pressing close to Jeremiah, calling for his death, singling out for criticism the charge that Jeremiah claims as YHWH's word the equivalence of Jerusalem with Shiloh, though distorting his charge by removing from it the conditionality.[17] We, reading, are no longer surprised by what the prophet is saying, thus able to note how deep indignation flares within and among his "setting" hearers. Where have they been, we may wonder, that they are so freshly outraged? What we are shown, arguably, is not so much the shock of new information but growing resistance to something hated and the receivers' distortion of it to make it even more unpalatable. The group arresting the prophet is joined now by palace officials who sit to hear the case, buttressed as it now is by a second call for Jeremiah's death, based on the words of his own mouth (v. 11).[18] Before that matter can be adjudicated, the prophet himself speaks up to reinforce his previous testimony: <YHWH *did* send me, but there *is* time to make a fresh choice. Kill me if that is your wish, but know that you are shedding innocent blood. I *was* commissioned as true prophets are.> Jeremiah, thus making light of—or strategically conceding the vulnerability of—his own fate, stresses rather that the choice being worked out is that of any who refuse what they need, who blame the messenger for what they don't prefer to hear.

Distinctively if not uniquely, Jeremiah's words find a home with some officials and people, who indicate to the priests and prophets that they recognize the words as God's and that death ought not ensue.[19] This openness is unprecedented in the long narrative we are reading, and hence noteworthy. Their discernment is made and offered readers with the aid of two precedents. First is the case of Micah of Moresheth, who spoke strongly about a negative fate for Jerusalem against the more hopeful words of Isaiah and still survived the event, thanks to King Hezekiah, who heeded Micah's unwelcome news as though from YHWH. <He listened and God repented. We might do the same ourselves,> Jeremiah's advocates seem to reason.[20]

More ominous but still pertinent is the case of the prophet, Uriah of Kiriath-jearim (unknown to us from other biblical material), also threatening shocking events as did Jeremiah and Micah, but to a king and his elites who sought his death.[21] Uriah's flight to Egypt availed him little, since Jehoiakim hauled him back to pay for his words with an ignominious death and burial. And finally the narrator concludes the unit, noting that it is only thanks to the patronage of the Shaphan family that Jeremiah survived, else he would have ended the same way as Uriah. The point seems clear: Not whether Jeremiah a YHWH prophet, but how will this YHWH prophet fare: like Micah or like Uriah? Not quite like either, we may suspect, but Uriah catches our eye as a sort of shadow fate of Jeremiah, demonstrating by his futile flight to Egypt something that needs to be made visible.

The impact of this whole section is to reinforce a number of things seen before and to make much clearer something previously only hinted. Newly described is that the presence of some formerly of Jerusalem now in Babylon accords with what God and Jeremiah together know is God's plan. We need not say that God is designing it but that God can be seen to use it, will not prevent what is about to happen in the neighborhood. The status of Jerusalem and Judah and the project planted and flourishing there for some hundreds of years has no survival guarantee against the might of the Babylonian empire. And yet the omnipotence of Babylon is not forever. The Hobson's choice is the reality Jeremiah extends as God's best offer: Not desirable, but better than alternatives. And now, consequence of the figs vision, the deity and prophet say that good will come from it, in time. The news is resisted strongly by palace elites, apparently willing to spend a prophet if his silence is the result. But their determination is not wholly successful, and some of their own number acknowledge that Jeremiah spoke well. Without (yet) pondering motives, what we have seen is that some (a somewhat undifferentiated group so far, except for the details given in 24:1 and plausibly the response described in 26:16–19) can accommodate themselves to submission to Babylon while others (some leaders) cannot, will not. We begin to witness some splintering, with at least one prophet generally agreeing with Jeremiah and some palace persons, people, and at least one scribal family willing to support what Jeremiah says. But though so far numerically ineffective, they are onscreen.

This section is matched below by C' chaps. 37–38, its three scenes detailing the last days of Zedekiah as he struggles against the fate of his royal brother,

Jehoiakim, but fails, ultimately, to choose well among options. Jeremiah's efforts to persuade him fail, though once again, his words fall fruitfully on at least some.

D 27–28—Prophetic Words Interpreted, Contested

This generally coherent unit narrates the episode called here *yokes contested.* Set in the reign of Zedekiah, it begins with God's directing the prophet to make a set of bars and straps for himself and for the kings of five nearby peoples, anticipated as convening in Jerusalem apparently at the behest of the king (27:1–3).[22] As the yokes are distributed, so is the prophet to interpret: God self-describes as creator of the whole earth and its creatures, all designed with strength and skill. God indicates, in what Brueggemann calls a highly unusual point of view, that Nebuchadnezzar's supremacy over all he controls and the consequent need for all to serve him is part of YHWH's *design,* with God is not simply coping with collapse but its architect.[23] To withhold submission, that is, to refuse to put necks into the proffered yoke, is tantamount to disobedience to God, leading to no good but rather to destruction of the yoke refusers by the three usual suspects: sword, famine, pestilence (27:4–8). God anticipates objection—occurring several times and hence possibly the main point to be heard: Those addressed will indicate that *their* prophets are telling *them* something different. But God says, <Do not listen to them, for they are lying, either so that or with the effect that disobedience to YHWH and the promised destruction will occur, and the refusing peoples will be dispersed and destroyed.> And, God reiterates, <To submit to the yoke is to survive, *even on one's own land.* This can still work> (27:9–11).[24]

Zedekiah of Judah is then given some words specific to him, though quite similar to what has been addressed more generally: <Submit and survive, accept the yoke of Babylon. Why court destruction?> He, also, is advised not to listen to his prophets who counsel him differently. Not sent by YHWH, they are lying, conniving at the destruction of Judah (27:12–15). And to the priests, a similar plea, though with their own special appeal: <Do not listen to those who promise you that the temple vessels carried off with the first exile will be back shortly, for that is a lie. Submit to the Babylonian.> Or, in a nice twist on the theme of fraudulent prophets: <Or, ask your prophets, so concerned for the plundered temple vessels, to beseech YHWH [speaking of self in third person as is frequent] that the rest of the vessels not be taken to join those already gone to Babylon.> Of course, to engage the objects of divine disapproval in a false inquiry will only serve to compound their fraudulent incompetence. <But,> the deity continues and countermands, <what was not taken the first time along with King Jehoiachin and his group will go eventually under my design. They will all return when I say so,> concludes YHWH (27:16–23). There is no immediate response to these words from any king, prophet, or priest to whom they are addressed and whom they critique.

But no, a prophet does respond, perhaps one of those mentioned by the deity three times in the advice proffered about the yokes: Hananiah of Gibeon approaches Jeremiah in the temple sometime later that same year and resumes the yoke discussion. Mark Bartusch invites us to read the narrative attentive to its detail as illuminated by social scientific categories as well as by its narrative detail.[25] Stressing the exchange as a contest of limited goods waged in public between persons of roughly equal rank, we see the issue is not abstract theology but the urgent issue of who speaks insightfully about what is happening, who misleads. Hananiah challenges Jeremiah's words, contradicts him boldly and clearly, claiming that God told *him* that the yoke of Nebuchadnezzar is already broken, and that shortly—in a mere two years—the temple vessels and the exiles themselves will return to Judah (28:1–4). Others are thus forced to choose between prophets, who cannot both be right on so starkly divergent a claim. Jeremiah, presumably conscious of their audience of priests and people gathered near the temple, ripostes (28:6–14), <Amen! I hope so but doubt it seriously.> And he follows up with his own sense of matters: <From of old, prophets have spoken far and wide about matters grim. To speak of peace, let's see when one of them says so how it will work out!>[26] Hananiah forgoes a verbal reply by offering a physical affront, striking off the yoke his confrère was wearing. Jeremiah matches that gesture with hard words, envisioning an iron yoke to replace what was broken, also repeating his original directions from YHWH (27:5–7): <I am the creator, the designer, and not to be thwarted in what is under construction in terms of Nebuchadnezzar's temporary hegemony.> Jeremiah announces also to Hananiah that God has designated him as a liar and a fraud, neither commissioned nor instructed by YHWH, fated to die within the year for his words. And, comments the narrator who manages this unit, Hananiah dies shortly thereafter (28:17).

We are thus drawn to watch a confrontation—not simply prophet versus leaders and/or people—but prophet versus prophet: Jeremiah proclaiming the unthinkable and undesirable (submit and survive), Hananiah offering something more palatable (some have briefly submitted, shortly all will not only survive but be free of the Babylonian yoke). John Barton, writing about "politics and religion," claims we do well to recognize that prophets like Jeremiah do not reason and preach *from* ethics *to* events: Judah is disloyal, and so the Babylonian presence is a punishment (which they often seem to be saying), but the *reverse*: the Babylonians are massively present and look liable to be dominant in a way Judah had not quite experienced heretofore, and so the best response is to show it as somehow in the pattern of God's plan, shocking though it may seem.[27] We glimpse Jeremiah as not a prophet meddling in politics but a political observer wading into ethics! Since no biblical prophet ever says, <These Babylonians are simply way too strong for us and our geographical location has put us at risk,> Barton's construction somewhat fills in the "reality gap" that seems in some ways obvious: Of course the Babylonians threaten the neighborhood; a big neighbor brings big trouble. This construction also saves Jeremiah from sounding reductive and naïve, God from seeming persistently petulant: <Bad behavior leads to annihilation.> The equation is not so simple. What Jeremiah has to make palatable is that God is somehow able to work with most undesirable events and urge that, counterintuitively, God has even had a hand in the design of what is experienced as so terrible. Another way to point out the difference between Barton and most other commentators is to suggest that even if "bad behavior" (idolatry, injustice) were to stop, the Babylonians would surely not pull back. The value of Barton's insight is that it intensifies the challenge of Jeremiah's preaching task.

Norman Gottwald puts it like this: "The 'inspiration' of the prophets consists in their authoritative synthesis of a tradition-drenched reading of history and a sharp-eyed reading of the sociohistoric horizon in which they stand."[28] The point I want to stress is not to reduce or eliminate the powerful role of religious intermediation from the scene or from the Bible, but to redefine the challenge that a Jeremiah faces. Gottwald adds: "Instead of despair, a pattern of redemptive possibility is wrested from the generations-long prophetic interreading of tradition and situation. God has again and again checkmated the atheistic and antisocial stratagems of Israel's leaders while nurturing belief and social caring among other Israelites who too seldom had power to shape the community. Though badly battered, the community retained all the necessary resources for a socioreligious healing process and a long arduous reweaving of the fabric of community."[29]

The match for this two-stepped yoke unit is two episodes in Jehoiakim's reign, where Rechabites demonstrate a startling but truthful interpretation of tradition—instructing even Jeremiah—and the king's refusal of prophetic words reaches its zenith as he burns the scroll.

E 29—Timing and True Liberation

As the topic has moved from whether resettlement to who, where, and how long, Jeremiah follows up with a letter sent in his own name—citing YHWH frequently—sent to the group just freshly under discussion and who I am suggesting we glimpse in chap. 26: those who went to Babylon in 597, addressed specifically to those elders who survived the process. The book narrator, in introducing us to the quite extraordinary and likely fictive document, reviews who was there: priests, prophets, people (including elders), the royal Josiah grandson and his lady (queen or queen mother), officers, princes, craftsmen and smiths—a microcosmic, substantial and resourceful community residing in Babylon (vv. 1–2).[30] Jeremiah's advice suits well both his general commission as a prophet and his immediate ministry to the one group who has heeded him: build, dwell, plant, eat, marry, beget, betroth—and let your children do so as well. Increase and do not diminish. Actively seek the well-being of the place where I (quoting the deity seamlessly) have sent you (stressing again the point that this *is* God's plan and not *simply* Nebuchadnezzar's strength), for its well-being is your own as well. Simply to be in Babylon is not enough: <Do not listen to your prophets, those diviners and dreamers in your midst, who make you dream as well. They are not from me but lie to you (vv. 3–9).>[31]

And then in what is, to my mind, among the most beautiful passages in the whole book, Jeremiah shares what he knows from God, laying forth God's perspective: "I know the plans I have for you, plans of well-being and not disaster, to give you a future and a hope," (v. 11). A long time coming, as suggested by the multigenerational advice and the stretch of seventy years, but YHWH will bring the resettled people back to the place from which Jeremiah sends these words. From where these resettled people of Judah dwell—and not from some other place—the prophet continues, they will call out to God, will come near in supplication, and God will listen to their words. "And you will search for me and will find me when you search with all your heart, I will be found by you . . . and I will restore your fortunes" (vv. 13–14). From the specific place to which they have been scattered, Jeremiah concludes this promise, God will gather them back. We hear the echo from the overture (10:19–22), where the hearts of deity, prophet, and people seemed to coincide in recognizing the necessity and fruits of resettling, of learning afresh and perhaps anew God's heart. And we recall as well God's resolution to take the initiative and transplant early some hearts able to be responsive, anomalous though that seem to all witnesses.

But back to a perennial concern of this unit: prophets who contradict what Jeremiah is saying.[32] The danger raised is that the resettlement process be short-circuited. Some, Jeremiah claims, quoting them, say that God has sent *them* prophets in Babylon, urging other advice. But, says Jeremiah, <Note the case of those remaining in Jerusalem—king and others: God promises to send them sword, famine, and pestilence, says he will make them figs beyond edible, will pursue them and make them proverbial in a whole set of ways among those who know of them, for their refusal to obey the prophets God did send and who, presumably, said what God has insisted through Jeremiah: submit, resettle, survive> (vv. 15–19). Time will sort this, Jeremiah maintains. Events are responsive to YHWH's design and not simply to Nebuchadnezzar's, appearances notwithstanding.

Jeremiah then moves on to address two situations of concern in Babylon, which we are able to construct to some extent and largely from what he says: First, he names two false prophets, affirming that Nebuchadnezzar will put them to death (the Babylonian's own reason not specified), because they behaved foolishly, lied, and made false claims about themselves. <I know and am witness,> Jeremiah says God declares (vv. 20–23).[33] The second situation involves both the community in exile and that in Judah, suggesting how tangled the groups remained (vv. 24–32): A certain Shemaiah is addressed and castigated for sending from Babylon letters to people and priests in Jerusalem, falsely claiming God's authorization and granting one of them (Zephaniah ben Maaseiah) status of or like that of the priest Jehoiada, able to place in stocks and collar all the renegades.[34] Hence Shemaiah's letter (quoted in Jeremiah's) scolds Jerusalem authorities for delay or refusal to rebuke "the renegade Jeremiah himself" (he refers to himself in the third person) for his "unpack and plan for a long stay" words (also quoted). Continues Jeremiah, <This harmful letter was read by Zephaniah the priest in the hearing of all—Jeremiah included—outrageous!> So, Jeremiah continues, citing YHWH's words to the exiles: <I do not endorse this communication, and Shemaiah can expect to hear from me concerning it, and can expect his family to be extirpated for what he has said.> Word is, what good lies in the future will not be experienced by all. Unworthy or harmful individuals are thus being peeled from the group, as will continue to happen.

The chapter continues several themes already on the table: submission and resettlement as survival, schism among prophets and those who hear them, the prevalence and danger of "false" prophets and those who claim authorization Jeremiah denies them.[35] It adds more clearly than before facets of God's commitment to reverse exile, thought time must not be construed as short nor the experience as all bad, and the project must not be seen simply as of Babylonian design. And this unit lays bare communication between communities and the effort of the exiles—some of them—to thwart what Jeremiah is saying to and concerning both groups. We see, more clearly than before, that the fates of the two populations are not the same and that even within each group, the outcome will not necessarily be common. The behaviors of the two communities are described in distinct terms, at least as God wills and designs: One is to reach out and beseech God—return in two senses of the word—and be accompanied in such behavior, while the other refuses instruction. That there are nefarious individuals in each group does not vitiate the main contours of each situation. What appears to be a negative thing can and must be seen as positive.

The match for this unit about the timing and credibility of liberation is the false language and behavior of the king to those enslaved—unreliable speech of

Zedekiah, who has little time left. Will the experience of the freed be brief or is that a false hope? Timing is to be queried.

F 30–31—Words of Hope

This set of material, some sixty-four verses of mixed poetry and prose, sounds quite different from much preceding it, though it may be simply the radical flowering of what has been worked out gradually in the book and in this unit: The dreaded can be fruitful, and experiences threatened and anticipated, suffered and endured, will be caught up into reality positive and sustaining. Suffering is not to vanish, as in fact the speaker underlines several times that it was deserved, inevitable, expected. But it is not the last word.[36]

These verses can be classified variously: a set of oracles alternating judgment and hope, a web of dialogical material heavily antiphonal, language laced with keywords and refrain expressions, cascades of polarized or reversing metaphors.[37] To be noted at present (since we will revisit this section) is the manner in which Jeremiah presents YHWH's words of reversal or consolation, written in a book, readied for later use. Fretheim points out that in the extant narrative, even before the worst has happened, its reversal is anticipated verbally, is underway.[38] As was prominent in chaps. 2–10, the deity addresses the people (mostly Israel/Judah though sometimes the nations), speaking of and to them in what seems a helter-skelter way. God's choice of language is densely metaphorical, the divine poet reaching for multiple ways to talk about the reversal of what has been endured while still referencing it. Trouble serves as backdrop for deliverance. Prominent by absence is specifically how certain scolded behaviors will reverse.

The narrator (either the book narrator or the prophet) speaks mostly to set the scene or tag a speaker. Beyond that, the prophet speaks just once in his own voice, at the most odd and anomalous 31:26, which I take as a reinforcement that the words being inscribed onto the scroll are not in "ordinary time" but remain in another dimension. That aside, the main and consistent speaker is YHWH, speaking of Israel and Judah, of Jacob and Ephraim—to them as well—and of and to Virgin Israel. The nations are mentioned as witnesses or commentators but otherwise play no important role. There is attributed speech, clear in certain instances (30:17; 31:6, 10, 18–19, 23, 29, 34), in other instances inferable (30:7, 12; 31:26). We have seen the deity do this before.

Two bracketing images (30:2; 31:36) are strong, solid, and nonreversing: Scroll words will come to fruition, be as reliable as the basic fabric of creation, claimed by YHWH as God's own, serving as witness to God's reliability for Israel. No more than creation's patterns can shift will God fail to accomplish these plans. Between those two posts, as it were, comes a series of some twenty-five metaphors of reversal, all sharing the pattern of a bad thing become good. Note the general one, the reversal of fortunes, where what was taken away will be restored (30:3, 10–11; 31:7–9, 17); fear and physical dread is resolved and grief assuaged (30:6–7; 31:12–13); the yoke of servitude is broken off (30:8) as the master is changed (30:9); a festering wound resulting from a cruelly inflicted blow is healed (30:12–17); former perpetrators are perpetrated against (30:16); the once disregarded and shunned are sought out (30:17); ravaged territory is rebuilt, enlarged, repopulated with produce and animals (30:18–19; 31:4–5, 8–9, 12, 23–24, 27–28, 38–40); mourning is changed to dancing (30:19; 31:4); an indigenous leader is restored to a position of honor (30:21); a pact broken is reestablished (30:22; 31:1); storming anger is spent (30:23–24); pursuit is thwarted (31:2–3); the captive is ransomed (31:11); the desiccated is rehydrated (31:12, 25); the hungry eat (31:14); the bereft are consoled (31:15–17); the chastised are reconciled (31:18–20); the route of exile is reversed homeward (31:21); a proverbial saying is transformed (31:30); the mode of instilling an ethos of relationship is improved (31:31–34).

The match for this piece is another text of consolation, corresponding in theme and image.

G 32—Land Deed Needed

The center of the structure I am sketching here needs to carry yet one step further what has been developed thus far by the rhetoric of the book. Given that we have just seen the reversal of the process of Babylon overwhelming Judah, the return of those who made a resettling journey and survived a sojourn, it is difficult to imagine what has been held in store. But here we have an enactment of the revaluation of the Judah heritage itself, making way, eventually, for the emergence of the postexilic people whose deepest roots remain in Zion. Though what we call diaspora Judaism will flourish and dominate numerically from exile onward, its center will be the community restored to the heritage land and working out a relationship with their deity and with each other around the worship center Jerusalem. The genre is enacted parable, aimed to demonstrate and effect the point it demonstrates.

The passage is set during the last days of the siege, where Zedekiah has reproached the prophet for claiming that the invader's success—concomitantly the Judean king's defeat—was God's plan and purpose (32:1–5). Rather than answer the king's complaint directly, the prophet narrates as prophecy a scene where he (imprisoned) is approached by his cousin to redeem the land of his father, Jeremiah's uncle (vv. 6–8). Recognizing the request as God's word, Jeremiah narrates that he made the purchase (v. 9) and then details the elaborate process by which a deed is produced (vv. 10–15). The transaction is followed by Jeremiah's prayer to YHWH—recall, we are still witnessing the prophet's reply to a royal reproach—a prayer reviewing the liberation deeds of the past and human failures to receive them, ending as the prophet points out to the deity the present beleaguered circumstances of Jerusalem (vv. 16–24). In the midst of all this disaster, the prophet reviews, <You, Lord, sent me to redeem ancestral land? Seems futile! But you reminded me why these things are happening> (vv. 25–36). But, Jeremiah continues, God promises reversal of degradation and defeat, speaks of return and renewal, and heritages will be resettled, revalued, reclaimed: So be sure you can lay hands on the deed when it shall be needed (vv. 37–44).

The uncle, powerless and clueless, has lost the land, but the fidelity of the nephew to the word of the prophet and the plan of the deity are to be counted on. The uncle will vanish in the present catastrophe, but the deed done by the nephew will stand. The community with Zedekiah's nephew Jehoiachin is the means by which the heritage will be reclaimed, the fidelity of that group to the prophet's narrative.

F' 33—Words of Hope

This chapter is a good match for its corresponding piece, since both include oracles detailing the reversing of the major problem under consideration: the conundrum of Judah's flourishing in Babylon. Both units are presented proleptically: the first written on a scroll and this present one addressed to Jeremiah while he is imprisoned in the besieged city. The book narrator confirms that this is a second communication of such information from deity to prophet, suiting my sense that it corresponds to chaps. 30–31, split from them by Jeremiah's land redemption narrative. Like its matching piece, this briefer set of divine promises is grounded at front and back (33:2–3, 25–26) with God's claim of being creator underwriting restoration, reminding the imprisoned recipient that the insight shared is something he has not heretofore known. We may suppose that the assurance comes in useful, given the gap between what appears to be happening and what is promised, between the looming defeat with implied capture exile and the blessings God promises may rise from it. But whereas the material in chaps. 30–31 seems to envision a return from exile, this unit seems received in Judah, suiting the piece we saw in chap. 32.

As before, we can note speaker, spoken about, parties spoken to, and language ascribed to them, as well as naming basic metaphors of reversal that make up this unit. The main speaker is, as expected, the deity, regularly identified. Spoken about is consistently Judah and Israel, or occasionally Judah and Jacob or "this people" (v. 24). Spoken to several times is Jeremiah, with sprinkled reference to a you (masculine plural: vv. 10–11, 19–22). Speech is ascribed less often than before: in v. 9 the nations are imagined as awed witnesses of God's doing with Israel and Judah; in vv. 10–11 the inhabitants of the place of desolation (plausibly

Judah) who spoke about the lack of habitation now are cited as giving thanks to God for divine goodness and love. The speaker of the words of v. 23 is uncertain: "The two families that YHWH chose he has now rejected." It is immediately contradicted by God, demonstrating again that what appeared to be the case is not so. That God had rejected his people is spoken against, as well as the inference likely attributable to the "speakers," that God's people should cease to exist as a people. All the ascribed speech demonstrates reversal.

Images function as before. Some are familiar: wounds are healed, houses rebuilt, profaned or unclean places purified, anger reversed, fortunes restored, sins cleaned up and forgiven. The land reverses from abandoned and desolate to repopulated, from wasteland to pasture. Those who commented in shocked tones now rejoice. The last few verses stress the change from no or bad kings to a David scion who will rule justly, to Davidic and Levitical personnel in place, to the progeny of the patriarchs (and matriarchs) as maintained.

E' 34—Timing and False Liberation

This unit, *slave reprieve revoked*, to be repositioned in our next chapter, offers a rough match, in fact an inversion of Jeremiah's letter to the exilic community in Babylon, providing them with instruction and insight as to the duration of their stay there and dealing with prophetic opposition to that word. Addressed to King Zedekiah in Judah, the communication dashes hopes for alternative futures he may envision and underscores the dangers of false interpretation of traditional values and of false prophetic words, never to be fulfilled. Perhaps the clearest point of comparison is timing. In unit E those resettled in Babylon, if hoping for a short stay, are advised it will be long. Those proclaiming falsely a brief sojourn of people or temple vessels are rebuked. Here in E', Judah's last king suffers from a related temporal fallacy. With a siege pressing, the king is rebuked for believing that it will not persist and prevail. The king's action of manumitting slaves—an apparently ancient custom carried forth when the siege seemed tight and the king sought responsibility for fewer people—he subsequently cancels, envisioning that when the siege should lift, slaves will be needed as before. But his hopes for a short travail are shown foolish, his refusal to credit the testimony of prophet and deity wreaking havoc on the lives of those he controls (34:1–11).

The king's broken promise is mimicked as God sets Jeremiah to relate an old narrative, with a new twist (34:12–22). <When your people, Zedekiah, were enslaved in Egypt, I freed them and then provided a related custom, to be obeyed, grounding the liberation of others enslaved. Oppression was not to last forever but to have a fixed term, after which the slave would go free. But that is not what has happened, not in the general case and specifically not in your case, Zedekiah. For you promised liberation when it suited your expectations and then reneged

on it when it no longer seemed feasible.> In a corresponding moment, God also piously delivers to Zedekiah false words, promising him a peaceful death, burial with ceremony, internment with his ancestors. But it will not stand: None of those words will come to pass. They will be reneged on and replaced by their inverse: defeat for the city, its destruction, deportation or death for the king and his adherents. Of course we may infer from the fact that communication is still happening that options remain, if implicit, unvoiced. Does Zedekiah heed sweet false words or harsh true ones? Does he have time remaining to choose? How will he use it?

D' 35–36—Prophetic Words Interpreted, Contested

These two units detailed in Jehoiakim's reign offer a match to the yoke contest between prophets, unfolding as did that event in two major scenes, with other details spilling out. Both sets of material show that reliable prophetic words are available, do not lack. The question is how to hear them, who will heed them. That some hear badly, notably here King Jehoiakim, with knife and flame refusing the word as dramatically as will ever be demonstrated, does not inevitably—yet—doom everyone else (36). His foil: the Rechabites, hearing skillfully (35). The prose teaching on the yokes showed clear speech from Jeremiah, refused by most of his hearers and certainly by the prophet Hananiah, shown speaking dangerously for his hearers and dying as a result of it. Here the piece works out similarly, but with greater emphasis on and attention paid to the diversity of hearing rather than simply to the diversity of preaching.

The detail: In the first narrative, God instructs Jeremiah to invite the Rechabites to violate their wineless heritage, an order the prophet duly prepares to enact. But the Rechabites, refusing drink, explain: What is licit for some is not acceptable for them (for example, drinking wine, building homes, planting fields [35:5–10]). But at the approach of Nebuchadnezzar, explains Jonadab, their spokesperson, they chose to move into the city, inhabiting a place they did not expect to dwell. They are not condemned for it, and in fact their discernment of fidelity to their own heritage is praised and made warrant for their survival. If any may have supposed that the Rechabites would be expected to remain helpless and exposed as the Babylonians came through their neighborhood, or would be condemned for seeking "strange housing," it is not the case. We do not hear how they chose so suitably, nor do we get much process over any struggle encountered when a reliable prophet offered them wine. Perhaps one thing was necessary (moving into a settled place) and the other not (drinking wine). But they are praised for seeing deeply into what they have known from of old, for adjusting when their plight became urgent. This is a brilliant *mise-en-abyme* for the larger storyline, providing another brilliant drama of unexpected behavior chosen and approved.[39] God instructs Jeremiah to point out their inverse behaviors to the people of Judah and Jerusalem, refusing God's ancient invitations to them and not engaging the Babylonian threat and its loophole for the faithfully attentive.

The next scene Jehoiakim's reign hosts is more complex and ramified, shows more nuance among players.[40] Jeremiah is told to record the words of his prophetic career on a scroll for eventual reissue, in case, God says hopefully, it may not be too late if intended and recalcitrant hearers have a second chance (36:3). Jeremiah, assisted by Baruch, carries out the assigned task, readying the scroll for reading, the words for reproclamation (36:4–9). Indeed, they are freshly proclaimed at least three times, arguably four. First, on a pilgrimage fast day they are read in the chamber of the Shaphan scribes, who appear to receive them with concern if not surprise (36:10–11). One of those men, Micaiah ben Gemariah ben Shaphan, undertakes to have the scroll read to other scribes, apparently part of the royal establishment (36:12–15), who also appear to hear it willingly and to decide that the king must be informed. They move to accomplish this next proclamation, taking the ominous precaution that prophet and scribe hide themselves (36:16–20). When the king and those in his chamber hear the scroll, we see several reactions: the king, most extreme, moves to destroy what he hates, cutting off the pieces as they are read and consigning them to fire (36:21–23). Less malevolent than the king are his attendants, some of whom listen with aplomb and presumably approve the scroll's destruction. But some, grieved and frightened, try to dissuade the king from his effort to destroy the proclamation (36:24–25). The king sends messengers to take Baruch and Jeremiah, who survive to rewrite the scroll, adding to it what has just happened (36:26–32) and insuring its ongoing survival to this day.

Resistance to truthful proclamation, though strong, proves ineffective. Refusal to hear does not shut down the power of God's words, though it may seem so to those attempting it. The choices are made manifest, with diversity among witnesses along a spectrum from the Shaphan scribes to the king. The king's refusal will be destructive for his partisans, though not all standing with him on the day of the scroll need remain there. Options exist for groups and individuals, and we see the suggestion—granted, it is not developed in detail—that some are taken up. Falseness is neither condoned nor obscured, and that Jehoiakim does not die at once (as did Hananiah) does not mean his day will not come. The question is, perhaps now, for the others, given the information provided by the Rechabites and the scrolls' adventures. Another way to put that is that the royal city is digging its own grave, but not all present are yet scheduled to die there.

C' 37–38—Demonstrations of Alternative Outcomes

We move from the days of the rebellious and defiant Jehoiakim to the final ones of his brother Zedekiah. Since these chapters will get careful scrutiny in our next chapter, here it must suffice to sketch the big picture. Their match was the decisive threefold demonstration of realities in C: the teaching about the figs (24), the demonstration of Judah and the nations forced to drink from YHWH's cup (25), and the temple teaching and trial of Jeremiah (26).

First we watch Zedekiah muster feeble hope that the Babylonians will back off from the siege and that YHWH's help might still be anticipated (37:1–5). The book narrator begins by reviewing the king's record with God's word as delivered by Jeremiah—not promising. Nonetheless, Zedekiah sends two messengers to ask for YHWH's intervention, but the word is similar to a previous moment when the king made such a request: <Don't even contemplate such a thing!> (37:7–10). But when, despite God's word and Jeremiah's, the siege *is* temporarily lifted, Jeremiah takes advantage of the reprieve to attempt a visit to his own home (*disputed departure*), but he is stopped on his way out and accused of deserting to the enemy, a charge perhaps understandable enough, given his "submit and survive" advice. Denial is pointless, and the end of the scene finds Jeremiah confined to the "Jonathan prison" for many days (37:11–16). The king, perennially indecisive and optimistic, summons the prophet in hopes of gaining a hopeful word, an occasion Jeremiah uses to get his place of imprisonment upgraded (37:17–21). The narrative thus continues to play the issue of viable positions, showing and then appraising them.

But finally the king delegates responsibility for Jeremiah to three others, with the result that once again the prophet is dropped into danger in *Malchiah's mud* (38:1–6), from where he is rescued, thanks to a brave and timely intervention to the same king from his palace servant, Ebed-Melek (38:7–13). Not free, Jeremiah is at least visible and less endangered in a city full of threats. Both scenes show the king, weak and dilatory, clinging to false hope, susceptible to manipulation first in one way and then in another while those around him make choices he is unable to manage—Jeremiah's fate swinging in the balance. The final encounter between king and prophet (38:14–28) seals the king's fate—the prophet's as well. Almost able to do what the prophet has long been counseling, at the key moment, he slips back from it and loses his life, for all practical purposes.

Scrutinizing the relationship between C' and C, we see the vast undertow of hopelessness that anything that God or Jeremiah can say will influence the king and elites to do their part to save the city. That there is a world of difference between Jehoiakim and Zedekiah is virtually moot, since each finds his own way to resist prophetic words. Nothing good will happen in the royal quarter of the city, and no heir of Josiah will be part of what lies ahead. Individuals are presented with greater nuance, and malevolent players outnumber benevolent ones, even with Ebed-Melek said to muster seven to help Jeremiah out. The prophet's location—in or out of captivity—becomes, now, the focus of the narrative—the point to be developed in our next chapter. If royal leadership represents one fate and the young exilic community another, still, for reasons needing clarification, Jeremiah's position comes to be important: where he will be and what he will do from where he is. Jeremiah's willingness to remain captive and to play out alternatives is part of his prophecy. Finally, that God is the designer of futures is also reinforced.

B' 39:1–10—Warnings to Kings and Other Leaders

The narrative winds down, quickly, tersely, and without obvious drama—spare twin to the longer unit B, where kings were shown to vitiate justice, prophets truth, priests authority. The book narrator succinctly catalogues the Babylonian siege of the city, an event actually lasting more than a year. Readers are left to infer the details of such a protracted and desperate situation, drawing our attention to how little we are told: The enemy breached the city walls and entered through a northern gate, last and urgent warning to the king and a few elites to flee ignominiously and desperately by night, through a gate accessed from the royal garden, and to head south. Pursued, Zedekiah is captured and brought face-to-face with Nebuchadnezzar himself at Riblah, where he witnesses the slaughter of his sons and companions before being blinded and taken off toward Babylon, after which note he disappears from our sight. The narrator concludes this tragedy by noting that the king's house and others were burned and the city walls pulled down. All those remaining in Jerusalem at the moment of its capture were managed in some way: some killed, we may imagine, though the text does not say so; some taken to Babylon; and a number left in the region and provided with land. All warnings refused, option of safe journey vanishes.

A' 39:11–18—Jeremiah Imprisoned and Freed

The final unit of this long set of material, like its fellow A, hinges or joins two major portions of text, one behind it and one ahead of it. The backward look: As Pashhur confined him briefly and then freed him, so Jeremiah suffers an analogous release here, much more serious, of course. And then the culmination: We understand that Jeremiah, in the city throughout the process of its defeat, is singled out for protection by the Babylonians, rescued, and given a provisional dwelling, amid the people of Judah. Having endured the fate of those refusing the choice he consistently begged them to accept, his lot is not quite the same as theirs, as the story will go on to tell in subsequent chapters. The flash-forward: We learn that Ebed-Melek is reassured of his own escape and survival, thanks to God's word delivered through Jeremiah. His life for booty, God explains, because the Cushite servant of the king put trust in YHWH rather than responding to the various pressures he will have felt in the days when Jeremiah's life was most threatened. We will catch the shape of this motif twice more, with libratory notes regarding Baruch (chap. 45) and Jehoiachin (chap. 52).

Conclusions

This large section, taken in concert with the prayers and prose of chaps. 11–20, lays bare the heart of the Jeremiah material, since as we consider it, narrated choices—good and bad—are extended, made, set, lived into. Surrounded by distinctive material—the call of the young prophet (chap. 1); the release of the old king (52); the mostly grim but briefly hopeful overture (2–10); the mostly hopeless finale (40–44), where the possibility of survival in Judah is rendered impossible—the main action of the book is enacted in these chapters 11–39. In the "early heartland" of 11–20, we saw God's and Jeremiah's collaborative efforts come to nothing good, witnessed their soliloquies diverge as Jeremiah remains largely caught in retributive anger at his foes while God, thwarted, undertakes to initiate and sustain relief of some sort for the Judah project. The texture of that divine resolve, the prophet's intense efforts to make it heard and seen, and the responses of various characters have moved into view for us, reading.

The loose and lopsided concentricity is not essential to my argument, so it may be more helpful to add the columns by topic: The first and only good news is that some, at least, in Judah have become convinced that their fruitful survival is in resettling from the heritage land to Babylon, have gone there, are being ministered to there, seem responsive to authoritative prophetic advice. We need to understand more about the literary portrait of that major turn and will study it more closely in our chapter 7. Second, other options, lethal in the view of this prophet, have been considered and shown wanting: To an unprecedented degree, the material of this central unit has excoriated Judah's leaders: kings, prophets, priests, virtually none of whom is shown to choose well enough. The kings as a set and then by name are shown wanting in many ways: They fail at justice, exulting in what is built from injustice; suborning others, they fail to serve needs of their people. Jehoahaz demonstrates the futility of going to Egypt. Jehoiakim is the most blatant abuser of his position and refuser of prophetic advice. Zedekiah, more weak and vacillating than determinedly villainous, nonetheless brings consummate disaster on the heritage land. Prophets, similarly, refuse their true role and preach falsely. Condemned as liars, thwarters, self-starters, and hence as missing the word offered to them, they confound themselves and others by harmful speech. In two cases they also demonstrate the fate of failed prophets, dying unprotected and shamefully. Priests are not so prominent, but we hear them named occasionally in the service of Jeremiah's opponents—Pashhur to Zephaniah—messengers and mouthpieces for kings. In addition, third, we saw brief and vivid imagery of fates chosen: The cup of divine wrath was filled, and all will be forced to drink. The warnings of overreliance on temple inviolability were ignored by most, as was the reply of all of Jeremiah's former prophecy rebuffed. The words addressed to the people encouraged them simply to mourn over what has become inevitable.

But, fourth, amid all this, there remain figures of hope: King Coniah (Jehoi-achin), a signet ring, was hurled away, not to return, his position as leader of re-settlers key. Figs are labeled, counterintuitively but unequivocally: out of the land is better than in, early selection better than late. New shepherds are envisioned. The foaming cup will be drained by Babylon as well as by others. Some individu-als and groups do well: Rechabites, Ebed-Melek, Shaphan scribes, and notably a group first angry at Jeremiah's temple utterances seems to listen. And, of course, we hear God's plans of well-being and the advice that must be followed if those are to come to fruition. With all these options in play, we will next lift out some of this material to scrutinize its texture in greater detail: ways that Jeremiah con-tinues to minister and prophesy in negative space, showing by his own positions what the king must see to do.

6

GOD'S DESIRES CONTESTED—THE CASE EMBODIED BY STRANGE RESEMBLANCE AND IN NEGATIVE SPACE

Chapters 21–45, 52

> The lives of prophet and king mirror one another in their limited choices and freedom.
>
> Mark Roncace, *Jeremiah, Zedekiah, and the Fall of Jerusalem*

The case developing in this book shows God and Jeremiah embarked on an urgent challenge of persuasion, aiming first themselves to see and then to show reluctant audiences that something apparently harmful may be good, that something vastly nonpreferred must be chosen. Their project continues to meet powerful resistance in diverse ways. We have glimpsed God struggling to invest in a salutary promise, tempering and converting a divine anger with its capacity, if not preference, for violent retribution. We have witnessed God, attributing distasteful speech to Lady Zion and the men of Judah—words showing all too clearly that they do not deserve a gift of mercy, are not ready to receive it. We have heard God soliloquize, reach out for insight in apparent isolation or in nonongenial company. As God contemplates the human heart and marvels at its capacities and deficiencies, we sense inchoative movement beyond hurt and reprisal to something more compassionate. But move God does. Jeremiah, though voicing his anguish and anger, commits his cause to God, whether he can yet be said to understand the implications of his choice very well at that moment or not.

The two character sets engaged early in the prophetic book—Lady Zion and the men of Judah—have in our hearing spoken harshly to God: to deny and alibi, to blame and counteraccuse. More recently, they have mostly fallen silent, in two senses: They made no clear response to the preaching offered them in chaps. 11–20, simply did not reply. And in the long section of 20–39, they mostly ceased being given discourse, underlining their refusal, or perhaps their powerlessness. But amid resistance and silence, we glimpsed a single scene (chap. 26) where Jeremiah's case was taken seriously by some listening, a moment to which we will return in our next chapter.

The main spate of speech, divine and prophetic comingling as they do in this genre of biblical prophecy, turned from people toward leaders, as reviewed in the last chapter. We heard priests accused of thwarting their role by abuse of authority, prophets distorting theirs by illicit blasts of language. Against the insistence of YHWH and Jeremiah that the only solution for the crisis facing Judah must be an urgent choice to resettle in Babylon and a willingness to remain there, other guild professionals have argued that such a choice is not necessary, or that the stay can be brief, or even that—since some have removed themselves—others can be held excused.

But the leaders most excoriated have been kings, both as a set and by name. The four kings succeeding Josiah exemplify, each distinctively in God-and-Jeremiah's constructions, disastrous choices: Jehoahaz, gone to Egypt and disappeared there; Jehoiachin, hurled to Babylon untimely, planning his descendants on the throne in Jerusalem; Jehoiakim, refusing, opposing, and thwarting Jeremiah and his deity in every way possible; Zedekiah, displaying not the determined refusal of his royal brother but equally resistant in his delaying tactics. The relationship between Jeremiah and this last Judean king is the primary focus of this present chapter, as the king provides the prophet with the opportunity to begin an intense phase of prophecy: enacting by unexpected analogy the situation of God's Judean project and making tangible in negative space the inevitable outcome of continued deferral of response.

Though there are some 350 verses in the book of Jeremiah set either directly or implicitly during the reign of King Zedekiah, the main subject of this chapter is seven narrative occasions on which king and prophet confer, with special attention given to the last of those sessions (38:14–28).[1] The units and their matrices on which I draw primarily, named (in the previous chapter and here) for easy reference are: 21:1–14: *wistful wish flattened;* 27:1–22: *yokes contested;* 32:1–44: *land deed needed;* 34:1–22: *slave reprieve revoked;* 37:3–21: *disputed departure;* 38:1–13: *in and out of Malchiah's mud.* Having just sketched and summarized the bigger picture in which these seven scenes are embedded, the purpose of this present chapter is to continue to show how Jeremiah struggles to make his "submit and survive" option viable to the king and to show how, at least in bold relief, he fails to do so.[2]

My root questions are three. First, how do these individuals relate so intensively that there may appear to be more interweaving one with another than separating them? How to understand fruitfully the ways ostensible opponents are actually collaborating and mutually implicated with each other, whether constructively or destructively? Second is the apparent failure of Jeremiah's prophetic ministry, his narrative inability to persuade his king(s) to act so as to avoid brutal defeat and destruction of Judah. But against the larger backdrop of prophetic purposes of persuasion, how does the literary character of Jeremiah succeed? And third, we return to a question raised earlier in this work: the challenge of talking about biblical prophecy and our appropriation of it that explicitly appreciate the difficulties of maintaining how certain humans—prophets—can claim to speak for God and be understood by others to do so, specifically in the direction of catalyzing compassion.

My hope here is to claim and develop three nested points. First, I will show the ways that the apparent opponents—the prophet Jeremiah and the king Zedekiah—deeply resemble each other and are in fact comprehensively interlocked. We will note their positions, apparently opposite but in fact quite similar. And we will observe the content and process of their discourse; how they engage, apparently as opponents but actually as helpers of each other, will establish their strange resemblance. Second, I want to suggest how their common striving makes visible a project larger than either of them: the characterization of prophecy and the survival of God's biblical people. The flailing pair brings into prominence this strugglous saving of something beyond themselves. And third, I want to name ways that the phenomenon of biblical prophecy and the challenge of seeing Scripture as God's self-disclosure can be made more complex and, at least to me, more helpful than we may sometimes construct it to be.

This chapter will also follow the storyline through to its finale, the end of monarchic Judah, as we watch Jeremiah fade from us in Egypt (chapters 39–45 and 52). I will suggest that the material of the final ministry of the prophet has a single relentless purpose: to show in multiple moments what is not God's plan of well-being for the people in hopes that the plans for well-being can be clear.

Demonstration of Characteral Correlation and Collaboration

Getting to the Final Encounter

Moving quickly through six scenes with king and prophet to reach their final disastrous encounter (at 38:14–28), we watch their literary character zones become heavily accreted. Insofar as literary characters are mobile speaking viewpoints and proffered ideologies (hence, zones), we observe how closely these two characters come to resemble and shape each other before we watch them interact a final time.[3] After offering the results of some close work on the first six encounters, I will sketch the overlap visually so it can be seen more emblematically.

Position is clearest to see. Jeremiah, who in the first twenty chapters of the book appears to come and go at will in the environs of Jerusalem, finds himself at the end of that large unit (20:2–3) placed in stocks briefly, rehearsal of a fate soon to intensify. In the large chunk of material under present consideration across which Jeremiah and Zedekiah interact, Jeremiah's position is as follows: He is, intermittently but relentlessly, trapped in the besieged city (21:2; 32:3, 24; 34:1), both when the siege seems relieved (37:5, 11) and surely when it intensifies (37:8; 39). However he has two forays out of the city: the first trek is hinted narratively, perhaps even imaginatively, as he—in response to a question from the king—enacts a transaction that involves his redeeming land outside Jerusalem (question of 32:3–5 generates the response of 32:6–44). The second journey is presented narratively as an actual event (37:11–14), where his effort to leave is thwarted and interpreted in a way the prophet refuses. Those journeys being noted, the rest of the detail on Jeremiah's position shows him nested in confinement: He places his neck in a wooden yoke which, when broken, he vows to replace with an iron collar (27:1–28:17). In the besieged city he is first at large and then restricted to the court of the guard (32:3; 37:21; 38:28).[4] He is removed from there on two occasions: first, taken to additional and more hazardous confinement in the Jonathan-house prison/pit (37:16); second, dropped into the mud in the Malchiah-house pit (38:6).[5] Sunk in the mud is Jeremiah's lowest and deepest position (thinking in terms where in/out and up/down represent extremes).[6] In the final portion of the book (starting at chap. 39:11 and continuing) Jeremiah will be ultimately freed when the city is taken by Babylonians. Presented with a choice—go to Babylon or remain in Judah—Jeremiah opts to stay in the defeated land but ends up in Egypt, whence he disappears from our sight. So although freer than he was, we may continue to think of him as still hedged to no small extent. What he urges for others he cannot manage for himself, making stark the choice.

Zedekiah, by contrast, never appears overtly in any place of confinement beyond being in the besieged Jerusalem (*supra*). He seems sheltered in his own royal complex, able to come and go at whim. It is odd that except that we are working on position and thus take none of these points as incidental, we learn at the end of the book (51:59) that in the fourth year of his rule, Zedekiah went to Babylon. The king also signals his position along a continuum of openness to secrecy in terms of communicating with Jeremiah: that is, sometimes openly sending messengers (21:1; 37:3) but ultimately needing to set up secret consultations (37:17; 38:14–28).[7] His fate is sealed once the city wall is breached and he flees Jerusalem, free only briefly, to be apprehended (39:1–7).

The contrasting positions of the opposing pairs are thus startlingly similar when looked at synoptically: Free at first, then increasingly constrained in Jerusalem, intersecting occasionally, resembling each other if briefly at the collapse of Jerusalem. Jeremiah physically prophesies, presumably for Zedekiah and any others listening, a set of prisons into which he drops and out of which he emerges, as though to show the king where *he* is, what *he* needs to do. Jeremiah enacts symbolically the journeys Zedekiah refuses even as challenged to contemplate them. The prophet demonstrates the options that the king might ponder as he discerns his future. Zedekiah, having tested the waters in Babylon but apparently without significant effect, finally flees, but not toward the choice he might have had. King and prophet each decline their best "go somewhat freely to Babylon" option, disappear from our sight, each in a dispreferred position. The two coincide nearly exactly at 38:5, when the king hands Jeremiah over to four men while saying that he himself is helpless to resist them, implying an existence surrounded by foes, a point Jeremiah shows visibly in his own position as well (for example, 11:18–19 and in the laments, *passim*). We will watch the two come to share sunk-in-the-mud-ness shortly (Jeremiah in 38:6 and Zedekiah in 38:22).

If we simply watch the action without being distracted by the identities of the players, we see that Jeremiah's positions are not so powerful and persuasive as are Zedekiah's. That is, Jeremiah's positions are improved by the king, while the king's position seems not helped by anything Jeremiah demonstrates.[8] King and not prophet is the agent of rescue; the king helps the prophet out—temporarily and thus repeatedly—not the reverse. Prophet petitions king more than king consults prophet. Zedekiah does Jeremiah's job of "helping out," and the prophet invites or condones it. But we can also see that these temporary fixes are the king's resistance to enacted prophecy, his royal thwarting of what God and prophet are trying to show him, with the hope that he will choose it for himself and thus for his people as well.

Before looking at their final meeting, we can also summarize as well the discourse manner of the pair's previous engagements, examining conversation in terms of its plain-spoken content, its accompanying enactment, and its reused or quoted discourse. There is considerable variation of "verbal staging" in the scenes that lead up to the ultimate encounter between prophet and king.[9]

The Plain Discourse

Jeremiah's discourse is prominent and consistent. To summarize his six speeches in these scenes (comprising nearly sixty verses) is to hear Jeremiah offering his two options (21:8–9 and 38:2 are concise statements of them): Plan A is "submit [to the Babylonians now] and survive," you, your house, the city (27:11–12; 34:4–5).[10] Plan B is "dig in and die," a fate elaborated in far more detail (21:4–7, 9a, 13–14; 27:5–10, 13–22; 28:14; 32:28–36; 34:2–3; 37:10). The overlapped quotation among deity, prophet, and narrator intensifies the impression that it is late in the day to make good choices; options, though still possible, are narrowing as scene piles onto scene, something we have already shown happening within this large unit of material.

The king, on the other hand, flails, commanding oracles he does not get (21:2; 37:17) while refusing to engage those he is given (21:3–14; 34:17; 37:17). He asks questions whose responses he overlooks (32:3–5; 37:17). He contradicts his own orders (38:5, 10). Resistant to the power of the "elephant" standing outside the city walls of which Jeremiah never ceases to speak, the king's capacity for avoidance is amazing. Dialogue proceeds at cross-purposes until the final meeting of king and prophet, where we will see that the king has listened better than he appears to have done. A common topic persists, consumes both: how serious and how long the Babylonian threat.

Crucial also to the verbal parrying of these scenes is the *enactment* that accompanies them, providing suasive background and interpreting each encounter of prophet and king. Jeremiah, to an extent surpassing other biblical prophets, constantly dramatizes his words, not simply to elaborate but to reposition them for deeper understanding. In their first exchange (*wistful wish flattened*, chaps. 21–23) Jeremiah casts the oracle of the destruction of the city over which Zedekiah now reigns in company with (non)dirges for Zedekiah's four royal predecessors, implying the same for the incumbent: dead and unmourned (22:10–30). The second set of oracles is made visible in *contested yokes* (chaps. 27–28), where the prophet himself wears the yoke he is urging others to submit to, even planning to replace his own when another prophet knocks it off him to counterclaim that Jeremiah is wrong about Babylonian hegemony and Judah's choice. The narrative *land deed needed* serves as Jeremiah's reply to Zedekiah's question "Why do you say such things?"; the detail elaborates not so much the reclaiming of the land from its danger but the delay of it, a point shown by the care with which the witnessing deed must be kept—so much time will elapse until it is needed (32:10–16).[11] The process of securing for a long time a deed that will eventually be relevant weights the words that signal return to the beleaguered land.

Enactment is particularly crucial to the fourth engagement of Jeremiah and Zedekiah (*slave reprieve revoked*, chap. 34), since it explains apparent discrepancy in Jeremiah's promise to the king about the manner of his death. In that passage, startlingly, Jeremiah advises Zedekiah that "you shall not die by the sword; you shall die in peace. And as spices were burned for your ancestors, the earlier kings who preceded you, so they shall burn spices for you and lament for you, saying, 'Alas, lord.'" But the matrix embedding that promise is Jeremiah's reproaching Zedekiah for his own broken promise to slaves (34:12–22). The prophet reminds the king that God and people had a mutual commitment: God had freed Israel from Egyptian bondage and had specified that Hebrew slaves had to be released periodically—a promise rarely kept. And when Zedekiah had himself freed enslaved Judean kin in view of the Babylonian danger and got others to do the same, he then reneged and reenslaved them. So the backdrop of false words sets the standard and colors the "release promise," consigning the reneging king from frying pan to fire, from sacrificer to sacrificed—from liar to lied to. The oracle ends with the more typical words of doom to Zedekiah.[12]

The fifth consultation between king and prophet, *disputed departure*, is made visual when Jeremiah attempts to leave the city, only to be stopped at its edge, accused of deserting to the Babylonians, arrested and imprisoned (37:13–14). This enacted parable suggests proleptically and dramatically that there is, symbolically, no escape for Jerusalem's entrapped.[13] Finally, the prophet's being allowed to be dropped into *Malchiah's mud* and then his rescue from it (38:1–13) make tangible the verbal contest accompanying the events: Are Jeremiah's words harmful or not? Who is powerful in the city? The discourse must be construed—is fruitfully construed—in context of the "backdrop scenery" against which the prophet casts it, remains incomplete without such consideration. Jeremiah speaks and he enacts that language so as to activate what might otherwise have been missed.

Zedekiah appears to speak without enactment—except insofar as the dire circumstances of Jerusalem make visible his refusal to take the Babylonian threat seriously. But in fact, both enact: Jeremiah goes in and out of confinement, while Zedekiah persistently enacts the outcome he wants to be true, proceeding as though the Babylonians were not a serious threat. It is not too much to suggest that—narratively if not historically—Zedekiah causes the fate of Jerusalem by "digging in" to the fate he refuses to see. Jeremiah's enactments (as constructed here) are clever and apt, but they fail to persuade. Are they too powerful for the man to whom they are offered? When we look at their last engagement, that suggestion picks up some support.

Lastly, while we are looking at discourse, there is a maze of *quoted speech* wending its way among these passages, voiced by king, prophet, and their surrogates.[14] The book of Jeremiah and the prophetic character are distinctive in the amount of material where the language of one speaker is picked up and made to function in the character zone of another.[15] Layered quotation provides a strategy for suggesting both similarity and difference: Characters resemble each other as they share speech, while varieties of reaccentuation distance or contrast their speakers. So again, our pair here is shown ostensibly at odds but quite startlingly conflated. We will consider three places where our main protagonists quote each other and examine those utterances in various ways. Germane is what topics are handled by quotation, how the discourse is truthful or not, what interpretive insights the language bears, and the perceptible effects of it, at several levels discernible by a reader.

In 32:3–5 (*land deed needed*) Zedekiah quotes Jeremiah's general dispreferred position ("dig in and die") to make several points: <Why do you say: <<YHWH has given this city to the king of Babylon and he'll take it; Zedekiah will not

escape but be taken and meet the king of Babylon face to face, eye to eye; Zedekiah will be taken to Babylon until YHWH is ready to deal with him; though Zedekiah et al. fight, they will not succeed>?> First, querying the quotation's accuracy, we can vouch for it, in two senses. It is what Jeremiah says (*supra*), and it is what ultimately happens (chap. 39–45). More urgent is Zedekiah's deeper question: why Jeremiah should say such things and why they should happen. These points lie at the heart of the prophetic book: intertwining agency of the deity, role of the prophet, fate of the king and people. We can next speculate about why Zedekiah chooses his "why do you talk like this?" question with its quotation and how he may receive the prophet's response of the land-redemption story with its claims about the seriousness of the Babylonian threat and the urgency of time. We might urge him to hear: Can "Uncle Zedekiah's" land be saved for his "nephew Jehoiachin" as apparently Uncle Hanamel's will be for Nephew Jeremiah? Can the nephew's early departure from the city—or the uncle's journey to where the nephew is confined—redeem the uncle's need?[16] Yes, but not effectively in the uncle's lifetime is what we have already gleaned from Jeremiah's enactment of the scene. As to effect: As we witness this interaction, we catch no narrative indication of royal openness to the prophetic persuasion; but when we reach their final encounter, we will see that the king has heard more than it seemed—increasing the culpability of the king who heard well enough to repeat the words, to sling them back over the net to Jeremiah. By the time we have understood the dynamics, the king shares the prophet's culpability for dangerous or unpatriotic words.

The narrative *slave reprieve revoked* is a bit more oblique, since the crucial language is alluded to as though familiar rather than being quoted; but the quotation dynamics are similar. Jeremiah brings traditional legal words of slave release (34:8–17) into relationship with the general noncompliance of Israelites/ Judeans over time and specifically with the king's deficient action during the siege.[17] Jeremiah charges that Zedekiah reintonated the legal language, first to obey it and then to renege when circumstances changed (34:8–11). That is, when the threat seemed serious, the king liberated slaves, as did others also; when the siege seemed less intense, all took their slaves back. The surface questions: Is the quoting valid? No character—including the king—contests it. Is the legal practice urged here condign with the king's situation? Commentators seem agreed that Zedekiah's act is unique in terms of biblical practice; but Jeremiah's aligning it with the general manumission practice, if unusual, is not opposed and seems well-suited to the point he wants to make about broken promises. Before this conversation the king may not have supposed that his particular deed was related to the general law of slave release, that link being offered distinctively—even uniquely—by the prophet. That is, we, reading, have been long "socialized" into

Jeremiah's connection, which may not have been obvious or imagined until he made it. Effect of the reused speech: The quotations (explicit and implicit) establish the king as unreliable and allow the prophet and deity to slide mimetically into that same role as they share the reneging strategy of the quotation. Jeremiah implies that God will be as faithful to a promise as was the king and then offers a promise that is manifestly not to be counted on. That point may be doubled as the king intermittently enacts his unreliability in the matter of Jeremiah's freedom/captivity.[18] Is Jeremiah simply blaming, or does he attempt to persuade? What is the effect of Jeremiah's quoting and resituating the king's utterance? The deity and prophet join the king here—all liars.

In a final episode, *Malchiah's mud,* the king's men overhear Jeremiah's preaching—which the narrator summarizes as though from what the four construct: Jeremiah has said, "Thus says the Lord: 'Those who stay in the city shall die by the sword, by famine, and by pestilence; but those who go out to the Chaldeans shall live; they shall have their lives as a prize of war, and live.' And 'This city shall surely be handed over to the army of the king of Babylon and be taken'" (38:2–3). Is the quotation accurate? Yes, generally so. Is it true? Shortly it will be fulfilled. Why the prophet continues to say such things is the next concern of the men who quote Jeremiah: motivation and effect. They appraise first effect and then motive: "This man ought to be put to death, because he is discouraging the soldiers who are left in this city, and all the people, by speaking such words to them. For this man is not seeking the welfare of this people but their harm" (38:4–5). They charge the prophetic speaker with malevolence, weighting his words as lethal. Their first claim about speaker intent is urgent in the whole book: Can "submit," "relocate," be good? The impact of the speech on diverse hearers in the city is impossible to know, but we can witness its effect on the four who—repeating the words—find them so dangerous that the speaker must be silenced. Their view persuades the king as well, who, however, had not acted on his own when he'd heard these words before. We may wonder why Jeremiah's words are worse now than before.

Into the fray steps foreigner Ebed-Melek to oppose this construction and persuade the king that his surrogates are wrong, misspeaking, malicious. Ebed-Melek makes controversial precisely what we need to assess: Is the prophet speaking against the city, his words evidence of a malicious intent? The issue of imprisonment and its fresh setting, brought forward to the king again by Ebed-Melek, counteraccuses the four men of harmful motive and lethal effect: imprisoning Jeremiah until he die of starvation in a besieged city. The quotation picks up a new layer of significance as it enters a third mouth, so to speak. The layered language puts the spotlight once again on whether the king is reliable, is a man of his word, will free a prisoner and stick to it, so that he not die of neglect and starvation in the bottom of a pit, sunk in the mud. Jeremiah does not speak here, but resounding aptly in the quotation slinging is his earlier question to the king in 37:18: "What wrong have I done to you or your servants or this people, that you have put me in this prison?" The king accepts Ebed-Melek over against the claim of the four, simultaneously contradicting his own royal assertion of 38:5. The servant acts to save both the prophet and the king, bridging them in his gesture. What is the agency of the deity, the role of the prophet, the fate of the king?

The complex battle of quotations we have so briefly considered may be summarized as follows: In virtually every instance, the topic is the duration of the Babylonian threat, with its attendant question of what YHWH plans for Jerusalem and its inhabitants. The threat from the Babylonians is either not serious or long term, claim Zedekiah and his people; or alternatively, it is both grave and enduring, counter Jeremiah and his helper, Ebed-Melek.[19] By their reaction to Jeremiah's words, the four officers denying the truth of them simultaneously give them importance by insisting that the speaker be silenced. Whose words save and whose destroy? Who speaks truthfully and who does not? Can YHWH contemplate destroying the city and those trapped in it? If destruction comes, is the deity its source? Is Jeremiah telling the truth over against other competing voices? Is there a way out for the king, for other elites, for Lady Zion and the men of Judah? If rescue is needed, who can accomplish it? Who needs rescue? Who is rescued and how?

Summary via Snapshot

Having pushed off from a default assumption that prophet and king are opponents at every level, we have shown them also as collaborators. Consider now that our two main characters are males, clothed in dark garments distinguished primarily by a small insignia scarcely visible: a small embroidered crown for the king's cloak, a roughly stitched scroll for the prophet's wrap. Aside from these traced markers, the two appear almost indistinguishable. Ponder now these short video clips and frozen stills composed from our textual and methodological work where we can now appreciate our pair as both thoroughly enmeshed while logically distinct, can appraise and appreciate their collaboration before heightening it in the last scene where they meet:

Once able to come and go at will, they are both confined in a besieged city, their plights worsening as the cordon tightens. Jeremiah's multiple places of particular confinement seem more obvious, but the king is as trapped as the prophet. Each also describes himself as surrounded by apparent friends who are in fact foes. Often linked by messengers, we also glimpse the pair, heads together, conferring as though colleagues. One topic absorbing them is: How serious and durable is the threat from Babylonian besiegers? We also see them with complex loyalties:

Royal Zedekiah is by definition God's man and by arrangement Nebuchadnezzar's.[20] Jeremiah is clearly God's man but is accused of collaboration with the Babylonians, a false charge, presumably, but one to gain credence when Nebuchadnezzar's men exercise such special care for him after the collapse of the city.

When each attempts to exit the city, their fates also collide. Neither is able to follow the advice of Jeremiah and go somewhat willingly into exile. The king may end up there, though not willingly, or perishing en route; and the prophet turns down the Babylonian offer and ends up, problematically, in Egypt. Jeremiah enacts their common moment memorably (*disputed departure*) when he attempts to leave the city and is stopped, accused, arrested, and imprisoned.

Each needs the other to help him out, literally out of the trap in which each is confined. They are locked into a matched vulnerability. And each does perhaps surprisingly attempt to help the other, with the king having far greater apparent success than the prophet. That is, in our snapshots we see the king helping the prophet out of a pit more often than we see the prophet assisting the king through an exit. Another way to view this collaboration is to say that so long as one of them remains trapped, the other stays with him, or that the king's refusal to leave constrains the prophet.

A crisp and clear enactment of their predicament is provided in *land deed needed,* as the prophet narrates for the king the vignette where Jeremiah—as Hanamel's nephew—leaves the city in order to rescue the threatened heritage of his uncle (or Hanamel comes into the city to see Jeremiah's action accomplished). The land needing help is in fact secured by the action of the redeemer, but with no discernible effect on the life of the uncle, who drops out of the story in favor of attention given to the document. Jeremiah acts the Jehoiachin role in this drama performed for Zedekiah, becoming "family" in order to suggest a path for the king. The nephew lives away from the heritage, and perhaps by doing so saves the family property, but not soon. The obsolescent uncle is otiose and can at best stand aside, enabling his nephew to act.

Listening closely, we hear them share words to a surprising extent. Though Jeremiah seems blunt, consistent, and to the point while Zedekiah flails and flusters verbally, in fact both the king and his surrogates quote the prophetic words they hate, testifying to and reinforcing their significance in their efforts to counter and eventually silence the words. And the prophet treats the king's inability to hear seriously by a constant stream of efforts to engage him in every genre imaginable.

To be specific, the pair shares broken promise language (*slave reprieve revoked*). The prophet quotes, rather allusively and messily, what the king said, attaching to that promissory language to slaves some language from what we call biblical law. In so doing Jeremiah calls the king unreliable while ostentatiously joining himself and the deity to that same circle, offering a promise that is manifestly unreliable. Three liars together: king, prophet, deity.

At three intense moments, we see the two figures all but coincide, first when the king, consigning the prophet to the Malchiah-house pit (*Malchiah's mud*), remarks on his own inability to act freely (38:5). Second, having thus consigned the prophet's feet to the mud of that pit, he will soon be told that he is in the same position. Third, in the most provocative moment, when Ebed-Melek acts to release both of the "prisoners" at once, the king from killing the prophet and the prophet from dying.

The point has been to show the careful sketching and suggest its impact, to allow it to deepen our sense of the prophetic challenge here. We will now consider in detail the last scene where they intersect and then move to say more about what is accomplished by seeing these more subtle patterns beneath the more obvious opposition.

Seventh and Final Encounter between King and Prophet: 38:14–28

With their strange resemblance in place from six encounters, we arrive at the final meeting of these contending and collaborating characters so mutually implicated in each other's fates.[21] We will use the same two basic categories of analysis as before, though in a more blended way. First, what to note about the *position* of the pair as we see them conferring face-to-face at the third gate of the temple, to which Jeremiah has been released and Zedekiah apparently comes unhampered— or constrained by nothing except the intensifying siege of Jerusalem.[22] Jeremiah arrives, narratively speaking, fresh from his lowest position, sunk in the mud at the Malchiah-house pit, where he had been first placed and thence freed, each time by Zedekiah's consent. Reprieved at least temporarily to the court of the guard, the king's destination underlies the main concern of this passage. Jeremiah has suffered his worst (the Jonathan-house prison or the Malchiah-house pit) and will not be consigned there again. Zedekiah, about to learn that his own feet are also trapped in mud, has his worst position ahead of him, virtually inevitable once he no longer engages with Jeremiah. So the two figures cross here. In this face-to-face meeting there are no near witnesses, though the king supposes that their clandestine sortie is observed—the fact if not the content.[23] Each needs something from the other while being vulnerable to what the other might do. As they bargain, their ostensibly uneven captor/captive positions take on a common resemblance in their need for reciprocal help.[24] As they part, which will be soon, each is still trapped and doomed.

Next we examine their *discourse:* as before, *plain-spoken, enacted, quoted.*[25] The king opens (38:14) with a compound request, *spoken more plainly* by him than we have heard to date: <I want something/don't refuse me.> (v. 15).[26] The prophet parries, in matched statements: <If I tell you true, you'll put me to death; if I advise you, you won't listen.> The king counters half of this prophetic rejoinder by persevering (38:16), sign of his determination here to proceed, reinforcing his request with an oath: <I swear I will not kill you or hand you over to others.> But he also confirms Jeremiah's word by withholding any promise to obey what he may be counseled. The king's oath offers safety for the prophet, but can Zedekiah deliver on this word, since we heard him say in 38:5 that he cannot land a word effectively? We have seen the king break his words to freed slaves, have witnessed royal equivocation on the handing over of Jeremiah, when pressed. Will a royal promissory word appeal on this occasion? Jeremiah is apparently willing to take a chance, whether it helps the main goal of "getting out" or not.

But, having grounded his own position and offered insurance to his interlocutor, Zedekiah does not, in our hearing actually make a specific request—a very tantalizing omission. The topic raging is how to escape the tightening fate, which is what the king just promised the prophet under oath. We can fill in the king's question only from what the pair discuss and from earlier requests: <How do I get out of here safely?> It is, of course, the question for both, for each: <*How* to get out of here?> It is what the king needs and now perhaps wants to know, wants help to do. It is also what the king has just reminded the prophet that *he* ought to be concerned with, will raise again. Previously Zedekiah has consulted the prophet about Babylonian withdrawal, about the particulars of Jeremiah's speech. Perhaps Zedekiah now senses events moving beyond those matters to something more urgent for himself. We can glean some verbal evidence that he has in fact listened to Jeremiah's words—as previously suggested both a good sign and a bad one. His capacity to have heard what the prophet is actually saying might have helped him but ultimately renders him more culpable when he refuses to heed it. The prophet offers the same choice as before (38:17–18): "Submit and survive," save yourself, your house, the city; or "dig in and die," causing defeat, destruction of the city by fire, and capture of the king and heirs.[27] We may now wonder whether Jeremiah's language is reliable. Is his proffered option still viable? Historically it is difficult—impossible—to say. Literarily, we have hints: Jeremiah, cast as Zedekiah's double, has already enacted a departure from Jerusalem that was thwarted, misrepresented, and distorted, resulting in accusation, arrest, imprisonment.[28] We have seen the king rescue the prophet several times by his word, though we have also seen him claim to be unable to manage his own men by words. We have not yet seen the prophet able to save the king. Who can assist the other in a truly salutary way? Neither, it will turn out.

But in any case and in a moment of great apparent candor, Zedekiah shares the reason he cannot do what Jeremiah counsels (38:19). First we note that he has in fact considered it, even if to reject it. This is an amazing moment in the long

Jeremiah book, with the king in effect reducing the whole matter of Babylon versus Judah and Jerusalem to his own fear of what might happen to him at the hands of others. He risks pulling down the venerable Davidic enterprise because he dreads a hypothetical outcome, though one wholly, dreadfully imaginable. He says he fears the people of Judah who have done already the very thing Jeremiah has been urging. This is a complex moment for all participating: The king cannot act because he fears abuse at the hands of those who have done what Jeremiah says he must do—presumably, go toward exile at Babylon, circumstances where he fears his reception. We are back to embodiment: the prophet stands before the king, abused for his own controversial actions, witness the present scene and those preceding. Once again, the pair overlap substantially. The king is either disregarding his prisoner's condition or else reading it all too attentively. The ethical/moral/spiritual question posed, ultimately, is whether danger and fear can—will—deter integrity or not. We may also ask to what extent the prophet's words can sustain and enhance royal courage. Jeremiah has voiced a consistent word in his life, and the king stands poised at his own defining moment. For an instant, again, they nearly coincide. But the king backs off (and some feel the prophet does too!). That is, Zedekiah looks in the Jeremiah mirror to find a man abused by his enemies, and he declines to risk inviting what Jeremiah's life embodies. We may construct a question from king to prophet: <How can I do what you say when in fact you are already showing me how it will fulfill my worst expectations?> That is, again in literary terms, the main disincentive for this whole catastrophe is the king's fear of the trap he has put himself in, specifically by his foolish relations with Babylon and Egypt that have boxed him into danger of defeat and exile.

Jeremiah then (38:20), perhaps fatefully, pushes this candidly poignant utterance aside—as has often been done to his own words—and replies, again with his best advice: <That won't happen. Obey and live.> But the dis/incentive now *enacted* is fresh and distinctive (38:21–23): The prophet paints for the king a scenario given him by God, he says, a proleptic vision of what has *not yet* happened to the king but, presumably, may or is about to happen (though we will not witness it in this precise way).[29] Jeremiah shares it: <If you dig in—refuse my advice—I see women led out to the Babylonians and they are blaming you (38:21–23) <<You are sunk in the mud, placed there by untrustworthy friends who, in any case, are deserting you.>> You and your women and children will be captured, and the false allies will escape.> Prophet and king face off at what is both climax and nadir of their relationship. The wifeless and childless prophet calls forth the reproach of the king's family to taunt or upbraid him for failing to do what Jeremiah urges him to do. But, as before and perhaps not surprisingly, the prophet is ineffective at this crucial moment and distinctive opportunity.

Astonishing is that this intense and honest exchange breaks off to wind down quickly. Zedekiah makes no response to what Jeremiah has shown him except to insist that their talk not be made public. That is, without engaging the content of the scenario the prophet has just shown him or making any sort of verbal response to it, the king moves to disaster containment (38:24): <No one must know what we have talked about.> This is yet another remarkable gap on the part of the king, inviting our interpretation. Perhaps we read the king as so shocked by what he is shown that he must suppress it from others' hearing, even from his own consciousness. Jeremiah, we may speculate, has used language so powerful that instead of providing the king an incentive, it frightens him into the same corner he was just emerging from. Each, having been vulnerable, is exposed. Each retreats. The king takes the initiative to seek cover for both, opens an escape hatch they can both take back into their prison.[30] Zedekiah says (38:25–26): <They'll ask you what was said and even threaten you, but don't tell.>[31] The king quotes his officials, apparently knows just what they'll say, and he tells Jeremiah what to say, quoting the prophet as well, though from a previous narrative moment (37:20): <Say you were begging not to go back to the Jonathan house.> Do we, does the Jeremiah of our constructing, hear that as a threat as well as a promise? Is Zedekiah's <Do this> also a <Better not do that,> his <If you don't do this> a veiled <know that I'll do that>? Does Jeremiah lose integrity here, as a number of commentators say? A Bakhtinian insight into the ambiguity of reused speech suggests no.[32] Jeremiah now falls silent, making no reply to this royal offer; perhaps we imagine him circling back to his opening remark at 38:15: <Our consultations never come to anything.> His discourse shuts down, and so far as we can see, he falls into the plan that Zedekiah makes for his own royal protection, for their mutual protection. And the narrator hints (38:27–28) that Jeremiah complied, since he was given the favor Zedekiah told him to say they had been discussing: No return to his worst pit, but no real reprieve, either.

Snapshot Just Viewed

We see the positions of the king and prophet even more closely overlapped than before as they confer as near-equals at the third gate of the temple, then share stuck-in-the mud-ness.

We watch the scene end with neither able to make a real escape, though each seems about to improve his worst possibility. Jeremiah does not go back deep in, and Zedekiah pushes away the vision of his kin reproaching him as they all fall to the Babylonians. Each has basically one move left: exit to the nonpreferred and fundamentally doomed choice.

Their mutual need and mutual vulnerability is intensified. The king is candid in a way he has not been before, and the prophet throws himself on the king's word—granted not worth much. But these two come as close to helping each other as ever happens.

The "nephew" cannot help the "uncle" here; their land will be lost, it seems, at least in the short term. The uncle, in refusing to be helped—or in resisting what he construes as harmful—dooms them both, them all.

The king's discourse is, among other things, characterized as consisting of a question he ought have asked and a reply he ought have given, but he fails at both moments. At arguably the key moment in Jeremiah's long engagement with the king, his language is counterproductive, frightening rather than encouraging Zedekiah, catalyzing exactly the wrong response.

In the end, the king dissimulates, if does not quite lie. And yet the equivocation selected is not fabricated but borrowed from another moment in the story. And the prophet, sometimes accused of acquiescing to royal dishonesty, allows the king's quote to stand without cavil or concession. It may not be his most transparent moment, but I don't find it to lack integrity.

The prophet remains silent to the end of the episode and well past it, allowing the king to urge on him his "old language" for reuse in fresh circumstances.

Implications of Characteral Correlation and Collaboration

If the substantial similarity and interdependence of these erstwhile opponents has been established and the literary artistry shown, the next question is why it matters. Let me return to the last two questions that opened this chapter: the apparent failure of the prophet and the complexities of speaking about prophetic ministry, specifically as we have it in this text.

Jeremiah as a Failure

It seems indisputable that King Zedekiah failed to protect the city of Jerusalem, over which his kin had ruled for more than four hundred narrative years. Insofar as Zedekiah's revolt against his overlord (2 Kings 24:20) provoked Nebuchadnezzar's retaliation and the Judean king's refusal to contemplate alternatives to submission sealed the fate of the Jerusalem heritage and inhabitants, the responsibility is his. Zedekiah enacts the basic charge of Jeremiah against the David sons in *wistful wish flattened:* that they abuse as well as neglect their trust (chaps. 21–23).[33] Jeremiah's main objective, at least in terms of the scenes where he deals with Zedekiah, has to be to convince the king to act such that destruction is averted. In that sense, Zedekiah's failure is Jeremiah's and the inverse as well: The prophet's failure brings down the king while the king dooms the prophet. The similarity of compositional figures brings into fresh relief Jeremiah's professional deficiency as well. As we watch the two figures separate at the end of their last conference in chap. 38—Jeremiah back to the house of the guard and Zedekiah back to his house—the story will soon move them to their ultimate destinations: the king to flee the breached city only to be caught, taken to Riblah, blinded after witnessing the slaughter of his sons, moved toward Babylon (39:1–7). The prophet leaves the city though under clearly less hostile circumstances, when—with Babylonian protection—he is offered multiple choices, including to go to Babylon with the "class of '87" or remain in the land (39:11–14; 40:1–6). It cannot come as a narrative surprise that Jeremiah fails to follow the advice he has spoken so consistently but remains.[34] In the construction we have been considering, he can't have done differently. He lives on, a largely failed prophet, persuading here neither his interlocutor nor himself, saving none. It is a provocative literary detail, however it may be resolved historically. What Jeremiah fails to convince the king to do, he himself also refuses. Their figures lock for a final time before separating to experience defeat in separate corners. King and prophet act in general synchrony, assisting and abetting each other's moves. They cannot be adequately treated in isolation. Rather, they demonstrate the intermeshed quality of virtually all moral activity. This is not to suggest inevitable malevolence; choices may be largely prompted otherwise—for example, fear, as seen with these two.

Another way to put that is to say that Jeremiah had one ministerial charge, becoming ever clearer in the final years of the life of royal Judah/Jerusalem: to encourage as many as possible to relocate. And he largely fails at it. The single pair of ears most needing to hear if the larger project was to be saved were not reached by Jeremiah's voice. My point is not so much to ascribe blame to Jeremiah as to gain insight into what the sketch we have proffered through him and his others. If we, living under siege and with diminishing/expanding options, need to contemplate failure, how will the literary persona, the prophetic calling?[35] What was required of Jeremiah, prophet? Several things to note, now, about the nature of his role as a prophet, though these will not be our final consideration of the topic: First, though there are prophets we meet *in medias res* and who vanish briefly in like manner, Jeremiah's narrative life is long and dominated both by his call and by his end. Prophet from the womb, he ministers as such for some forty years and is prophesying as we take leave of him in Egypt (1:2–3; 51:64). Jeremiah is a paradigm for those who give their life wholly to God, who has taken it over already. He is completely consumed by his call to preach and prophesy, with no apparent remainder. If he fails at this calling, it is difficult to know where to turn for him, except that we know that humans like Jeremiah have lives hidden with God. But if we are assessing professionally, the prophet cannot expect a high score in terms of pragmatic effect. We can't balance his signal failure, claiming that, after all, he was good at 'x'; there is no 'x.'

Second, his prophetic calling challenges him to listen attentively to what he thinks and feels God wants and needs him to say to the people and then to communicate it, choosing and using whatever modes seem best. As suggested in the introduction to this book, that process is far from simple. If we make appropriately problematic the ways by which prophets discern God's word and ready it for reissue (think of Moses, Isaiah, Ezekiel, Jeremiah himself, and even Jesus having their flawed speech apparatus—mouth, lips—attended to, or a more eloquent helper provided to assist), we recognize that the reception and redelivery of God's word and especially the transition between receiving and sharing them is deeply, vastly challenging. That the Bible makes it seem fairly straightforward does not change things. Jeremiah must be understood to blend life experience with what he "hears," to transpose it fruitfully for preaching. Jeremiah comes, at least in the material considered here, to a consistent certainty that he proclaims repeatedly, "submit and survive," or "dig in and die." In more nuanced terms, we have seen that polarity's positive edge to inspire some sort of choice to resettle to Babylon. In Brueggemann's terms, YHWH is agent of both judgment and possibility.[36] We understand from the book of Jeremiah (if not necessarily from what likely happened) that one choice only was valorized, with other options deemed pointless, destructive. Was Jeremiah correct to limit options to one—and it inherently unthinkable by a proud nation and venerable kingly line under threat? Did he do well so to privilege one option that there seems no negotiating room? We need to appreciate how unpalatable would have been Jeremiah's "Babylon bent" as he hammered on it while the siege tightened and alternatives looked so urgently attractive; how unlikely such an urging that the leaders of Judah in effect capitulate to the menacing foe. It may be that Jeremiah was too tightly narrowed in his hearing, too short-sighted in his vision, too rigid in his formulations.[37]

Third, having heard and absorbed God's urgency through the sieve of life experience, a prophet like Jeremiah needs to help others come to an enhanced point of view, to assist hearers to appraise what the prophet sees and accept it as urgent, offering more potential for change than those listening might have supposed. There is no shortage of effort for Jeremiah. When one medium runs dry— words—he turns to enactment; when certain pronouncements seem to bypass or bounce off their targets, Jeremiah finds parabolic paths. Able to threaten and denounce, at times—most ominously at the end of his last meeting with Zedekiah— Jeremiah falls silent. Jeremiah needed to weigh situations, calculate outcomes, and preach those to hearers unfamiliar with, or offended and threatened by, such intensity, to convince those heavily invested in alternate outcomes. It is not so much a matter of forcing a choice but of catalyzing one. A prophet must enable his people to see as well as hear, help them to contemplate what can be imagined.[38] Jeremiah and his biblical peers attempt this by authorizing God to threaten reprisals or to tender rewards. Brueggemann says bluntly: "YHWH's governance is [shown] comprehensive, massive, and irresistible." All must submit in "willing obedience or in disastrous judgment."[39] Moderns, even committed believers, may draw back from this massive club of overweening agency and violence. "I can't listen to any more of that violent language," is a frequent and not unjustified complaint of Jeremiah students. But that exact point is made, perhaps startlingly, in our biblical material: Jeremiah does not succeed in convincing Zedekiah by threats of what God will do if the king does not conform to the prophet's ukase. We see, rather, that the overwhelming negativity of the prophet frightened the king from a choice Jeremiah urgently wanted him to make. At the moment of Zedekiah's greatest vulnerability, Jeremiah bullied rather than enticed, offered a threatening rather than a consoling image. Instead of preaching to the king's tiny openness, the prophet pounded on his vast fear. No go.

But, fourth, we recognize that a prophet must pitch to multiple ears/hearts, since not everyone needs or can receive the same information. The prophet presumably discerns to whom he or she can most appropriately speak—calculates the needs of others and the prophet's own capacities—and invests in that project. Complicating, no doubt, is when the ears and hearts are both diverse and needy—not to say resistant. Elsewhere in this prophetic book (and even in the Zedekiah material [for example, 38:1–4]) Jeremiah has a wider audience than one—granted, he spends a good deal of time on one pair of royal ears. Zedekiah becomes his main audience, is the most crucial person to persuade.[40] There, it appears, he fails. Would he have done better with a different audience? Who preached to Ebed-Melek, that he acted so fruitfully in his moment of challenge? And, to raise a point to which we shall return, how are we to understand our prophet's relationship with the group that we understand did resettle in Babylon? Before settling, too satisfied, on a simple sense of Jeremiah's failure, we can consider a few points to reweight our assessment.

How, then, to appraise Jeremiah's skill amid all we have seen, or at least drop a few markers before returning to the question at a later moment? First, he consistently makes the choice clear, or clear enough that we can discern his proclaiming as time moves on that no good lies in any choice save a quasi-voluntary resettling in Babylon. Second, he helps us understand how prophecy is thoroughly a team effort: God, prophet, people; hearing and speaking; catalyzing and cooperating; resisting and refusing. The responsibility is shared, and it is not easy, perhaps impossible, to ascribe blame confidently when things do not go well. Third, he makes clear that the main point is not the valorization of the prophet. That things end badly for Jeremiah is part of what we need to see, to understand. Fourth, Jeremiah demonstrates to us the limits of harsh divine sanction, shows us massively how God's threats and punishments are insufficient to inspire or even conduce obedience. And finally, fifth, Jeremiah offers us an elusive and valuable insight when he shows us how close can be one human and his opponent. That king and prophet are drawn with the same crayons, resemble each other pervasively, are locked codependently in their choices is an insight crucial for the growth of compassion.

There is more to say on this topic, but the remaining task here is to extend our negative space further and examine in what variety of ways the prophet makes vivid what choices are never to bear fruit. That prophetic enactment takes place in chapters 39–45 and in 51:59–52:30 (broken apart now by the oracles against the nations). While briefly discussing that material, I will also suggest how it functions as a finale to the long performance of Jeremiah, a match to the overture that introduced the piece. As the small unit of the prophet's call (chap. 1) prefaced the overture, so will a brief note of exilic hope (52:31–34) serve as a coda to the finale.

Finale

The challenge of this last section is to continue to construct Jeremiah persona as preaching, even though at a certain angle his main responsibility may seem ended. We will witness the filling out of choices still minimally and theoretically viable as the events of 587 unfold narratively. The prophet continues to demonstrate, whether with direct usefulness to intended audiences we construct or not, that there is no fruitful path for God's people but to have already entered into a consistently dispreferred and unpalatable choice with hope and receptivity. No alternative will accomplish the same purpose. This material includes the fates of various individuals and groups at the collapse of the city (chap. 39): some killed, some exiled, one given his life as booty; the establishment of a local community of poor under the Babylonian-appointed leadership of Gedaliah: first attracting some Judeans who had taken refuge in the small peoples surrounding Judah and then foundering when Gedaliah was killed—with a remnant of that group taken to Ammon but then opting for Egypt against Jeremiah's word (40–44); the last words of and to Baruch (45); and a narrated reprise of the events of 587 (52). Jeremiah himself embodies multiple possibilities, challenging us to plumb why he did not choose better than he seems to have done. Hearing this unit as a finale, we will look at it in five sections, rough match to the overture of chaps. 2–10.

A. 39: four immediate fates: The quickly moving storyline, dominated now by the book narrator, sketches four fates: Jeremiah's begins the unit, contrasting with those of Zedekiah, two sets of Jerusalem people, and Ebed-Melek. Sprung from the prison where we last saw him (38:28), Jeremiah was protected by those involved in the capture of the city: <Be sure nothing bad happens to him, and whatever he asks, see to it,> came the word from Nebuchadnezzar (39:12). As this brief note concluded, the prophet was remanded to the new governor, Gedaliah, whose patronymic identifies him as one of Jeremiah's partisans.[41] The postcollapse fate of Jeremiah is thus considered in this short scene from the angle of the Babylonians, adopting their limited viewpoint, as it were.[42] Jeremiah remains silent, his last extant words having been those fatefully spoken to King Zedekiah.

Alternatives are shown: The king escapes only to death, after he is witness to terrible things. Implicit, if in negative space, is the situation of Jehoiachin, jailed in Babylon, to whom the narrative will return at its very end. One king resettled early and survived, with his group; one delayed and perished, destroying others with him. For we see people loyal to the king either perish with him or in some cases taken captive to Babylon, in either case demonstrating what is *not* the main plan, where there is no life available (39:8–9). Shown also by way of inversion or foil for all the others—individuals and groups—is the king's servant Ebed-Melek, who rescued Jeremiah from the mud (39:15–18). Analeptically, we learn that at the time of the man's brave action, God notified Jeremiah that Ebed-Melek was to be delivered from enemies he dreaded, to receive his life as booty in thanks for his reliance on YHWH.[43] This narrative crumb, coming not in chronological or story order but at a time we can appreciate it, is offered us at the moment we are contemplating various fates.[44] Their lives as booty had been available as well to others as Jeremiah preached, but most evinced no interest. The contrast is clear: The lone foreign slave trusted exclusively in God, while the Judean establishment invested in imperial allies, in fortifications, in human beings, in lies—none of which proved reliable.[45] Not demonstrably part of Israel/Judah, he disappears at this moment, except insofar as we have his story.

B. 40–41: roads taken and not taken: But there now develop at greater leisure and in more detail additional possibilities. First (40:1), we learn that Jeremiah has somehow after his rescue become bundled with those slated for deportation to Babylon, as though that most obvious option but road refused must be marked at least narratively. Without much detail we see him removed from that set of prisoners—taking on a quick resemblance to Ebed-Melek and to the royal-in-exile. Still in communication with God though in a "quiet phase," Jeremiah shares none of what he may be learning with any, ourselves included. A Babylonian surrogate of Nebuchadnezzar interprets for Jeremiah a not inaccurate view of what has happened and claims the event as God's. That is, since we are not (yet) hearing from Jeremiah, Nebuzaradan plays that interpretive and theological role, briefly. Is he to be seen as reliable in what he says? I think generally so, though he may also caution us to rethink our own theology here, in which case he is drawn deliberately unreliable. Is it realistic that a Babylonian be the bearer of the information he provides? Though this general viewpoint has been imparted on numerous occasions by Jeremiah, Nebuzaradan is the first person to state the matter unequivocally on the other side of the defeat and destruction of the city: unexpected but needed in our narrative.[46]

Jeremiah is, now, given two choices: put broadly, go to Babylon under protection (not the same as going shackled with others from the defeated city), or remain in Judah. The first option sounds similar to the one Jeremiah has been urging, though of course the defeat and destruction of the city has changed it substantially. We learn that when the prophet, so addressed, signals no choice, the Babylonian rephrases: <Stay in Judah under Gedaliah's protection or name something else,>—a sort of wildcard placeholder that will ramify into the lot that ends up as Jeremiah's, though against his will. From the point of view of the narrative, we are seeing more figs, more fates, with only one of them genuinely and straightforwardly good but alternatives not yet quite foreclosed.

Jeremiah now seems to choose, though nonverbally: Again, the narrator supplies information that the prophet came to Mizpah of Judah under the responsibility of the Babylonian-appointed governor, was released with a food allowance (40:6). It seems, perhaps, a good selection, though we might speculate why Jeremiah does not choose to go to Babylon, either as a captive or as a protégé.[47] But this selection is brilliant for the character of Jeremiah, who will briefly participate in an option that might have been shown workable but soon turns rancid. We also learn, now, that not all the people of Judah were killed or expelled; some are allowed to remain in the land, under the care of a Babylonian-appointed Judean official: princes, fighting men, poor people, named individuals, among whom are members of the royal family.[48] The newly appointed governor encourages and reassures them about safety from their erstwhile foe, providing them (astonishingly under the circumstances of protracted war and siege) with land ready for harvest. A cult commences—we learn shortly—nonblood, of course, since the temple to support such a liturgy is inoperative if not destroyed. Again, the point is not realism but the implication that the new beginning might be viable (40:7–13).

Lest we feel too encouraged by that choice, we learn at once that the group is threatened by rumors, factions, conspiracy, assassination of the governor and the slaughter of others—Babylonians included—thus offering an affront to the powerful captor. As we watch players regroup and be manipulated, Jeremiah himself remains silent during what we may call the collapse of that possible viable future, not speaking for sixty verses! The governor's assassin, a Davidid, entices fresh arrivals into his net, killing most and plundering the rest. Seizing as captive some of those who had gathered under Gedaliah, he attempts flight to Ammon. But at least his hostages are freed, while he himself disappears, another shadow or lookalike to his royal kin. The detail of plan and counterplan suggests possibilities, but born of and perishing of violence. The assassination of Gedaliah (narrated in 40:13–41:18) ends in the dissolution of the possibility that any will survive and prosper in Judah.[49] That the life of those remaining in Judah seemed hopeful, briefly, provides more "figs" for consideration. What is being presented to us is not abstract alternatives but those filled not inappropriately with ideological (as well as theological) viewpoint. The primary interpretive stance proffered here via Jeremiah persona has been a quasi-voluntary resettlement that seems likely to have been the seedbed of the Babylonian *golah*, with no other option deemed ultimately valuable. Such, we may understand, was the experience of at least some who went to Babylon and eventually returned from there, whose voices and hands provide us with the basic biblical viewpoint. So Jeremiah—prophet and prophetic book—underwrites and endorses that point of view. To live in the land under Babylonian protection was most likely precisely the lot of some, but it is not presented here as possible, once Ishmael's deed of assassination has happened. But then another choice is made.

C. 42–43 **Jeremiah's last words in Judah**: Faced with consequences of the murder of a Babylonian-appointed leader, the beleaguered and officially leaderless community (princes and some named people [42:1]) approach Jeremiah, virtually a first in this long book. With the exception of the last king hoping foolishly to conduce a favorable word, we have not seen the prophet importuned for advice or intervention. Has Jeremiah's credibility increased in the eyes of this group, given the truthfulness of much that he said? The setup hints of it, briefly. The speakers ask, even implore, intercession of God from him and promise in several expressions that they will heed whatever word the prophet might bring them from God. This is a most important unit, not only because it comes at the end of Jeremiah's active life but because it provides startling information. Brueggemann is particularly useful here and in the analysis of this unit (42:7–43:7).[50]

Jeremiah indicates his willingness to consult, doing so with no specific process that we observe (as has consistently been the case). At the end of ten days, he communicates what he has learned to the assembly of the people.[51] In short, his answer is, <Remain here where you are.> But the specific language is more revealing. The speech comes in a series of conditional (if/then) clauses, both positive and negative, options real and unreal, starting in vv. 10–12: <If you remain here, then there will be good things and not bad—building and planting, not overthrowing and uprooting—because I [God] regret what I did.> That is, unequivocally the words of the prophet and deity promise good to the community remaining in Judah. The divine change of heart about the destruction so recently experienced is expressed in terms of future policy. The community's choice to obey and remain may prompt God to change the heart of the Babylonian conqueror. Brueggemann says, "God now pines to do good for Israel, but God's goodness will require obedient residence in the city."[52] As if anticipating such fears, God addresses the primary concern of the group, a sensible concern on their part, given the recent assassination of the Babylonian-appointed Gedaliah. <Do not fear the one you have dreaded so long, up to this moment, for I am with you to save you, to enable a merciful return to your land for you.> This seems a fresh and creative possibility not previously entertained in the book, though we must recall that all options have been thoroughly reshuffled since the defeat and destruction of the city. The "remain" option becomes different on the other side of defeat. As has been its consistent bent, the book shows the prophet teasing apart options and evaluating them for YHWH's people. Jeremiah indicates that God can deal with the nonexiled community fruitfully, can manage his powerful tool, Babylon, the thing the consulters seem most panicked about. "Do not fear," they are advised, twice, ringing an echo of Jeremiah's own initial call in chap. 1. Again, Brueggemann: "The oracle gives every thinkable theological warrant for not running away from the trouble."[53] But in the drama of our book, it is another road not taken, another poor choice on the part of the hapless and past-it figs we know so well.

For the offer is balanced immediately by its alternative, spoken with threat and vilification (42:13–14): <But if you are even now deciding you will not obey and remain >—and here God quotes their hypothetical but about to be enacted decision that indicates their determination to go to Egypt and their reasons: to escape war, trumpet, famine—<then just those very things will meet you there: sword, famine, death, pestilence, nonsurvival.> And God reinforces these words again: <The wrath poured out on Jerusalem will follow you to Egypt, and you will become a byword as you perish there> (vv. 15–18). To not remain is to refuse obedience. Unequivocal. As we have seen many times, God attributes speech, projecting or assuming the worst.

Jeremiah follows up in his own words, reintonating God's words—rarely a successful strategy, we may note: <God has spoken, as have I: do not go to Egypt> (42:21–22). And the deity/prophet language, indistinguishable, interprets additionally, indicating his assessment that the petitioners set themselves up—YHWH/Jeremiah as well—by asking about something when they show themselves unwilling or unable to hear what might be said. The flight to Egypt appraised as an escape from death is actually an approach to it, the people are cautioned. The prophet's grounds for this accusation are not clear in the narrative as we have it, except insofar as he has always maintained that to refuse obedience to God-and-Jeremiah is the root of all troubles. His point seems to be to insure that they have no misunderstanding as to what is in store for them, that point possibly more important than his attributing false motives to them. Indeed, he may not be doing so but rather underlining that since they asked and received a word, they are not free to disregard it but will suffer the consequences if they do so. But then Jeremiah narrator changes tone and characterizes the petitioners as deceitful, and we may surely understand that they are panicked and pressed.[54] But the point is clear: No survival in Egypt, no figs to thrive there. We may wonder whether, as was the case with Jeremiah and Zedekiah, the language is too harsh, too accusatory, too threatening. Brueggemann summarizes the significance of what has been said: "The theological claim of this prophetic assertion is enormously important. It affirms (1) that new commandments are given; (2) they are given through prophetic authority, the voice of newness, even when the command is not rooted in old tradition; and (3) the new command concerns concrete issues of public policy in the midst of public crisis. . . . The danger is double. It is wrong to go to Egypt. It is wrong to vow to listen to the prophet and then to disobey. On both counts, this remnant community has placed itself in profound jeopardy."[55]

But as the conversation winds on (43:1–3), the tone deteriorates. On this occasion as sometimes before, God's speech ends up in the mouths of opponents. We hear precisely the belligerent communal disobedience described. The leaders, without apparent warrant, accuse Jeremiah of lying, of claiming falsely to speak for the deity, of having gotten his advice from Baruch. The somewhat unexpected charges—except as we have seen Jeremiah disbelieved consistently—are not particularly well grounded. Baruch's reappearance seems unprompted and is not so easy to understand in narrative terms. Is the claim that the prophet is too dependent on his scribe, speaks for a scribe rather than for the deity? But in any case, the narrator concludes that the whole group—every individual left in Judah by the Babylonians—disobediently goes to Egypt, including Baruch and Jeremiah, presumably against their will (43:4–7). Like Moses, Jeremiah dies outside the land of promise, and indeed may be seen as reversing the journey of Moses, a most ominous trek.[56]

But YHWH is not finished, as he and Jeremiah collaborate for a final time in another lesson, apparently no more fruitful for its intended recipients than were any of the others (save those in chap. 26): God commands the prophet to take stones and embed them in mortar at the palace of Pharaoh at Tahpanhes, the marked pavement to serve as the base on which Nebuchadnezzar will plant his throne when he gets around to conquering Egypt. We hear the directions and the language of death, captivity and sword claiming their victims. Destruction for all (43:8–13). Again, unambiguous. No surviving or thriving in Egypt.

Considering this passage, we may ponder the sketched motivations of the group asking, receiving, and repudiating the advice. The laconic narration allows a variety of options: They asked insincerely; they did not expect the reply they received; they were split in some way, falling into disarray when a strong answer came. The relevant point from the perspective of the present study is that at so late a date (587 or slightly later), the prophetic persona suggests that God would bless and prosper a vital community in the land of Judah—but there was no group willing to accept that challenge. In the imagery of baskets of figs, a potentially healthy basket turns putrid. It is understood, of course, by the time of the production of the book, that only one basket of figs is approved for survival, those in Babylon. But the recital indicates that such was a human choice, not a divine given.

D. 44: stranded in Egypt: We come, finally, to chap. 44 and Jeremiah's last prophetic words delivered viva voce, as it were (thus distinct from the OANs clustered afterward). The discourse is presented as YHWH's, addressed through the prophet to all Judeans in Egypt, wherever and whenever they have arrived settled variously (44:1–25): YHWH addresses first the past events—evil, ruin, desolation in Judah as a result of false worship (vv. 2–6); next, the present situation—an ongoing commitment to such false practices (vv. 7–10); and finally the future—God's acceptance of the determination on the part of Judeans to be in Egypt and now a divine commitment to hold them there even when they may wish to return to Judah (vv. 11–14). The language is familiar except for its bounce against Egyptian rather than Judean walls. The discourse braids destruction for the many with escape for a few.

The passage is well discussed in various contexts, not all of which are relevant here. In the context of the book of Jeremiah, we have two characteral viewpoints, each distinct, though generally discussing the same recent cataclysmic events, interpreting them as foundationally causative in those recent doings. Jeremiah's viewpoint is consistent with what he has said before, and I think we can take it is at least roughly compatible with the Deuteronomic YHWH-alone view of theology and worship—and more importantly, I think, with the perspective of the book of Jeremiah. The prophet's interlocutors, whose narrative function is to voice resistance and refusal, see "the same" events somewhat differently, or to be more precise, understand the causality propelling them differently from the prophet (who speak by turns: God directly in 44:1–14, Jeremiah in 44:20–23., until the voices blur again). Jeremiah maintains that all the recent disastrous events came about as a result of false worship offensive to YHWH, with such offenders knowing God little and thus digging into stubborn error. The community leaders addressed counter that what they have suffered comes about as a consequence of neglect of the Queen of Heaven, thus seeming to sidestep the YHWH issue. The discussion here is somewhat frustrating for us if we spend too much time wondering, specifically, what deity is so referenced.[57] But with our eye on the rabbit rather than the hat, we catch two irreconcilable views of the same events. This is not confusion or weakness on the part of people but clear-headed determination, marked in this prophetic book as a culpable error. God-and-Jeremiah are answered by the bluntest language we have heard from any of Jeremiah's opponents except possibly Jehoiakim as they make their case against their prophetic and divine accuser (vv. 15–19)—a case not without merit. Explaining their commitment to the Queen of Heaven as long running and carefully chosen, they aver that they have no intention of abandoning it. They additionally claim that she favored them in the past, and only when they abandoned her cult did things go poorly for them. It is a piece of theology thrown right in the face of all that God has claimed: <Your troubles are from abandoning me and worshiping falsely> is met with <Our troubles are from abandoning the Queen of Heaven!>

Ellis reminds us that we need not assume that the question must be resolved into two absolute discrete positions: YHWH alone versus all other deities. We may and often do read it that way, but Ellis suggests that we allow the possibility that the issue is more subtle: YHWH *and* other deities or YHWH alone, with the question being whether worship of the Queen of Heaven is compatible with Yahwism or not, how it may or may not be.[58] Her insight offers a valuable reminder insofar as our concern is to understand the nature of religion in pre- and exilic Judah, but it is actually not the main thrust of the present passage, I think. From the angle of the book of Jeremiah and the "character zone" projected by the prophet, worship of the Queen of Heaven is thoroughly false and illicit, and the fact that its adherents present their view without giving quarter counts against them. Thus is life in Egypt once again painted in negative colors, valorizing silently the group resettled in Babylon. The argument cannot be decided or won simply by its content, since of course it is not possible to know how deities act. But being part of the consistent view in canonical Jeremiah means that the YHWH-alone position is officially accepted. It is a viewpoint likely relevant for most discussions of worship that have filled the book to this far point, reflecting, as we assume, perennial disagreements in late pre-exilic Judah.

In any case, the literary prophet abandons the arguments about the past to urge that this one will be settled in the future (44:20–30). Jeremiah persona, buttressing his argument no doubt with some *ex eventu* information, before turning on his heel, provides specific information about how Nebuchadnezzar and the Babylonians will visit on Egypt the very things they have done to Judah, and the acts will serve as validation for what deity and prophet are claiming here.[59] As Brueggemann emphasizes, this is a discussion about power, and the upper hand, holding the stylus, is that of the Babylon *golah* community, itself most likely not unanimous on such a fraught issue.[60] The deity-prophet team replies not with argumentation but offering the sense of a fate sealed (vv. 26–30): <So be it! Do what you will. Nothing good will come of it.> God maintains that he will continue—at least for this group—to be the agent of evil and not good, offering a sign so that the truth may be known: Pharaoh Hophra will experience the same fate with Nebuchadnezzar as did Zedekiah, as indeed historians testify occurred.[61] This exchange between deity and prophet and those Judeans in Egypt writes off any hope that the survival of God's people will be in Egypt. No healthy figs there.

E. 45; 51:59–52:30: **wrapping up**: The discussion and elimination of viable group options continues in its somewhat haphazard though basically relentless way as we reach a final unit, comprising three odd but coherent and correlated pieces, all rooted in past events, providing information we either had or could have had sooner but demanding fresh consideration now. In chapter 45 we find a short piece on Baruch's outcome. Scholars have been most interested in the issues tangled in the placement of this information.[62] The question relevant for us here is not historical or redactional but literary: Why is this the place for the Baruch information to be provided? Several possibilities: One, the dating of the event; these words to Baruch from Jeremiah and YHWH are said to have been delivered to Baruch at the time of the scroll episode, Jehoiakim's fourth year. But similar to—indeed a match for—the words addressed to the individual Ebed-Melek in chap. 39, we hear them only later. Baruch, lamenting (as Jeremiah did also throughout his prayers of chaps. 11–20) that things are not going well, is challenged by the deity and told that these are times for God's work of overthrowing and uprooting, and Baruch is not to anticipate anything greater. Scholars since Calvin have tended to see Baruch reproached here and often for "self-aggrandizement," but that strikes not quite the right note.[63] God's responses to Jeremiah's laments are bracing as well, a cold splash of water rather than warm washcloth. Indeed, in the year we call 605, there was still much catastrophe to come. What we have learned of his words since then is the allegation in 43:3 that Baruch is accused of urging *against* the resettlement to Egypt. It is impossible to verify the claim from the information we have; and since the characters who accuse are cast in a somewhat negative mode, it is difficult to assume they are speaking well, except perhaps once again in negative space. But that their view is a sentiment worth slinging suggests it was plausible, thinkable, to at least some group of intended readers of the book, whether we can pin them down or not. We do recognize it as a sentiment of which YHWH firmly approves. Since Baruch spoke well, he, like Ebed-Melek, will have his life as booty. As before, the point is about options for the future: one good, the rest not. Brueggemann, rehearsing the issue about the historicity of the figure with all its attendant matters, underlines the sense of Baruch representing an ideology, a viewpoint, specifically carrying the Deuteronomic portfolio forward within the surviving community—a possibility. Baruch may also represent the scribal position, the commitment to write the tradition down—clearly enough his role in chap. 36. In a book so filled with individuals, we do well to consider not only viewpoints but experiences, and Baruch here does not coincide quite exactly with either Jeremiah, with whom he agrees substantially, or with the Egypt refugees, in whose company he seems to walk. But since we hear the scribe given his life as booty in all the places he shall go because of his good words, that gift cannot be equivalent to disappearing in Egypt. Perhaps he can be thought of as breaking off from the Egyptian group and ending up somewhere else, his life as booty. For Jeremiah, there is no such word.

With the OANs intervening (46–51) one more legacy is noted, this one to Seraiah, brother of Baruch, also given to us out of order (51:59–64).[64] In the fourth year of Zedekiah's reign we learn that the king, accompanied by Seraiah as caravaneer, traveled to Babylon. Jeremiah had provided him with a scroll detailing the evils that would come on Babylon and instructed him to read it aloud and then to sink it in the Euphrates, suggesting the downward fate of Babylon that YHWH was committing to—witnessed, presumably, by the group of resettlers. And so, having now heard multiple detailed verses about the deeds of YHWH toward Babylon, we learn that they were prophesied by Jeremiah and proclaimed by Seraiah to ears in Babylon before being accomplished by YHWH. Placement is for the reader, verifying that what YHWH promises is reliable.

And then, as is familiar both from Jeremiah 39 and from 2 Kings 25, the final days of royal and first-temple Jerusalem are repeated. Zedekiah is pronounced responsible for the final anger of YHWH against Judah and Jerusalem, not least in rebelling against Babylonian Nebuchadnezzar. The long siege of the city resulted, with its attendant suffering. And when the walls were breached, the king fled, to no avail, captured, taken to Riblah, deprived of sons and eyesight, detained in Babylon until the day of his death. The temple, palace, and portions of the city were burned, its walls torn down. Some people were exiled, others left in the land. The destruction of the temple is elaborated in detail (vv. 17–23), a sort of sad parody of other texts that linger lovingly on their beauty and detail when they are being crafted, again negative space. Certain priests were taken to Babylon, beaten, killed. "Thus Judah went into exile from its land," summarizes the narrator succinctly. Those taken are counted according to the three waves in which they went, 3023 in the first exile, 832 next, and finally 745, making a total of 4,500.[65] It is clear that not everyone who went will thrive and survive, since we are told bluntly that some are put to death for their deeds, at once or eventually. Exile of itself is not necessarily redemptive. But the best chance is to have gone early and remained in healthy relationship with YHWH.

Conclusions

Since this long chapter with its two diverse sections has been summarized already (the prophet/king resemblance passages by me above and the collapse of Judah, here by the narrator), there is little more to say. Though the choice to consider this material as a set was somewhat arbitrary, the consistency of the prophetic ministry has emerged dramatically, Jeremiah's speaking and enacting remain in existential if not theological solidarity with those who resist him. Whether we see him as simply underlining the survival choice by his accompanying the doomed, or whether we imaginatively construct him in urgent dialogue with those God has hinted will emerge from Egypt (44:14), we see the multiple poor options making stark the one that—retrospectively—was salvific. And so what remains yet to unfold are the plans of well-being spoken to those who chose to be part of them in Babylon.

7

GETTING OUT

Chapters 30–33, 24, 26, 29

The only chance of newness is due to God's radical and undeserved action.

Walter Brueggemann, *Commentary*

In the previous pages of this book, my argument has singled out and valorized the reluctant readiness of some in Judah and Jerusalem to relocate to Babylon in order to survive. I have tried to show how counterintuitive and dispreferred that decision would be for any steeped—as I presume the people of Judah and Jerusalem were—in the importance of God's project for the people of Judah dwelling in the land itself. A prompt to choose otherwise would have seemed perverse. The gift of heritage land would have been assumed and considered to be inherently part of God's deep desire. I have shown the possibility, and I hope plausibility, of the deity's coming to this exile-insight via soliloquy, then communicating it to a prophet who did not welcome it but came eventually to invest in his responsibility to preach this sojourn to resistant contemporaries. And preach exile Jeremiah has done in multiple ways: verbally and visually, by plain language and with imagery, in positive and in negative constructs. Part of his ministry, as we have just examined, was Jeremiah's enacting the refusal he was meeting in order to confront resisters with the outcome they are choosing, perhaps before it is too late to opt differently. That is, Jeremiah's own self in and out of confinement made visible the futility of nonresettlement in Babylon.[1]

The purpose of the present chapter is to examine Jeremiah's dealings with the particular group who appear to have heard, understood, and heeded his prophetic preaching and relocated to the east well before the final days of siege. Though the main focus will be on the chapters that celebrate most prominently the gift given to and through this resettling community (chapters 30–33), we will also draw together from elsewhere within the prophetic book what we can learn of these citizens: pushing off from chaps. 10, 17–18, slowing a bit at 24, 26, 29, reviewing 34, 45, 51 (its last verses), finally to look once more at the final words of the book (end of chap. 52).

The point to explore and establish here is the whole movement of going to, staying in, returning from Babylon. It is not simply a matter of temporality and spatiality, though it is that. It is also a matter of imaginative relocation and transformation, at a deeper experiential level, a change cultural and spiritual that requires but transcends time and space. Though we lack the detail we would like about life in exile, still we can sense that it will have been vastly different from life lived at home. Insofar as we, at a great historical remove, think exile a simple and easily grasped matter, we reduce it and deprive it of its power to address us. We must touch back on the analogy with which we opened this book, the choice of our own elders, at the end of productive lives, urged to forsake all they have known for what seems and is in many ways a diminishment. Or perhaps it is time to think of another analogy, the vast and uncertain challenges of climate change and our reluctance—even on the part of the most convinced of us—to make substantial and far-reaching changes in our ways of life, changes that we know will not reverse for the situation for us. The stakes are the highest imaginable, and yet we delay to change, hoping it won't be necessary, at least for us.

Glancing Back: 10: 17–18

As we recall the commissioning of young Jeremiah, we know that amid his assignment of uprooting and destroying, overthrowing and pulling down, was also the charge to build and to plant (1:10). It is not difficult to associate the so-called destructive verbs with prophetic events, to see that much of his language articulates those four negative processes. But we recall that he is assigned to build and plant, and so we are ready now to see how this step goes. And we also sampled in the book's overture, if fleetingly, a proleptic and imaginative moment (10:11–16) where after many painful and discordant utterances exchanged among characters, the deity, the prophet, and the relocated community blended voices in harmony, appear to have come to agreement on the importance of the exile experience, painful and dreaded as it continues to be. It was not, in chapter 10, a developed narrative moment but a fleeting impression, like a dream. This may be the place to emphasize how far from "pro-Babylonian" this insight on the part of characters is, and of course on the part of the producer(s) of the book of Jeremiah. It is not pro-Babylon but prosurvival of God's dealings with Judah in the land of Yehud: chosen with tears, with regret, with trepidation. It is likely that the mature awareness took years to become fully appreciated.

After the overture, as we would expect, the task of the book is to work out in detail how such an insight as to common weal can have come about, to show it both and simultaneously nigh unthinkable and also indispensable—no easy blend. In the material of chaps. 11–20 we witnessed the failure of the deity-prophet team to provoke so much as a single tangible response from the people among whom they labored and to whom they spoke—until the priest hobbled the prophet over-night. And we witnessed laments by the prophet—virtually bereft of any sense of compassion for those resisting him. In his soliloquies the deity, too, struggled through anger and bitterness at his people, but unlike the prophet, seemed to have come to the insight that the divine self must take the initiative if any with mortal hearts—tortuous beyond even God's comprehension—were to be salvaged (17:9–10). And God's poetic and imagery-rich discourse turned to the consideration of things inexplicably going out of their expected and accustomed places, but for the good (18:13–17).

Going Out: 24, 26

We need now to reexamine several moments in the material subsequent to the deity's watershed insight about hearts and change in order to see how the proclamation of the necessity of resettling became clearer and more impelling. This is material we have examined previously but now will consider in fresh detail and with the specific focus of the present purposes of this study: How did it come to pass, according to this book of Jeremiah, that a small group early went into exile to Babylon?

Strangely the book seems to assume rather than narrate this moment. When Jeremiah and God are scolding kings for their so-flawed leadership, the Josiah-grandson, Coniah, is characterized as a signet torn from the divine finger and hurled away—valuable but cast off—and hoping for a return (22:24–29). Then we are told more bluntly and less suggestively how Jeconiah came to be in Babylon: King Nebuchadnezzar had taken this son of Jehoiakim—succeeding to the Jerusalem throne at the death of his father but not remaining there long—off to Babylon with some family, elites, and artisans (24:1). But the information is provided primarily so that we can negotiate the enacted parable that follows, Jeremiah's discernment of figs (24:1–10). Shown two baskets of fruit, one at their prime and one past it, Jeremiah readily diagnoses the two sets of fruit.[2] But the crucial point is to attach their identities: God assists the prophet, presumably because the teaching is difficult, to recognize the early and ripe as the group in exile, able to anticipate a return to the land eventually, but not soon. Those figs putrid and past eating are those refusing to accept or even contemplate a sojourn in the land to the east. If the labels were obvious, God would not need to point them out. We need to imagine that most of the prophet's and the book's intended listeners would have ascribed identities differently. Insofar as the setting seems to suggest this parable is exclusively for the prophet—in that he is not told to proclaim it, nor does he—we are thinking of his reception of the news and those intended readers of the book: Are the figs and their assessment demonstrating punishment or position?[3] God promises return to one set of people but extirpation for the other.

But we still do not know, at least chronologically and plainly, how this early exile came to be. Our best hint comes, I think, in the drama of chapter 26, where Jeremiah himself preaches, finally, the words God rehearsed from him in chapter 7. Clearly unconcerned to put the story in chronological order, the narrator of the unit backs up into the reign of Jehoiakim, that arch-refuser of prophetic pronouncement. The prophet is sent to communicate to those entering the temple in Jerusalem, is dispatched with the hope that they might listen while allowing us to suppose that God thinks they might not heed. <But try, Jeremiah,> we may hear. The communication centers, as it did in chap. 7, on the inevitability of destruction of the holy place—Jerusalem to suffer the fate of Shiloh—if its patrons do not heed divine instruction, minimally elaborated here (26:4–6) but developed persistently elsewhere. The scene indicates that the words were heard but hated, resisted, refused: <How can you say that these are God's words?> is the point of contention (vv. 8–9).[4] As discussed earlier, the prophet is placed on trial, with leaders calling for Jeremiah's death (v. 10–11), while the accused proclaims his innocence, underlining that his words are indeed those of the deity but spaciously conceding his opponents the power to kill him if they so choose (vv. 12–15).

The group of citizens in attendance then splits, with some elders recalling both the case of Micah the prophet and his words to Hezekiah—harsh about the fate of Jerusalem but heard and responded to by royal ears—and also the precedent of Uriah the prophet—sounding like Jeremiah and opposed, such that he fled to Egypt but was hailed back by the king and put to death (26:17–23).[5] The narrator ends the unit by noting that Jeremiah, avoiding both Uriah's Egypt and immediate death and also Micah's royal assist, is sheltered under the protection of the Shaphan family (v. 24).[6] The question left hanging is, who is this group of elders that sides with, perhaps believes, conceivably obeys the prophet? As noted earlier, Louis Stulman identifies this scene as the first in the book where the prophet is listened to with some indication of acceptance.[7] What are we to suppose they will have done, in heeding?

Pushing Stulman's insight that here, that *for the first time* a group listens favorably to the prophet, I will construct that this group—virtually the *only* set of Judah/Jerusalem citizens that *ever does accept* a Jeremiah word—stands as narrative marker for the resettlers. It puzzles me that we do not know more about them, but we will work with what we have. The first exile, so-called, that of 597, remains strangely general, as a comparison with the more detailed events of the second exile of 587 illuminates. This pioneer group to go to Babylon is discussed in 2 Kings 24:10–17 as well as in Jeremiah, but the information is not different.[8] Nebuchadnezzar is said to be the impetus for the population shift, and the group of elites selected to go included the young Jehoiachin, who apparently had just begun to reign after the death of this father. However, in Jeremiah 29:4, the deity claims or is claimed to be the agent—major difference in viewpoint and well utilized in this book. Some questions: Under what conditions of warfare and diplomacy was such a deal as the 597 population transfer struck? Who decided which people would relocate? Was there any choice or negotiation space, since this moment seems to predate the absolute defeat of Judah by Babylonians? What was the understanding of those resettlers about why they went and what would ensue? What was the view about their fate of those who were not selected/did not have to go to Babylon? Were these exiles of one mind, or were there factions among them? What was the role of the displaced king in their community? If we review the question of naming the figs—which desirable and which past their prime—to whom might Jeremiah and God's enacted viewpoint have come as a surprise? And for whom was it a pleasant insight, and for whom quite jarring?

Sojourning Out: 29

We return, next, back to a scene where Jeremiah writes to the community in exile, a group again introduced to us by vv. 1–2 as though we know who they are but need reminding—while also calling attention to the fact that we might not know because we have not been told very explicitly. Having discussed this letter previously, we can offer some fresh points here. First, the tone of it—its insistence on the addressees remaining where they are—helps us appreciate that their desire and the wish of some regarding them must have been for a quick return. The point of at least the first portion of the letter (29:1–7) is to insist with a variety of images that the resettled group should anticipate a sojourn of more than a single generation, should think long term, not short. The community is urged to seek the good of their new home and told that only in such a matrix will their own good be rooted, neither apart from nor in spite of it.[9] And then God's word stresses that this viewpoint will be opposed by prophets arising in the Babylon-sojourning group to offer an alternative and clothe it with words and dreams in the manner of prophets. God distances self from these liars and their view, reiterating that the stay will be long (seventy years). Only then will return be made possible (29:8–10). Jeremiah then elaborates one other thing needful for the return to remain possible: that the community move into coherence and cooperation with God's plans of well-being and hope, remain faithful to the constant and perennial process of seeking God who longs to be found. That mutual relationship—the deepest and tenderest desire of God's heart in this long book—is the condition under which the gift of replanting and rebuilding will be accomplished: given, received, planned, implemented, enjoyed, made fruitful (29:11–14).

Lest we think such communication obvious, the speaker reiterates and reemphasizes the reality of prophetic opposition among some in the resettled community and of those who will be convinced by them and hence encouraging them.

As we listen to this slightly general warning (vv. 15–20), we can discern that the fulcrum issue seems to be that those remaining in Judah are envisioned as prospering, or at least surviving: <Why should *we* stay *here* when *they* are doing fine *there*?> may be the sense of it. And the response to the hinted question: <They are doing less well than you think, and it will get worse for them, and their lot will be far worse than yours: death, dispersal.> The "Babylon zipcode" is not the only fate available and not the worst. As noted previously, the letter moves on to discuss the fate of two resettlement prophets: execution by the Babylonians vv. 21–23) and the condemnation of the advice they sent back to the group in Judah, to the effect that Jeremiah should be discouraged specifically from talking about the length of the sojourn in Babylon and the necessity of being there rather than seeking other circumstances (vv. 24–32).

So we have learned three things: The resettlement advice given comes as an unwelcome surprise to diverse ears; the time spent must not simply be endured but entered into synchronistically with God's plans; and there was opposition to this preaching and not simply in one place.

The Plans of Well-Being: 30–33

And so we come to the heart of this prophetic book, the elaboration of God's plans for well-being and not disaster.[10] These four chapters are generally recognized as consolatory in a way distinctive from what surrounds them. Scholars order them variously, but my choice is to split them into two large units: the poetry of 30–31 and the prose of 32–33.[11] The first two chapters offer in short, intense images a reversal of the past, words addressed to various personages: male plurals, or Zion as female singular, but also to a male singular: Jacob, Ephraim, and so forth. An old situation is referenced and then God promises to reverse it. Underlying all the reversals is return to the land and restoration of joy and fruitfulness. The second half of the consolation is to be articulated in longer prose strands, a royal question, a prophetic response, God's address to Jeremiah. The whole unit catches chapters 24 and 26, where the centrality of a resident and faithful group is made known.

A Closer Look: 30–31

This first half of the discourse includes a set of ten poems, bounded by a rather generic introduction ordering the prophet to gather God's words onto a scroll in advance of the days of return (30:1–4) and a fuller and comprehensive conclusion (31:27–40), moving beyond what will change to how it will—this time—endure. The word for "return" includes acceptance, forgiveness, a commitment to live the new covenant, presumably on the part of both parties.[12] God's promises are described, certified, bonded. The first half of this intense pledge, then, is edged by its inscription in a scroll, on hearts (30:1; 31:33)—witness to the reliability of the return and the repossession of the land of Israel and Judah—and certification that the language is as reliable as that of creation.

The first subunit, 30:5–11, begins in panic, with speech attributed to those suffering from an enemy; the aphorism—surely men don't bear children—is contradicted, as it were, by human speakers watching males in grave physical distress, hands on loins, skin pallid.[13] But the image is quickly reversed by the divine speaker, who promises Jacob and Israel that the yoke of slavery will be broken and the bonds of slavery burst by God. Fear and distress will give way to deliverance with its calm and quiet. Though punishment will occur, it will not be complete, promises God, as return will happen with the diminishment of the one among whom God's people was dispersed. The second poem, 30:12–17, speaks with Lady Zion about her wound and the reason for it as well as its healing. I take the first few phrases to be language ascribed to her peers and hurled derisively at her: <incurable wound, no point in crying over it,> a diagnosis contradicted by the divine speaker: <Of course it was severe. I did it, you deserved it, but all those who are discouraging you over it will be confounded as you were. I'll heal your wound,> promises the deity, <putting an end to silly utterances of those who know no better.>

In 30:18–21, the divine speaker promises a rebuilding of shattered tents, dwellings, cities, fortifications. Destructive noise will be replaced by sound arising from many celebrating. No opponents will threaten, since Jacob will be his own ruler, confident and bidden to approach his Lord. The most brief unit of 30:22 restores the particular relatedness of deity and people, turning the storm of divine anger on others, part of God's plan and to be witnessed by God's own. Perhaps building on the preceding verse, 31:1–6 details how the restoration happened: those fleeing the sword found grace in the wilderness, unexpectedly, and en route home they learned again, afresh, of God's ongoing love. Addressing Lady Zion, the speaker promises her rebuilding and replanting, vows that she will dance and her men will plant and successfully guard vineyards and enjoy their produce. Again, what has been devastated, abandoned, and wept over will be repopulated, replanted, and celebrated within.

In 31:7–9, the journey of return is itself sketched, with people brought home from afar. Though they come blind and lame, pregnant and weeping, they will be guided gently to springs of water and eased along a level road. The speaker claims and shows paternal love to Ephraim, God's firstborn. Similar is 31:10–14, where the scattered are regathered, the flock reassembled, powerful predators put to flight. Joy again will attend those who experience bounty: grain, wine, oil, sheep, cattle. The land will be watered. Mourning will turn to dancing, grief to cheer, sadness to consolation. The unit of 31:15–17 has a slightly fresh cast: The deity, speaking as throughout, recalls Rachel's lament for her children, vanished. She is bidden to cease her outcry and her tears since her children are streaming back toward her, filled with hope. And in 31:18–20, her strayed grandson Ephraim speaks of his experience, owning that he deserved what he got. He seems abashed, filled with compunction but hears himself welcomed by a parent who maintains that the child has never ceased to be thought of with love, has been missed when absent, and is welcomed back with nothing but love. In 31:21–25 Lady Zion is assigned the task of erecting markers and signposts, presumably to help others behind her walk the way she has found. Return, do not delay. Is God not doing a new thing, as fortunes are restored and the deed is recognized and articulated? Farmers as well and those with flocks will return; there will be water sufficient for all.

The odd note of 31:26, where the prophet claims to wake up and reflect on what he has been experiencing, marks the fact that this material is still in the future. Narratively, Jeremiah is still stuck in Judah and the moment for return cannot be yet. Awaking from sleep, he implies his language is like that of dreamers.[14] Finally the conclusion (31:27–40), reviewing all that has been said, promising that it will come to pass: The four destructive verbs Jeremiah was handed in his call will be replaced by the two hopeful ones. How people used to talk is not how they will speak in the future. The new covenant will override and overwrite the twisty human heart. Past lapses will not recur, nor will the process of teaching and learning about God be laborious: All will know, in their new hearts. And, God says, how can you count on these so unlikely promises? If creation's laws and patterns should shift, these reversals might be unstable. Foundations are reliable, witness the new shape of Zion.

To sum up this first section: The most consistent utterance on God's part is that journey- suffering will be reversed—that process detailed in multiple images. We also note that the people are not assigned any active part of the process, except to respond with joy to what God does for them. God learned some time back that human hearts struggle mightily with goodness and are likely both to cling to the security of the past or to lapse back into it, and so God resolves to be the primary agent here. The passage stresses in a variety of ways that the preaching is given early and must be stored, believed, remembered against the unlikelihood of the moment of its setting: the final days of Jerusalem's siege.

A Closer Look: 32–33

The second half of the oft-called Book of Consolation is a rough match to what precedes it, though correlating primarily in terms of content. Where 30–31 comprises short poems, 32–33 is a prose passage, split in two major parts with subsections. As with the first half of the material, this second portion is introduced by the extradiegetic narrator (32:1), who also provides a scenario narrated as backdrop and pretext for what then unfolds (32:2–5): The king asks an accusatory question—raising again the specific issue of how Jeremiah can claim YHWH's authorization for words of defeat, destruction and death. Though we can look at this text unfolding here in projected time of consolation, we also need to recall that it has another job to do—to show something important and almost unimaginable about the future at the moment of persuasion.

What follows is Jeremiah's response to the question of the king: <How can you claim this is God's doing?> (32:3–5). The prophet tells a story, in fact, a parable (the land deed needed of 32:6–15): He relates: <God told me that my cousin would appear with an offer and in fact a charge from my uncle. Sure enough, as God was just finishing the directions, Hanamel came in and said his father, my uncle, needed me to redeem some land of theirs. Since I recognized this situation as being from God, I did as asked, in fact as I was obliged. My uncle got some silver, and I got two copies of a deed, one of which I had duly signed and witnessed and handed over to Baruch for safekeeping. I stressed the importance of keeping the record, since—contrary to appearances—property will be worth something here again, and my family will want to have the deed. God has said so: "Houses, fields, vineyards will again be purchased in this land"> (32:15). The prophet has responded to the king's question, in effect, narrating and enacting a correlating scenario that maintains the inevitability of the loss of land: God's word, foretold, happened as promised.

But with all that confidence seeming to fade, or perhaps moving from prophetic proclamation to prayer, Jeremiah examines the matter more deeply (32:16–25). He opens to address God with a statement we may take as either a question or an assertion—perhaps a word of praise—"Nothing too wonderful for you to do" (32:17), adducing as proof creation, the saving deed in Egypt, the granting of land (vv. 18–25). But, as frequently reviewed, refusal on the peoples' part to heed God has culminated in the siege-mounds all too visible: <All as you have said would happen. And in this neighborhood, filled with Babylonians, you put me through the process of conspicuously redeeming one little plot of ground. The point?> Jeremiah raises once again the major issue of human hearts. And God replies (32:26–44): <Too wonderful for me indeed! You are correct that I am handing this city and this region into the hand of the besieger who will destroy it, for all the reasons I have enumerated before and that you just noted> (vv. 29–35).

But, God continues (v. 36), <Despite all that, this city that you see is so doomed will once again be inhabited, as I return to it those who have been taken from it for their survival. They will be my people and I their God. A new covenant will help us do better with each other: I with them, they with me. So as I have said, and as you have just testified aloud, Jeremiah: "Houses, fields, vineyards

will again be purchased in this land" (32:44). And you will want your land deed.>
The whole discourse is about the prophecy that defeat, destruction and death will
not be final, will, in time, be reversed. And the timing is stressed: What seems
unlikely—impossible—at the time of utterance must be remembered as foretold
when it comes to pass.

Next comes chapter 33, appended again by the book narrator (33:1, 19, 23).
Perhaps we can best understand it as continuing the previous conversation of
reassurance, as though the prophet can hardly accept what God has promised in
view of the scene from Jeremiah's own prison window. The content is all spoken
by God, with numerous bracing reminders of who is talking (33:4, 10, 12, 14, 17,
20, 25). The address is to a masculine singular, as though God beckons Jeremiah
closer to hear more: "I will tell you wonders, hidden things you have not known"
(33:3). The imagery repeats: Healing for the city, restoration, rebuilding; purg-
ing and pardoning from sin, fame and glory, hope and prosperity (vv. 4–9). The
desolate places will be filled with praise, the land devastated by years of war will
once again host animals to graze (vv. 10–14). The culminating verses make specific
mention of the houses of David and of Aaron, who will not lack descendants or
those descendants their traditional roles (vv. 15–22). And this unit, like its sibling
(chaps. 30–31), winds up with God's guaranteeing the basis of these all-but-
incredible promises, at least from the perspective of the one hearing them in the
final days of monarchy: <This is like my agreement with day and night, sun and
moon> God explains (33:21). Reliable. Count on it.

Conclusions: First, again God is the one who will act to accomplish the reversal. Those to whom it is offered are to accept it, participate, rejoice. The community, however named—Israel, Judah, Jacob, Zion, Ephraim—is not envisioned
as needing to do anything except respond wholeheartedly, though that is no small
feat.[15] If I am correct in my construction that a small group trusted in Jeremiah's
word and sought to refuge in Babylon early, then it is primarily to them that these
words are addressed. Their challenge, as they have been told, is to prosper in exile
until the return should come about—not to mope, rant, resist, refuse to unpack.
Second, since one of the major issues of the book is whether or not Jeremiah is
speaking for God, whether it can be that God can be saying such dread things,
care is taken that the words are recognized as true before they happen. This is a
complex thing for us to work out: The character Jeremiah, in the book as we have
it, is told many painful things before they happen, things mostly not believed by
those with whom he is described to share them. But now, narratively speaking
still prior to the year we call 587, he is prophesying a return from the place most
have refused to go, and the book is insistent that those words be respected as
having been spoken well before they happened. The words of consolation are as
unexpected, possibly as unwelcome, as the words of accusation. That the book

was produced substantially later should not prevent us from availing ourselves of the scenario it paints for us.

So to fill out the title of this chapter: Getting out of Judah is urgent, and a small group, responsive to Jeremiah's preaching as well as to existential events, refugees prior to the collapse, because they accept that God's people will survive in no other way. Getting out of Babylon is also envisioned, by some group of those resettled people or their descendants who have lived faithful to God, eventually and likely because they trust the words of their prophet, whoever he or she may have been. We, reading, understand that a historical Jeremiah likely did not work all this out ahead of time. It will have taken strenuous communal theologizing and meaning-making to have arrived at such insight. We hear, as well, that this point of view will have grounded and justified a group of early Babylon settlers over against those arriving later or those never arriving at all, certainly disqualifying those who attempt to survive in Egypt.[16] In order to clarify this doubled referent, it might be useful to consider that when late-twentieth-century Jews are exploring the vast phenomenon of the Shoah in order to deepen understanding, there are various ways to do it, including to focus on the 1930s—of course from the perspective of decades later. In a sense, the book of Jeremiah—produced in exile—nonetheless chooses to draw most of its material from the events of the days leading to defeat. The book is not composed literally for those living before 587, though it is pitched as though that were the case. The concern, I think, is about prophecy and the discernment of truth and falsity among such speakers and about the mystery of God's purposes and the challenge of living into them.

I would say that the pitch of this material is twofold (similar to what we saw in chapter 10 of the overture): one angle is to those in exile promising them a reverse of what they have suffered and endured with fidelity; the other view is before destruction though on the edge of it, to hope that some Judean group— clearly not the king—can understand that return is not possible until departure has taken place, departure again being different from deportation. It is in this context that the deity promises more kings and priests. If we think in terms of exit strategy: in 30–31 God says <I have one,> and in 32–33 the exit strategy is <Go there and then, in time, return will be provided.> The other exit strategy is in the words written on a scroll (30:2). For an alternative to my sense but a powerful reading of the resonance of Jeremiah's strong words to the exile community, see Kathleen O'Connor's claim that the language enables survival.[17]

Coming Back: 34, 45, 51, 52

Though it may seem to the reader as it does to the writer that an almost disproportionate amount of space and time has been invested in the book of Jeremiah's effort to get some representative group healthily out of Judah and Jerusalem before the collapse and defeat, that objective still does not quite suffice to explain the material. Even the previous section, stressing the need for the resettled group to remain away long enough for the transformation of heart to take place—not simply individual hearts but the corporate or "popular" heart—the key destination of the book of Jeremiah is to envision return. How, specifically, is return to happen? Having imaged it in the language we just reviewed, we note also that there are four other brief and cryptic scenes where the journey back to the land is previewed. Those moments are articulated very briefly, as follows.

First, the narrative of chapter 34, discussed above as *slave reprieve revoked,* may be constructed to support the belief that the term of servitude is not forever, and that no matter the broken promises and disappointments along the way, liberation is God's plan and goal.

Second, the brief chapter 45 (simply five verses), also introduced previously, provides reversal in words addressed to Baruch as though around the year 605, indicating God's intention to bring full circle the building and planting that represent the community transplanted with some cooperation to Babylon. Though a community will remain there, yet a portion—arguably the group with which the book of Jeremiah is most concerned—is also to be uprooted from their resettlement and transplanted to the land of Yehud. Baruch, representing in this book the survival of the words of Jeremiah and the efficacy of his ministry (such as it was), has yet another step to take.[18] If Baruch needs to allow his status and role to move beyond his managing the scroll, God encourages him to do it, though it may also be that return to the heritage land and survival of the scroll go together.

Third, perhaps, and surely as brief, is a short address (51:59–64) to Baruch's brother, Seraiah.[19] Placed between the OANs (chaps. 46–51, with their spate of verses condemning Babylon) and the somewhat repetitious summary of the 587 fall of Jerusalem to the Babylonians (52:1–30), this is an analeptic piece, dragged way out of the chronological order that the book editor is clearly not much concerned for.[20] It offers almost pointlessly information to us and advice to one of King Zedekiah's men, accompanying and assisting the king with supplies when—we only now discover—he himself went to Babylon midway through his reign (around the year 594). It seems, perhaps, an important piece of information to have known when we were scrutinizing the actions of that king, but now is when we learn of it—still without gaining much information, at that. Jeremiah had confided into Seraiah's care some words, analogous, perhaps, to the words handed over to Baruch and his scroll-making part of the story we are reading. Seraiah's bundle of words from the prophet were those involving the disastrous fate of Babylon—perhaps those just reviewed in the concluding OAN (50–51 concerns Babylon)—to be read aloud when the quartermaster should arrive in the aggressor city. Read to whom, we may ask, but the simplest assumption is to or in the hearing of the resettled community, the only group present who might begin to understand them. Then the words were to be consigned to the Euphrates to await their time of filling. Seraiah was commissioned to enunciate the last of Jeremiah's prophetic words: "And thus shall Babylon sink and never rise again, because of the disaster that I will bring on it. And nations shall have wearied themselves for fire" (51:65). Things are not what they seem, but even words must be patient in exile and await their time. That note has been stressed here as not previously.

Finally, fourth, the book ends with the few and cryptic verses that tell of the release of the resettled king Jehoiachin from his prison (52:31–34).[21] The narrating voice turns once more to catch us off guard as the book ends with now a proleptic hop. As is well noted and thoroughly discussed, the material of chapter 52 is strongly reminiscent of the final chapter of 2 Kings, reviewing the ending conditions of the long story it has related, with grim statistics.[22] In no rush to conclude, the book of Jeremiah finally comes now to its last four verses though without making those easy to understand.[23] But in these final four verses, anticipating its storyline by some years, we are informed that the Josiah grandson—leader of the first exile and of those Jeremiah characterized as good figs, taking up, if perhaps not wholly willingly, the choice the prophet preached as necessary—has emerged from prison. Commentators agree that this is not jubilant news in any clear or unrestrained sense, and some decline to speak of it as good at all. In the context that has been urged throughout this book, it is undeniably hopeful, if not for the monarch and monarchy, surely for the survival of his group. But to emerge free is better than to die inside, and so Jehoiachin becomes a figure of survival if not radical hope, of adequacy and not dishonor, of well-being and not disaster. It is not the purpose of the book to relate the future, but the sighting of the old man is hopeful for his people.

Conclusions

Since it is nearly time to conclude this whole book, let me simply make seven summary points about the consolation material under consideration here. First, we can see more clearly than before that the book of Jeremiah has had in mind the whole process of *šub*/turning, with the book mostly but not exclusively concerned with going out; crucial as well is staying in the new land while expecting that some group of survivors will emerge, eventually, to return to the land of promise. The ticket issued has included a round-trip, in fact with a lengthy stay at the nonhome destination. Each step, each phase is important, granting the unevenness of their treatment. Second, hearts have been consistently important. From the moment that the deity has understood and articulated, so to speak, his insight that human hearts are not capable of much initiative toward the good nor faithful persistence in it, God seems to have shifted the weight of frustration and blame about what his people cannot do toward undertaking what he must do. Hearts, as is well known in Hebrew Bible anthropology, combine what modern Westerners split as heart and head. God has appeared to bend toward the fashioning of a gift that can be received by such human hearts, can be responded to, engaged, appreciated, entered into. The dominant tone of shaming and blaming, accusing and blustering has given way, largely, to something more gentle, respectful, gracious. The attributed speech, as it occurs, is less defensive on everyone's part. Something important has been understood.

Third, we must ask whether this fresh relationship—the terms of the covenant inscribed on hearts—will be different. Is it new? The terms of relatedness seem basically the same: God demands and expects, desires and anticipates, the love and loyalty of the people, undiluted by other commitments. That is not new. Jeremiah's God's innovation of writing the reality on the heart, as distinct from whispering it into the ear, is also not really so different. If the image implies that the binding knowledge, the bond of relation, is inset deeper than before so that less effort is required to remain mindful, we have to ask how that might be so. To simply announce a new metaphor does not suffice to create new reality. But God is ever-new, and so surprises and fresh starts are to be anticipated.

So we arrive at point four: If we turn that last question a bit, and ask what might make YHWH's people more deeply attentive to God than had been the case, what emerges is the matter of experience. If it has been urgent to leave the land of Judah and journey to Babylon before the final destruction of the monarchic state, as I have been arguing, we have to ask why. If to remain in Babylon for some extended length of time has been stressed by deity and prophet, as it has been: again why? For some reason, not stated explicitly but perhaps understood by those participating, it was considered vital, urgent, required. We may think of the long story of Joseph concluding the book of Genesis, which urgently and with both consistent and diverse motifs draws the children of Jacob relentlessly into their land of exile and stalls them there, until it is time for them to leave. What is learned by those living "outside"?[24] There are many ways to answer that question, and some of them are likely known to us from our common experience of "being away," whether by choice or not. God's people learned something in Babylon that they had not known before, or they internalized it differently. We can surely say that diasporal Judaism is a different creature than the older kingdoms of Israel and Judah. It is possible to speculate on the cultural exposure that seems to have occurred, the incredible enriching of the tradition as touched by prolonged exposure to its ancient Near Eastern siblings. The exile communities going back, whenever and however they did so, did not return the same as they departed. The sojourn in Babylon was transformative, even if we can scarcely detail how that was so.

A fifth point: Jeremiah scholars are, most appropriately, deeply interested in what happened after the year 587, how the tradition was shaped, filled fuller, and so forth. I have mostly sidestepped that matter, having made other choices of angle. Jeremiah scholar Kathleen O'Connor has recently written of the biblical book as taking some of its character from its role in enabling the survival of disaster. Her question, pursued in various venues over the past several years and culminating in her recent book, has argued well that the book's language must be sturdy and bold enough to enable those traumatized to be able to see and say what they have gone through, to resist internalizing the blame hurled at them while engaging the vigor of the discourse to articulate their painful experience, to mirror chaos without giving up on the possibility of making a future of well-being. However I want to emphasize as well the importance of hearing the damage done by some of the violent language and urge that contemporary readers like ourselves have a responsibility to problematize it in a slightly different way than O'Connor has done, though to supplement rather than counter her valuable insight. Coping mechanisms are vital, and yet they can also delay healing. Coping is not a long-term strategy, nor a place to remain longer than one needs to.

Sixth: Related is the question of what God learns from the whole exile experience—beyond the fragility of the human heart. This, of course, is another way of asking what the prophetic tradition appears to learn or how it seems to change over time. What the character God learns in the book of Jeremiah is, arguably, the pointlessness of the violence directed toward the people as an incentive toward better behavior. This is a question with which the present study began and to which it will return shortly. Here it suffices to point out that God's broken and suffering people, if chivvied into exile by brutally vivid language, have the opportunity to heal when the harsh language stops. The language of love and compassion is more salutary than that of anger and accusation, vitriol and violence. If that is true in our own experience, it has to be true on a more cosmic level as well. God can "learn" this point insofar as it is more deeply grasped by us who talk about God.

Finally, a seventh point: What of Jeremiah himself? Is there something here for him, beyond his role in speaking helpfully to the community that heeded him by going early to Babylon? That role is no small thing in itself, enabling the prophet to extend to that group what it needed: the advice proffered outside the temple (chap. 26), the insight as to how the "firstborn figs" were appraised (chap. 24), the important instructions about how to live in Babylon (chap. 29), the consoling images of return (chaps. 30–31). And yet, and yet: Is there nothing for Jeremiah except to survive the defeat of Jerusalem only to fall into the hands first of assassins and finally of the Egypt bound? After the prophet's bold and parabolic words to King Zedekiah (chap. 32)—irate at what Jeremiah had claimed—our prophet says to God, in effect: <But all these Babylonians, and you want me to believe that the land can blossom again?> (32:16–25). And God consoles Jeremiah with the words of chap. 33, addressed to him, language and imagery we heard before, from the lips of the prophet himself. But these words are spoken by God to Jeremiah, responsive to the trusting doubt voiced to the deity. Jeremiah will need to take the path that is his, and it does not go to Babylon. But he also has been addressed by words of tenderness, has heard the plans for well-being and not disaster. Surely Jeremiah's heart is refreshed as he learns of God's plans for the future.

AFTERWORD AND IMPLICATIONS

> Narrative, in short, is more than literature, it is the way we understand our
> lives. . . . Great literature speaks to the deepest level of our humanity; it
> helps us better understand who we are.
>
> Robert N. Bellah, *Religion in Human Evolution:*
> *From the Paleolitic to the Axial Age*

It is time to return to the questions with which this book began: *Can* a responsible, coherent, compelling book on biblical Jeremiah result from a study of the
vast complexity of issues that make it up? *How* can a classic, gathering shape
from the sixth century B.C.E. and then thriving under interpreters for more than
two thousand years, be freshly addressed? Can such an ancient religious document pose issues *for twenty-first century readers*? Since I have summarized each
chapter's material as I have gone, I choose here the challenge to review not so
much content but process, methodology, and underlying assumptions grounding the construction attempted here. Let me name five major frameworks that
bear primary responsibility for my interpretation of this biblical book named for
Jeremiah.

First, the basic choice was to cue from and work with primarily literary
issues rather than historical ones. Though I have consulted and attended to
pertinent historical and sociological data and count on the general reliability of
the clash of powers great and small near Jerusalem at the turn of the seventh to
sixth century of the previous era, yet I also maintain that the book of Jeremiah
recomposes its events fictively, to suit its own purposes. Consistently—whether
for good or bad—I have etched the prophet as a literary persona rather than as a
historical one and, to an extent surprising to me, have seen the deity emerge distinctively as well. The prophetic book draws suggestively and skillfully prophet
and deity working together, shows them blending their efforts toward the persuasion of other character sets. Both YHWH and Jeremiah are shown radically capable of every feeling known to our human species—God is anthropomorphized
in this book—and they meet a range of responses from other characters as well.

Though they come to work as a team, their shares of the project overlapping, the deity is surely a central figure of the book, receding primarily as he hands over the responsibility of implementation to the prophet once Jeremiah has confirmed his allegiance to the project in his last soliloquy.

Other characters are shown with great variety as well: the blatant Jehoiakim and the conflicted Zedekiah, with their more shadowed kin, Jehoahaz and Jehoiachin; we see Baruch and Ebed-Melek emerge memorably and distinctively; Lady Zion and the men of Judah take on recognizable profiles in the ruminations of others; the Shapan clan provides a cadre of positive figures amid many others.[1]

Varieties of discourse have provided the main pathway for investigating the characters in this book, with tremendous diversity of utterance. Spoken language and not inferred psychology has provided as the primary data for teasing out these various literary *personae*. My choice has been consistently to bypass previous influential criticism on form of the prophetic speech—useful though that has been—to work with more flexible literary genres as they actually have impact in this biblical book, rather than as their form may signify in the abstract, across or within biblical books. So we have attended to quotations and questions, to attributed speech and ascribed motivation, considered soliloquy within and speech without, pondered the impact of proverb and proclamation. How the characters have been given to talk and be spoken about has been our primary access to them.

Without in any way denying that the book was produced much later than the events on which it spends its time, and surely not disregarding that its insights are the fruits of mature reflection, I have not focused on those compositional processes in this book. The prophetic book spends almost all its actual words on the events before 587, and I have chosen to do the same.

The choice, then, has been one of assigning proportion: Some historical work, considerable literary method, and a bold reader entry point. The experienced reader will miss in text, notes, and bibliography some scholarly participants and issues normally attending Jeremiah study. It seemed best to attempt a fresh approach rather than to be led along smoother paths defined by the more usual assumptions.

Second, I have discerned while working and hence invested in a basic order for the book, again, literarily rather than historically derived. That is, I am not reducing the book to the patterns that I see and claiming them as authorial but underlining them as fruitful for interpretation. Though I did not start with the possibility of the book's having a demonstrable thesis, over time it pressed itself too firmly for me to disregard. Again, I am not claiming that the author's intention has been uncovered but rather that amid the undeniable disorder of the book, there is a distinct momentum that repeats tangibly. Analogy: Though San Francisco is a city taking physical shape in complex patterns—even containing "the cookedest street in the world"—there is a vantage point across the bay from the ferry slip in Tiburon from where San Francisco's streets appear in a perfect grid, climbing the hills on which they lie. From that angle, the streets align, though they don't when viewed from other places. An urgent insight accumulates.

The base plan of the prophetic book is manifestly not chronological, does not report events in the order beloved of moderns (and even sometimes of ancients). There is occasional order of that sort, but it does not predominate. I have suggested that the main trajectory is gradual and temporal, aiming to make visible over time and to various characters in particular ways the possibility that God envisions plans of well-being that seem nigh unthinkable to any encountering them amid danger, defeat, and destruction. That is, over against the pincers of Egypt and Babylon promising the disaster of the removal of God's heritage people from the beloved garden in which they had been invited to live, the book's urgency has been to make a "choice" of quasi-voluntary relocation seem viable enough to undertake. To quote Walter Brueggemann once again, "The primary work of the book of Jeremiah is to speak Israel into exile."[2]

The deity depicted shows up as outraged at the abusive trashing of the divine garden by guests who remain beloved to God. Indeed, among the provocations of divine anger is that those so cared-for would behave so badly. Human-like, God vents that massive indignation but eventually is shown—or can be seen—to come, by degrees, to another insight, though only on the far side of extensive violent discourse. God's outrage bears the turn toward something gentler. The brutality of the language also hides, poorly, a pervasive fear that those addressees will fail to take seriously enough the circumstances of the situation God sees. This is not a phenomenon mysterious to us humans: When we are fearful for the well-being of others or sense dire danger, we tend to shout rather than cajole. The deity and prophet each participate in this trap of anger and blame, threat and retaliation, but the deity is the one shown to come to a fresh insight: Human hearts have, over time, shown a vast incomprehension about their own health. They—we—choose badly, relapse readily, adhering stubbornly and destructively to the most perverse behaviors. God can continue to rant ineffectually, but if change is to come and the unlikely good be chosen, God will need to take the initiative in amending behavior. In the divine soliloquies, we are privy to God's process of turning from anger toward a resolute compassion. Jeremiah, with less insight, climbs on board the project in time and enacts his commitment in his own distinctive way.

If God comes with difficulty to the awareness that he must make the decisive move from anger to compassion, and if Jeremiah somewhat reluctantly overrides his own apparent good and possible gain to labor for other hearts (while, of course, strengthening his own in the process), other characters are not so easy to persuade. Most of those addressed—notably kings, elites, prophets, and some priests—cannot and will not adapt their perspective to what is demanded. Again, there is great variety in the depiction of this refusal. Some is blatant and malevolent: King Jehoiakim comes to mind. His brother, the royal Zedekiah, embodies his refusal with greater subtlety and prompts, I think, a fuller hearing from us. We watch others hesitate, or act with apparent sincerity: In the end, we watch a single shadow detach itself and move away from Judah and Jerusalem before the end comes as a group goes east under the leadership of Josiah's grandson.

A great set of options for survival is explored, each presumably viable at least for a time, but eventually all are eliminated except the single group that can be seen to agree to relocate some years before the cataclysm. So we are given the perspective of those who see no need for change, and we hear the futile challenge offered those who would stay to amend their ways. We watch the fate of those who delay until the city falls and then suffer either death or brutal banishment. Other survivors of Jerusalem's defeat seem to be offered a reprieve. They dwell in the land, then refugee across the Jordan once the governor is assassinated, finally journey to Egypt. But clearly enough, none of those options proves sustainable. So far as the early exiles are concerned, even they are not automatically safe: At first the early removal is spoken of by God as a harsh punishment; we know it is perceived by participants and witnesses as undesirable, since some wish to return prematurely from it and have to be dissuaded from doing so—or perhaps they don't heed. Only the group that can participate responsively with the plans of well-being that the deity discloses to them through the prophet can be said to benefit, at least from the perspective of the prophetic book. The plans of God's heart cannot be reduced to a zip code but are a process of deepening trust and cooperation in ways that surely remain mysterious.

That the deity has to come to fruitful insight with difficulty, followed by the prophet and finally by a few people—with most refusing—is given us on a huge canvas for our study. Another way to put that point is to suggest that the book offers numerous and subtle mirrors into which characters peer—and readers behind them—in order to find the way to the place and process of well-being valorized in the prophetic book. It seems obvious that this sifting is ideological and theological, a literary construct rather than a historical accuracy. The gift is not primarily geographical, though it is that; it is primarily relational. Nor does the prophetic book pose this possibility as simply a one-time offer, as though God has only one set of well-being plans that have long since expired. The deity, we may all learn, has multiple gardens, not just one.

So though disorder is acknowledged, still there is some clear order to the book of Jeremiah, as I tried to show on the map provided and by proceeding basically with the present study in narrative order, moving steadily along but also revisiting and reviewing material from a fresh angle as it seems to want and repay.

Third, it should be clear that this interpretive project participates as deeply in biblical spirituality as it does in classical modern biblical studies, making manifest that the choices of the interpreter are not objective and inevitable—even should she wish them to be, which is not the case here. In so vast a project as interpreting and exegeting this complicated book, some starting places have been preferred to others and held more influential than alternatives. If biblical spirituality can be understood as project and process of orienting one's life toward what is of ultimate concern, which for those appreciating the Bible as Scripture will be an orientation toward the compassionate heart of God, then the urgent starting point and in fact basic project will be to make God's heart more known and our own more like God's.[3] My starting point does not strike me as alien to the book I am interpreting but condign with it. Biblical studies, as featured in this book and in many others familiar to readers, overlaps the concerns of biblical spirituality as well as those of reader-alert and cultural studies in recognizing and in fact rejoicing to name a clear and values-oriented starting point and lodestone for their endeavors. It is not fortuitous or meretricious that the present study is taken up with how God language works, aims to show how that treasured biblical discourse can be salvific. At a time when the world scriptures are not well known and when the particular writings held canonical by Jews and Christians are considered suspect by many and virtually unknown by more, the project of interpreting such religious classics well is urgent.

Fourth and related: A support beam of this reading has been my strong sense and construction of the impotence of deity and prophet to persuade sufficiently that their viewpoint is good news, can conduce to the good. We see this point in the book and hear it witnessed among commentators, scholars, students. The scandal of the violent language in the prophets, not least in Jeremiah, is well explored in our era, appropriately so. The harshness is perhaps most evident in the gendered constructions and insults emerging from the mouth of deity and prophet, divinely attributed threats to visit sexual violence on Lady Zion. Such language has been profitably uncovered and indignantly declaimed, not simply verse by verse but cumulatively across a canon that is arguably racist and sexist. Beyond that, the prophetic tactics of blame and shame, of accusation and reviling are prominent and increasingly jarring to moderns, not least when the Bible continues to be heard as Scripture, for example in liturgy and prayer. How, many readers ask, can this vengeful portrait resemble God, can these words be claimed as Scripture, can this cumulative experience of reading be healthy and productive? This indeed is a Jeremiah-sized problem.

And yet, we see as well—even as clearly if we look critically—that the book is honest enough to own that the violent language is not persuasive, is not helpful, does not inspire reform or repentance on the part of any hearing it. Violent language is not effective. God and Jeremiah can see that, or can learn it over their shoulders, as we can in their company. The deity cannot shout the people into compliance, and the prophet, at his most intense and urgent moment of persuasion, fails by blaming instead of understanding. He does best at a moment where, less defensive, he concedes some space to his hearers, explains. This is a major insight of the book, available to us if we are open to it. It of course brings challenges in its wake, and those are not always welcome.

One of the implications of such construction is to recognize that Jeremiah's deity who must learn how to convert anger and disappointment to compassion through suffering may not offer an exact overlap with existential God, certainly not with the deity of classic systematic theology. It is, again, an anthropomorphic portrait. Language, and particularly language about reality as mysterious as God, is not strictly representational but imaginatively suggestive about what exceeds precise discourse. A modern default impulse to prize facticity and verifiability does not serve us well when we are reading old texts. It is a mistake to assume that the bedrock of truth is "happenedness." To confuse these categories is not true, not necessary, not best.

The book of Jeremiah, deeply reflective about many realities, opens up to us God's people narrativizing their experience of that relationship at a particularly painful moment, brings forth in language the mystery of God's offering the people of Judah and Jerusalem—and Babylon—what they most ardently desire: plans of well-being and not of destruction. Insofar as we, reading, assume and count on that God's deepest desire is the well-being of creation, then we are challenged to look beyond the surface of the abusive language, to listen more deeply. The language is more malleable than it is literalistic. The challenge holds for readers of ancient texts, of poetry, and surely of Scripture. The book of Jeremiah is not a snapshot of God any more than it is a video of political events. The slippage, if we can call it that, is not bad news but good.

Finally, fifth, the focus on the language of the prophetic book, on its powerful discourse as catalyzing meaning, rather than on its containing reliable and specific historical data, has also invited us to understand in a more complex way the phenomenon we call prophecy, whether we are talking about the ancients or about their descendants, our contemporaries. Insofar as our default toward exact linguistic precision and verifiable correlation between entities has made us naïve about what prophecy entails, this biblical book showing failed intermediation invites us to think more deeply. Prophets we know—classic and contemporary—are those who most intensely and skillfully struggle to know what God may desire and to share such insight with the rest of us. The dance entailing intuition and persuasion, discernment and recognition, analysis and disappointment is not readily chartable. The quest for learning the deep desires of the divine heart is primordial to humans (perhaps to other creatures as well, for all we know). Jeremiah's God has learned that our species, at least, discerns hearts rather poorly, for all our good intentions and efforts. Some ancients and a few moderns are deemed to be good at hearts, skilled enough to be reliable for the rest of us. Jeremiah is such a book, is such a figure. And yet what a struggle we see. There is nothing automatic or simple.

So how does it, does he, read the events of the turn of the seventh century into the sixth to learn and articulate what God desires, intends, initiates, and accomplishes for Judah? How does God communicate such realities, and how does God's prophet perceive them? We are back to the mystery of divine agency—collaboration of creator and creatures—with which the biblical prophets are filled. Jeremiah, arguably, sees it more simply than we may do, or at least in terms other than we would use to talk about what God can do. Can God's plans for the beloved community sustain a radical relocation, an ignominious defeat, the collapse of revered institutions? Can the language of Jeremiah show us how to widen our vision so that we can, with integrity, contemplate what has seemed impossible? Can this intense language and the vivid *personae* available in the prophetic book catalyze a compassionate growth in our expectations, push us past our narrow prejudices and preferences to accept gifts of well-being? Insofar as we recognize the difficulty of being asked to choose and cooperate with plans larger than our favorite screens, we learn something important. The struggle of Judah with YHWH is not so much about alien statues, shrines, and sacrifices as it is about something far more subtle.

If Jindo is correct to draw our attention to the reality of the garden of the gods, the beloved heritage the creator deeply desires to share with creatures, a signal contribution of this prophetic book may be to remind us, reading, that such a metaphor and symbol is wonderfully and urgently available for us as well. Though it is not simply spatial but deeply relational, we have heard the characters in the book of Jeremiah specify to us that place matters, that care and respect for the garden and its hosts and guests coincides with God's plans of well-being. The shared garden is perhaps the most powerful symbol available for our age, the invitation to live there joyously made clearest, perhaps, as we visit the gardens of the book of Genesis; of the Song of Songs; and of the Gospel of John where Jesus meets Mary of Magdala. But Jeremiah has told us of it as well. So, in the end, literary Jeremiah—fragile, fallible, faithful Jeremiah—can show us the path to the place where we will thrive, enact for us the compassion we need if we are to move well into God's plans of well-being.

NOTES

Introduction

1. There are two early editions of the book of Jeremiah, one Hebrew and one Greek, with unusual discrepancy between them. Consult Terence E. Fretheim, *Jeremiah*, and Jack R. Lundbom, *Jeremiah 1–20: A New Translation with Introduction and Commentary* (hereafter Lundbom, *1–20*), 57–62.

2. See A. R. Pete Diamond, "The Jeremiah Guild in the Twenty-First Century: Variety Reigns Supreme," for a trenchant discussion of the impasse reached by biblical scholars on whether, to what extent, and how we may gain precise, reliable historical detail from a book like Jeremiah, or if the character is fictional and the quest to retrieve him ill-considered.

3. Jerome T. Walsh, *Old Testament Narrative: A Guide to Interpretation*, 6–9.

4. A useful discussion of these factors can be found in Barbara Green, "This Old Text: An Analogy for Biblical Interpretation."

5. These events receive substantial and responsible attention in Göstra W. Ahlström, *The History of Ancient Palestine from the Paleolothic Period to Alexander's Conquest;* J. Maxwell Miller and John H. Hayes, *A History of Ancient Israel and Judah;* and Lester Grabbe, "The Lying Pen of the Scribes? Jeremiah and History."

6. There is vast discussion on virtually every aspect of Josiah's reform. For briefer summaries by historians, consult Ahlström, *Ancient Palestine*, 764–81, Grabbe, *Ancient Israel: What Do We Know and How Do We Know It?* 204–7. For fuller treatments from a variety of methodological perspectives, see Marvin Sweeney, *King Josiah of Judah: The Lost Messiah of Israel;* Uriah Kim, *Decolonizing Josiah: Toward a Postcolonial Reading of the Deuteronomistic History.*

7. It is impossible to achieve certainly about numbers of exiles and those that remained. For a consideration of the biblical material provided, consult Miller and Hayes, *History*, 480–81.

8. For a general survey of this vast issue, see Mark S. Smith, *The Origins of Biblical Monotheism: Israel's Polytheistic Background and the Ugaritic Texts*. Scholarly disagreements are many but mostly more nuanced than what will engage us here.

9. Smith, *Origins*, 77–80, observes, for example, that Israel does not pick up on the family aspect of its likely parent religion, nor on the deity as lord over the realm of

the dead. Yahweh emerges with no divine peers, fewer divine subordinates than was typical, no sex, no death, no kin.

10. Consult Martii Nissinen, ed., *Prophecy in Its Ancient Near Eastern Context: Mesopotamian, Biblical, and Arabian Perspectives;* David L. Petersen, *The Roles of Israel's Prophets,* 9–19; Hans M. Barstad, "Prophecy in the Book of Jeremiah and the Historical Prophet," 87–100.

Chapter 1: Womb and Workshop

1. See William L. Holladay, *Jeremiah 1: A Commentary on the Book of the Prophet Jeremiah Chapters 1–25,* 26–31 for a standard exposition of this form-critical feature.

2. I will use angled brackets to offer my paraphrases of character speech, leaving quotation marks for precise quotations.

3. Though it is early to pin down specifically the referent on this foe, for a useful discussion, see David J. Reimer, "The 'Foe' and the 'North' in Jeremiah."

4. Louis Stulman, *Jeremiah,* 37–39.

5. For a nice chart of this set of resemblances, see Brent A. Strawn, "Jeremiah's In/effective Plea: Another Look at נעד in Jeremiah I 6."

6. Stulman provides this information efficiently in *Jeremiah,* 41–45. See also David L. Petersen, "The Ambiguous Role of Moses as Prophet."

7. Carolyn J. Sharp, "Embodying Moab: Jeremiah's Figuring of Moab (Jer 48) as Reinscription of the Judean Body."

8. Lundbom provides these appraisals in *1–20,* 121–22.

9. See Lundbom, *1–20,* 67–68.

10. Lundbom, *1–20,* 57, drawing from the summary at the end of the Hebrew Masora, notes that Jeremiah extends to 21,835 words.

11. Lundbom is a pioneer in Hebrew rhetoric. In *1–20,* 68–101 and 121–40, he lists and describes the tropes, providing as well a brief glossary of some of them in *Jeremiah 37–52: A New Translation with Introduction and Commentary* (hereafter Lundbom, *37–52*), 586–94; he also presents these features as a set in *The Hebrew Prophets: An Introduction,* 165–207, and notes them throughout his commentaries. See also Yehoshua Gitay, "Rhetorical Criticism and the Prophetic Discourse"; Roland Meynet, *Rhetorical Analysis: An Introduction to Biblical Rhetoric.*

12. Lundbom, *1–20,* 122–27, names these and provides some examples.

13. See Lundbom, *1–20,* 127–29. I add drama to this category, where he has it separate.

14. Lundbom, *1–20,* 129–32.

15. Lundbom, *1–20* scatters these and does not mention reused speech, which I draw more from my familiarity with the work of M. M. Bakhtin: Barbara Green, *Mikhail Bakhtin and Biblical Scholarship: An Introduction.*

16. For example, the first oracle we will examine is unambiguously focused on the battle of Carchemish; it makes little sense to think it was not crafted at the time of that

event, though it does not appear now in the section of the book where other similarly dated events occur. The final oracle in our study claims a setting in Zedekiah's reign.

17. Lundbom, *37–52*, 181–84. He observes that the form existed more broadly than simply in Israel and Judah. Scholars differ as to the setting that produced the OANs, and it is possibly best to assume it is not a single setting; see Robert P. Carroll, *Jeremiah: A Commentary*, 753, for that point. War is obviously prominent but may not be sufficient to account for the rise of the form. Generally useful is the short report by Thomas G. Smothers, "A Lawsuit against the Nations: Reflections on the Oracles on the Nations in Jeremiah." Stulman, *Jeremiah*, 350, makes the point that the oracles are not all the same but differ from each other in various ways. The oracle concerning Babylon draws that nation quite different from its appearance elsewhere in the prophetic book.

18. For alternative scholarly proposals, consult Lundbom, *37–52*, 185, 206. He prefers to see small independent units, whereas I am cued by elements that correlate sections.

19. Walter Brueggemann, *A Commentary on Jeremiah: Exile and Homecoming*, 424. Egypt represents what Judah desires and dreads as well as seeks and is swamped and eventually deserted by, in any case standing for a partner profoundly unreliable and unsatisfactory. John Hill, *Friend or Foe? The Figure of Babylon in the Book of Jeremiah MT*.

20. Lundbom, *37–52*, 203, calls the figure where apparent and ironic support and encouragement is offered but for a futile task *epitrophe*. Note another example in v. 11. Holladay *Jeremiah 2*, 316–22, stresses the taunting of Egypt for its lack of prowess at the battle.

21. Jared J. Jackson, "Jeremiah 46: Two Oracles on Egypt," 137–39, comments on Jeremiah's particular use of liking "how" statements to express mockery, satire, taunting, and anger as well as asking for information. The sarcastic "how"s serve as virtual negatives, a distinctive mode of divine discourse in this prophet.

22. Lundbom, *37–52*, 200–202. Brueggemann, *Commentary*, 426–28, points out Jeremiah's penchant for battle detail with its brutalizing impact.

23. Commentators differ on precise referents; there is also wordplay here, with the bull's name sounding like the Pharaoh Hoprah's: Holladay, *Jeremiah 2*, 327, or puns on Egyptian geography: Lundbom, *37–52*, 210–12. Carroll, *Commentary*, 770, points out Jeremiah's fondness for theriomorphic imagery (deities as animals). It seems clear enough that Pharaoh is being mocked, implicitly by the negative comparison with the rival king and also by wordplay: in v. 2 the *nkw/hkh* assonance (strike/Necho), surely when he is given the ridiculous name of v. 17.

24. Catchwords unify this material while chiasms and *inclusios* mark its edges.

25. Lundbom, *37–52*, 221–22. Jeremiah will reuse some of this material, e.g., healing balm, slithering serpents.

26. Lundbom, *37–52*, 224, with a six-fold repetition of the preposition *'al*.

27. Lundbom, *37–52*, 312–18, makes the case for boundary disputes and notes that Nebuchadnezzar was in the neighborhood of Ammon and Judah in 604, 599–98, 594, 588 (when Ammon escaped Judah's fate) and implicated in the assassination of Gedaliah after the removal of Zedekiah.

28. Holladay, *Jeremiah 2*, 366–69, comments on other instances of Jeremiah's use of multiples.

29. For an analysis of rhetorical features that stresses some other aspects, see Duane L. Christensen, "'Terror on Every Side' in Jeremiah," who notes the *inclusio* that attends the deity's explanation for Ammon's punishment.

30. Christensen, "Terror," 500–501, on the contrary, finds it somewhat sympathetic.

31. See Linda Haney, "YHWH, the God of Israel . . . and of Edom? The Relationships in the Oracle to Edom in Jeremiah 49:7–22." It is part of her argument that the prophetic diatribe against Edom likely occasioned around the exile ought not eliminate the positive regard for Isaac's eldest son in Genesis, a point she claims Jeremiah recalls here in not accusing Edom of anything that was not also characteristic of Israel/Judah. Lundbom's useful analysis is in *37–52*, 324–47.

32. Haney, "Oracle to Edom," 80–86.

33. Both Lundbom and Haney consider a variety of issues to sort the arrangement. How do the stichs of poetry work? How do chiasms and *inclusios* do their job? How is repetition effective, including the key- and catchwords? Lundbom, *37–52*, 324–47, opts for divisions into three units with subparts: I, vv. 7–11 split into vv. 7–8, 9, 10–11; II, vv. 12–18 divide into v. 12, v. 13, vv. 14–16, vv.17–18; and III,: vv. 19–22 are composed by vv. 19–20a, vv. 20b–21, and v. 22. Haney, 90–92, likes four units: vv. 7–11, 12–13, 14–19, 20–22. Consult their work for rationale.

34. Haney, "Oracle to Edom," 89; Lundbom, *37–52*, 333, 340–41, 347.

35. See Lundbom, *37–52*, 330–31, for discussion of the passage.

36. Lundbom, *37–52*, 347–51, says that before the rise of Assyria and Babylon, Damascus and other cities in the region were the most persistent foe of Israel and Judah and reminds us that in 2 Kings 24:2, Damascus assisted the Babylonians to savage Judah. This piece may assume that but does not so specify.

37. Lundbom, *37–52*, 349, reminds us as well of the nautical imagery used in the oracle against Babylon, specifically 51:34–45.

38. Lundbom, *37–52*, 351–59 reminds us that this is not the Hazor within Israel but a nomadic merchant group farther to the east and apparently noted in the Babylonian Chronicle, according to Holladay, *Jeremiah 2*, 382–86.

39. For some speculation about the historical background, consult Eric Peels, "God's Throne in Elam: The Historical Background and Literary Context of Jeremiah 49:34–39," 217–20. Lundbom, *37–52*, 359–64, fixes the setting to 596-95. No other prophet has an oracle against Elam.

40. Holladay, *Jeremiah 2*, 387; Peels, 223. Cf. Lundbom, *37–52*, 361, who says there are no catchwords to Babylon's oracles

41. Lundbom, *37–52*, 361.

42. Holladay, *Jeremiah 2*, 388.

43. Peels, "God's Throne," 221.

Chapter 2: Overture

1. Lundbom, *1–20*, 306, observes that the only temporal indicator in all of 1–20 is at 3:6, setting the piece in the time of Josiah.

2. Joseph M. Henderson, "Jeremiah 2–10 as a Unified Literary Composition: Evidence of Dramatic Portrayal and Narrative Progression."

3. Henderson, "Unified," 117.

4. Versification varies here: the Hebrew runs 8:4–23 and 9:1–25, whereas some English texts number 8:4–22 and 9:1–26.

5. By way of example: God quotes himself at 7:23, tags his speech at 2:4 and elsewhere, and quotes the people at 2:6 and many other times. Jeremiah quotes himself, tags his own speech, and quotes God, all at 4:10. Jeremiah paraphrases other characters at 10:11–16. We may know from forensic process that attributing speech and motives to others—hearsay—is not the same as eyewitness accounts. Lest we lose sight of the dominance of the deity's voice here, recall that most of the words are God's self-presentation to the prophet, who then tells us.

6. The verses where the speaker is uncertain include, in my opinion, 4:11; 4:23–26; 5:17; 6:10; 8:18–9:1; and 10:11–16.

7. The prominence of quoted speech or dialogic discourse has been noted though not much discussed by most commentators. See Robert P. Carroll, "The Polyphonic Jeremiah: A Reading of the Book of Jeremiah"; unlike me, he supposes that the voices represent various live viewpoints. John T. Willis, "Dialogue between Prophet and Audience as a Rhetorical Device in the Book of Jeremiah," makes a number of excellent observations about them, though in my view without taking their dramatic character as seriously as he might.

8. There is room for disagreement on various pieces, depending on what cues a reader takes. But my point is that, in general, YHWH talks to/about a female singular and male plurals, intermittently and shifting abruptly, though of course inflected endings make this clearer in Hebrew than in English.

9. The conditional sentence at 4:1–2 is complex and discussed in its variables by William L. Holladay, *Jeremiah 1: A Commentary on the Book of the Prophet Jeremiah Chapters 1–25*, 126–27.

10. Thomas W. Overholt, "Jeremiah 2 and the Problem of 'Audience Reaction,'" raises the basic set of questions about this discourse, wondering if—and we might say to what extent and with what effect—it is real or not. His conclusion is that we ought not take the content too seriously, ought to be leery of reading too much into (or out of) it. But to plumb the rhetorical impact of the dialogue is exactly what I want to do.

11. Holladay, *Jeremiah 1*, 137, noting that Micah and Habakkuk had included simple voicing, maintains that the plurality and complexity of what Jeremiah does with speakers was "stunning" for his hearers.

12. Henderson, "Unified," talks of them on pp. 124–33. His identification of the agent as being from the heavenly council fits in well with information suggested below about the provenance of the root metaphor, though the agent is usually seen as a human enemy.

13. For intertextual citations of God's anger as burning, see Lundbom, *1–20*, 337–38.

14. Females addressed at 4:7, 4:14, 4:18–21, 4:30–31; 5:7; 6:24–26; males at 4:8; 5:18, 5:21–30; 6:20–21, with much toggling between "you" and "they" reference.

15. Ten questions come at 4:14, 21, 30; 5:7, 9, 22, 29, 31; 6:10, 20. Brueggemann has worked carefully with some of these to show a consistent pattern where the speaker uses double questions to oppose another view, whether by contrasting something human with what is "natural," to question the inevitability of the default outcome, to make a new alternative seem prompted: "Jeremiah's Use of Rhetorical Questions."

16. Brueggemann, *A Commentary on Jeremiah: Exile and Homecoming*, 84, reminds us this is still imaginative rhetoric.

17. A second stimulating article by Joseph M. Henderson, "Who Weeps in Jeremiah VIII 23 (IX 1)? Identifying Dramatic Speakers in the Poetry of Jeremiah," becomes a dialogue partner here. Henderson wants to distinguish the speakers here, as do I.

18. A short but perceptive article by Robert M. Paterson, "Repentance or Judgment: The Construction and Purpose of Jeremiah 2–6," points out the repetition between chaps. 4–6 and 8–9 (my sections B and D) while also noting that since circumstances are altered, the "same" language is also fresh.

19. As Leslie C. Allen points out, *Jeremiah: A Commentary*, 65, the name "Babylon" is not provided until chap. 20.

20. The initial verse, 10:11, is in Aramaic, anomalous in the whole book, and baffling to commentators.

21. Job Y. Jindo, *Biblical Metaphor Reconsidered: A Cognitive Approach to Poetic Prophecy in Jeremiah 1–24*.

22. Zoltán Kövecses, *Metaphor: A Practical Introduction*, chap. 1; Jindo discusses these points on pp. 33–50.

23. Kövecses, *Metaphor*, chap. 2.

24. In my opinion much of the "marriage metaphor" work, though insightful and important, is myopic in this way and hence overreaches.

25. Here I argue against others, notably Diamond and O'Connor, who assert that the marriage metaphor is a root image. See "Unfaithful Passions: Coding Women Coding Men in Jeremiah 2–3 (4:2)," 289–90: "We claim that the marital metaphor functions as a root metaphor, organizing the disparate pieces of the composition and providing a narrative frame designed to guide the reader in the management of the twists and turns of the tradition."

26. See his chap. 4 for this careful and comparative work, summarized quickly here. One of his crucial sources is F. W. Dobbs-Allsopp, *Weep, O Daughter of Zion: A Study of the City-Lament Genre in the Hebrew Bible*.

27. Jindo, *Metaphor Reconsidered*, 90–150.

28. Consult Jindo, *Metaphor Reconsidered,* chap. 4 and more specifically in his chap. 5.

29. Jindo, *Metaphor Reconsidered*, 239. He explains that it is Zion theology vs. a view where the nations may be used by God to accomplish God's purposes.

30. Jindo, *Metaphor Reconsidered*, 239–40.

31. For a fairly compact treatment of these political and economic arrangements, see D. N. Premnath, *Eighth Century Prophets: A Social Analysis.*

Chapter 3: Resistance

1. Commentators are not so split over the extent of the general unit as might be supposed. One disagreement involves the length of the unit: Starting at chap. 11, does it extend past chap. 20, even as far as chap. 25? See the views of Louis Stulman (*The Prose Sermons of the Book of Jeremiah. A Redescription of the Correspondences with Deuteronomistic Literature in the Light of Recent Text-critical Research,* and "Jeremiah the Prophet: Astride Two Worlds"), who has specialized in the prose passages whereas others have been more interested in the poetry. Stulman likes chaps. 11–17 for the unit while describing it as "bumpy, disjointed, and stitched together," in his commentary *Jeremiah*, 115. In "The Prose Sermons as Hermeneutical Guide to Jeremiah 1–25: The Deconstruction of Judah's Symbolic World," Stulman asks some good questions (e.g., p. 36) while perhaps not taking the prose passages seriously enough in terms of what they actually accomplish.

2. Kelvin G. Friebel, *Jeremiah's and Ezekiel's Sign-Acts*, 20–24.

3. Lundbom, *1–20*, 614–29, puts v. 14 with what follows, points out its covenant vocabulary, and names an *inclusio* stretching from 11:3 to 20:15; he also says, 624, that v. 12 restates 2:27–28, useful in terms of my saying 2–10 is an overture. He calls the unit three oracles, atomizing it, without asking what else the unit of thirteen (for him) verses might be. He is also concerned here, as others are as well, to stress the relationship between Jeremiah and the language and viewpoint of Deuteronomy. William Holladay, *Jeremiah 1: A Commentary on the Book of the Prophet Jeremiah Chapters 1–25*, 348–49 splits it into four YHWH utterances, again, true enough so far as it goes. The point to note is the general lack of scholarly consensus about how these materials are ordered.

4. In order to attend to these layers of speech carefully, we can think of the "delivered words" as emerging from a series of envelopes into which the speakers successively insert them, penning the sender's name as though a return address. Here we have the book narrator at v. 1, the deity addressing the prophet who is to proclaim to the people, with God sometimes using more than one envelope, or quoting earlier speech to intensify the point.

5. Walter Brueggemann, *A Commentary on Jeremiah: Exile and Homecoming*, 111, thinks Jeremiah is recommissioned.

6. Holladay, *Jeremiah 1*, 346–53, calls the unit 11:1–17 and notes the hierarchy of quotations, seeing four YHWH utterances, with the pronouncing of the curse the main point.

7. Lundbom, *1–20*, 660, says this passage anticipates Jeremiah 30–33 and 46–51, which is the case, and he comments on presence of wordplay (661). Brueggemann, *Commentary*, 123, draws our attention to wordplay of heritage/*nahalah* and weary/ *nahal.*

8. There is some hesitation among commentators to accept that the destination of the garment is the Euphrates (in Hebrew, *Parah*), since it seems too far a journey, especially given the presence of a location with the name *Parah* only a few miles away from Jeremiah's presumed location (Lundbom, *1–20*, 668, and Holladay, *Jeremiah 1*, 398). But this reading seems too literal. In a narrated symbolic action, the details need not be realistic nor the journey practical.

9. Lundbom, *1–20*, 671–74, calls it a symbolic act, with key words and *accumulatio;* Holladay, *Jeremiah 1*, 401–2, puts the first words of v. 12 with what preceded but puzzles a bit as to how it matches other units; he raises (402–4) lots of questions about how the questions work.

10. Brueggemann, *Commentary*, 129–30, stresses that this is not a sign-act, and he reminds us that the drunkenness metaphor brings in its semantic field loss of equilibrium, dizziness, loss of balance, and so forth. Terence E. Fretheim, *Jeremiah*, 206, likes the *nebel/nabal* wordplay: wine-jug and moral fool.

11. Lundbom, *1–20*, 703, puts v. 10 with the preceding unit, though he grants it is poetry. He thinks without it, vv. 10–15 make a chiasm (704); he sees lots of *accumulatio*, with catchwords; he calls it a two judgment oracles split by a dialogue (703) and a symbolic action (706–7); he also says it is speech about, not to (709); Holladay, *Jeremiah 1*, 419–21, makes the unit longer (to 15:9), recognizing that scholars are mixed on what it is made up of.

12. Holladay, *Jeremiah 1*, 434, notes that this is the first of thirteen times Jeremiah employs this triad.

13. Mark E. Biddle, *Polyphony and Symphony in Prophetic Literature: Rereading Jeremiah 7–20*, chap. 3 calls our attention to the web of such references: 7:16; 11:14; 14:11; 16:5–9; cf. 15:1; 17:16; 18:20; 21:2; 37:3, 7; 42:2, 4, 20; 15:11; 27:18; 29:7. He summarizes (53–59) that Jeremiah intercedes fourteen times and is forbidden to do so four times.

14. Lundbom, *1–20*, 718, says that Jeremiah is rejected as a covenant mediator, a point I cannot see, at least in any permanent sense.

15. The Manasseh reference is interesting and somewhat distinctive. Elsewhere in the book of Jeremiah, there is still evil for kings to do. Manasseh may have been decisive, but he is not definitive. Kings will emerge as main villains in this prophetic book, and here one is named, with others to get their parts made explicit in the material ahead.

16. Lundbom, *1–20*, 752–5, calls this set of verses a small collection, divides it differently from me, names lots of rhetoric, and senses a connection with 7:1–8:3.

Holladay, *Jeremiah 1*, 467–75, also seeing no major links, splits it differently while noting what correlates. Brueggemann, *Commentary*, 151, sees triads. Friebel, *Sign-Acts*, 82–95, sees the section differently still. Clearly these unit choices are not settled yet among scholars.

17. Lundbom, *1–20*, 765, splits it into two sayings, allowing one to be more positive and the other negative. He provides biblical intertexts for fishers. Brueggemann, *Commentary*, 155, says the object hunted and fished is not clear.

18. Brueggemann, *Commentary*, 154–55.

19. Lundbom, *1–20*, 801, splits this at v. 23, noting significant divergence among commentators: he sees that catchwords unify it; Holladay, *Jeremiah 1*, 509, calls it a covenant unit like 7:1–12 and 11:1–14; Brueggemann, *Commentary*, 165–66, finds the change of tone after v. 23 odd.

20. As before: Jeremiah, narrating, says he was addressed. Then he distinguishes among directions he is given, what he is to proclaim, how he is to identify his proclamation, and how he is to call for general hearing of those addressed—all in vv. 19–21.

21. Lundbom, *1–20*, 801–5; Holladay, *Jeremiah 1*, 509.

22. Lundbom sees the unit unified by catchwords, which common vocabulary of course it needs to ramify its points (*1–20*, 805). He (810–11) likes the unit but splits off the last two verses, shows this similar to several others in this set: a call for reform (812–13); he calls it a *similitudo: k/ken* (814–15); for Holladay, *Jeremiah 1*, 512–13, it is a covenant speech, similar to 7:1–12 and 11:1–14, a symbolic action actually carried out, with speaker of v. 12 not clear (517). Brueggemann, *Commentary*, 168, calls attention to the two if/then sequences at vv. 7–8 and 9–10. Stulman, *Jeremiah*, 181, thinks 18–20 is a whole new unit, not linked to what has preceded.

23. Note the clear allusion to Jeremiah's ministry, with his "signature" verbs.

24. A similar expression is attributed in 2:25.

25. Lundbom, *1–20*, 833–36, makes a break at v. 13, sensing a link between this unit and 7:30–8:3, suggesting four oracles buried in prose, with twinned units or echoes discernible. Holladay, *Jeremiah 1*, 534–36, has my last two units as a set. Brueggemann, *Commentary*, 174, splits them at the chapter break and finds v. 11 incredible (177). Fretheim, *Jeremiah*, 283, suggests the audial link between the jar (*baqbuq*) and the voiding of the plans and commitments God had anticipated (*baqqoti*). That the border between the two pieces is not obvious is clear. Various scholars stress the similarity between this set of material and 7:1–8:3, though the differences are as many.

26. Friebel, *Sign-Acts*, 115; see pp. 115–24 for his additional views on the unit.

27. Holladay, *Jeremiah 1*, 544, reminds us that Jeremiah formally pronounces, is not just emoting spitefully.

Chapter 4: Deep Learning

1. Mark S. Smith, *The Laments of Jeremiah and Their Contexts*, 1–2, identifies six prophetic confessions or laments: 11:18–23; 12:1–6; 15:15–21; 17:14–18; 18:18–23; 20:7–13.

Pete A. R. Diamond, *The Confessions of Jeremiah in Context: Scenes of Prophetic Drama*, 11, sees eight, splitting Smith's third and making a pair where Smith has one. Kathleen M. O'Connor, *The Confessions of Jeremiah: Their Interpretation and Role in Chapters 1–25*, v–vii, discerns five (joining Smith's first pair into one). In biblical studies terms, this is substantial agreement!

2. O'Connor, *Confessions*, 24, names the formal elements as follows: address to deity; complaint indicating speaker's situation; plea of speaker's innocence; statement of speaker's trust in God to respond; petition that God intervene; oracle of assurance; vow of thanks or praise.

3. This "poetic unit" includes prose at vv. 17–19 and 21–23, a matter able to be addressed in various ways. Here, I simply accept it and make no effort to justify or account for the anomaly, if such it is.

4. Walter Brueggemann, *Like Fire in the Bones: Listening for the Prophetic Word in Jeremiah*, 4.

5. Consult Fretheim, "Caught in the Middle: Jeremiah's Vocational Crisis," 356, for consideration of the relationship between Jeremiah's anger and what he says of God's wrath, how the prophet's strong feelings become entangled with God's. See also James Crenshaw, *A Whirlpool of Torment: Israelite Traditions of God as an Oppressive Presence*, 49, who wonders if Jeremiah's basic concern is whether he can remain God's spokesman in view of the issues he is raising.

6. There is considerable discussion as to how 20:14–18 fit the seven preceding verses. For a summary, see Joep Dubbink, "Jeremiah: Hero of Faith of Defeatist? Concerning the Place and Function of Jeremiah 20:14–18." I hear them as discordant in form but not in content, providing a suitable climax to these laments.

7. Jack Lundbom, *1–20*, wants to include v. 14 with this piece (see his argument, 627); but v. 14 is addressed to the prophet and suits the context of the preceding prose unit and does not fit here, where the prophet is typically not engaged in these divine outpourings. The final verse here is held by Lundbom, *1–20*, 627, to be prose, but semantically it fits with this unit, and so I place it here. Holladay, *Jeremiah 1: A Commentary on the Book of the Prophet Jeremiah Chapters 1–25*, 349, wants the basic unit to be 11:1–17 with vv. 15–16 being a piece of it, though he acknowledges the disorder (and reconstructs substantially).

8. Some commentators identify this as a YHWH lament (and not an oracle) though insisting that it does not use lament language (e.g., Lundbom, *1–20*, 651; Holladay, *Jeremiah 1*, 385). Lundbom says it is one of a series of eight judgments running to the end of chap. 13.

9. Lundbom, *1–20*, 655, argues for the predator as a speckled bird of prey, possibly dappled like a young deer, with the adjective referring to its color, perhaps both the attraction to predators and the safety of camouflage.

10. Some commentators want a change of speaker at vv. 12–13, doubting that YHWH speaks of self in the third person, a point I contest.

11. For Lundbom, *1–20*, 615, the large unit is 11:1–13:27, with the possibility that chap. 13 stands somewhat independent of the previous two chapters. Commentators typically give the opening lines (vv. 15–17) to the prophet. Though noting various key and catchwords threading the verses, Lundbom opts discontinuous rather that continuous pieces. Holladay, *Jeremiah 1*, 405–6, though also open to unifying verbal and thematic links, also splits this unit into thirds, argues for individual poems, exactly the sort of exegetical reasoning I am wanting to counter.

12. On the oracle that starts oddly, see Lundbom, *1–20*, 678.

13. There are many textual and translation-related issues generating a wide opinion of understandings and translations here; see Holladay, *Jeremiah 1*, 411–17, for a sampling.

14. Lundbom thinks, *1–20*, 677, this verse marks Jeremiah as the weeping prophet. That may be so, but must it be? That he may (or may not) weep elsewhere does not mean God cannot do so as well. I am indebted to Lena Sophia Tiemeyer, "God's Hidden Compassion," 191, for the quotation from Isaiah 22:4: "Let me be, I have to cry. Do not try to comfort me when my people are being destroyed."

15. There is an imperative, "say," at v. 18, which could be repointed as a first person imperfect, a sort of self-direction or note of progress: <next I say to the king. . . .>

16. Judah, all of them, gone into exile in integrity? Commentators vie to name specific referents of these verses, but I would rather stick to the image itself. Have some gone quasi-voluntarily, the position I am urging that the book ultimately recommends? Such a move stands between refusal to go while continuing to try to make deals of some sort with the imperial powers . . . and being dragged away in ignominy and defeat if siege and final battle are survived at all.

17. The imagery here is of removing clothing, which, though bad, is not identical to rape (the way marital infidelity is not to be conflated with harlotry). Ignominious, surely; rape, not necessarily. If "someone" removed from Elizabeth II of England her hat, coat, and purse and forced her away from the throne in her slip (or in pedal-pushers, a T-shirt, and a backpack), the point of firing her would have been powerfully, humiliatingly, made.

18. Lundbom, *1–20*, 691–92, names the large unit as 14:1–15:21, unified by the theme of drought but split into four units: v. 1, vv. 2–6, vv. 7–9 (with v. 10 placed with the next section rather than with this one). Holladay, *Jeremiah 1*, 421, also sees it as part of 14:1–15:9, while noting that any order discernible is secondary. There is a general and loose consensus that the verses are best classified as a communal lament, the superscription that they are God's word notwithstanding. Fretheim, *Jeremiah*, 217–19, sees laments of God (vv. 2–6) and of people (vv. 7–9).

19. Lundbom, *1–20*, 693–94 and 699–700, catalogues lots of them and comments on their effect.

20. Lundbom, *1–20*, 126–27: Triads: Judah mourns, her gates droop, they lie dark on the ground. Nobles, servants, farmers represent the humans in missing water. Water

is not found, cisterns are empty, the ground is cracked. Three kinds of animals—doe, ass, jackal—are in distress. Sin is triplex: iniquity, rebellion, sin. God is named as a stranger, a passer-by, a weak warrior. God's decision is rendered in three moves: not accept, remember, punish.

21. For a lengthy discussion on the identity of the speaker see Timothy Polk, *The Prophetic Persona: Jeremiah and the Language of the Self*, 75–91. Lundbom, *1–20*, 699, opts for its being the prophet, though without explaining why.

22. In speaking of self in the third person, the pronouncement nonetheless fits here rather than with the prose unit that follows.

23. Wandering feet occur in Proverbs 11:6 and Isaiah 59:7. More broadly, the path is a common wisdom trope, with feet leaving it an obvious metaphor.

24. Opinion varies among commentators, ranging from those who seem to hear no problem with the mix of claims to those who problematize the speaker's odd theology. Fretheim, *Jeremiah*, 219–20, takes the language as basically sincere; Brueggemann, *Commentary*, 135–36, hears it as more accusing than requesting; John T. Willis, "Dialogue between Prophet and Audience as a Rhetorical Device in the Book of Jeremiah," 74–75, hears it as unfeeling, formalistic, or formulaic, by which I understand him to mean prompted by a liturgical form as distinct from being uttered more spontaneously. He urges that we attend to the context of what is being said rather than simply to the words themselves.

25. For a rich set of ways in which a basic metaphor like water may be read, see Else K. Holt, "The Fountain of Living Water and the Deceitful Brook: The Pool of Water Metaphors in the Book of Jeremiah (MT)," 99–117.

26. Tiemeyer, "God's Hidden Compassion," 202–6.

27. See Lundbom, *1–20*, 710–15 for a discussion of its components.

28. As the people reply, God's use of a passive verb is changed to an active verb: from God's "is struck" to the people's "you struck."

29. On this as divine soliloquy, see Crenshaw, *Whirlpool*, 55–56. Stable edges: The upper limit seems clear enough, with the shift to poetry from prose. The bottom limit is more disputed, since though it becomes clear that this unit runs into a lament of Jeremiah, it is not so clear when the prophetic speech begins. There is a tendency to begin the prophet's confession in 15:10, though commentators recognize the anomaly of having the deity respond. O'Connor, *Confessions*, 31–39, discusses various scholars' views, summarizing that they either leave vv. 10–12 (or 10–14) as a very awkward part of the prophet's lament or else excise them.

30. There are many other ways to perform the imagery of this unit, indeed to correlate it with other language of divine soliloquy. Lundbom, *1–20*, 728, and Holladay, *Jeremiah 1*, 443, agree that noonday dark suggests unexpected timing. It is not really the sun that goes down but the woman's world that grows dark because of what she has just experienced.

31. Michael H. Floyd, "Prophetic Complaints about the Fulfillment of Oracles in Habakkuk 1:2–17 and Jeremiah 15:10–18," 397 and 407–15, speculates fruitfully on the

possibility that the speaker (for him, Jeremiah) is quoting the deity, and antagonistically, pointing out divine claims that have not been borne out. Floyd also draws attention to the possibility that the quote of 15:11–14 is drawn from 17:3–4 and that this is rhetorical strategy, not redactional clumsiness.

32. This interlocutor becomes even less likely to be Jeremiah when we listen to God's reply.

33. The asseverations in v. 11 may be oath language rather than questions. See Holladay, *Jeremiah 1*, 450, for that discussion.

34. Fretheim, *Jeremiah*, 235–38, brings out the ambivalent quality of even these ostensibly simple questions, pointing out that elsewhere God is not always so righteous and unconflicted about Jerusalem's suffering.

35. See Fretheim, *Jeremiah*, 226–33, for good discussion of these theological issues.

36. I did not find any commentator except Robert Carroll (and his sources), *Jeremiah: A Commentary*, 327, who does not assume that God is speaking with Jeremiah. Given that assumption, commentators have to make sense of such a dialogue. For such discussion, see Lundbom, *1–20*, 732–33 and Holladay, *Jeremiah 1*, 450–54.

37. The complaining son may, of course, be Jeremiah. See the discussion in Lundbom, *1–20*, 735–36; Holladay, *Jeremiah 1*, 454–55. In Jeremiah 6:28 unrepentant Judah (male plural) is thus referenced.

38. Lundbom, *1–20*, 752–94, splits what he construes as a loose, large unit of 16:1–17:18 into fourteen small bits (the large unit titled "prohibitions, prophecies, puns and psalms"), of which these present verses make six brief poetic compositions and part of a seventh: 16:19–21; 17:1–4; 5–8; 9–10; 11, 12, with v. 13 going with the next verses. Holladay, *Jeremiah 1*, 484–503, breaks it up similarly to Lundbom though ending it at v. 13. Fretheim, *Jeremiah*, 255, also sees a miscellany here. Brueggemann, *Commentary*, 161, quotes John Bright's view that it this material makes up Jeremiah's miscellaneous file.

39. For choices of "fear" and "see," consult Lundbom, *1–20*, 779, 782, 785. The words are related paronomasically, of course, with the second tree not *fearing* what the first refused or was unable to *see*.

40. Reading Lundbom's translation work, *1–20*, 787: Not perverse so much as desperately sick, or desperate from perversity. The idea may be that it is split from its singleness, so of two minds.

41. Some commentators, e.g., Fretheim, *Jeremiah*, 260, think these inscriptions are easily erasable compared to the inscriptions referred to in 17:1, but I doubt it. This is not light matter.

42. Lundbom, *1–20*, 780–86, sees the voices quite differently from what I am proposing. He prefers Jeremiah as the non-YHWH speaker, e.g., for the reflection on the trees (vv. 5–8), though not for any discernible reason (presumably because this resembles a psalm: humans say psalms, and God does not).

43. There is no consensus among scholars as to where or whether the prophet is part of the conversation of vv. 9–10, though in none of these eight of these I am

construing does the prophet have any role beyond that of silent witness to and eventual transmitter of the words.

44. Possibilities include arguably just about any verse: 16:19–20 (praises), 17:1–3 (bad worship formula), 17:5–8 (macarisms, the two ways and tree choices), 17:9–10 (assessment of the heart), 17:11 (animal and human foolishness), 17:12–13 (praise and warning). The whole unit sounds proverbial.

45. Mark E. Biddle, *Polyphony and Symphony in Prophetic Literature: Rereading Jeremiah 7–20*, chaps. 2–3.

Chapter 5: Well-Being or Disaster

1. Terror roundabout: Jeremiah 6:25, 20:10, 46:5, 49:29 (Lundbom, *Jeremiah 1–20*, 847).

2. 1:1–14 is one of the units that will be considered in more detail in my next chapter. Others are 27:1–22; 32:1–44; 34:1–22; 37:3–21; 38:1–28. Some of these will get additional attention in my chapter 7: chaps. 24, 26, 29, 30–33.

3. Christopher R. Seitz, "The Crisis of Interpretation over the Meaning and Purpose of the Exile," 83, says the object of the speech is the city and not its people, a distinction that seems unlikely to me.

4. For an extensive discussion on various characterizations of Jehoiachin, both within and without the Bible, see Jeremy Schipper, "'Exile Atones for Everything': Coping with Jeremiah 22:24–30." He asks questions like what the last king can be understood to have deserved, whether he repented, and so forth, most of which are not explored within extant material. Noteworthy is the tendency of commentary to see the fates or options under discussion as predominantly moral and personal, a viewpoint I consider incomplete.

5. Walter Brueggemann, *A Commentary on Jeremiah: Exile and Homecoming*, 204, finds the deity's rumination poignant here.

6. Lundbom, *21–36*, 173, raises to dismiss the possibility that Jehoiachin is the righteous shoot. The tradition (Jeremiah at chap. 52:31–34 and 2 Kings at chap. 25:27–30) reflects interest in the fate of the last king, but there is nothing in the enigmatic account they share of him that suggests the description of Jeremiah 23:5–6.

7. Terence E. Fretheim, *Jeremiah*, notes, 325, that the scattered and gathered are never not God's.

8. Lundbom, *21–36*, 201, says God expects a "no," not far off but near, while Brueggemann, *Commentary*, 213, says that God distances self here from royal temple manipulation and from other efforts to limit God's freedom, assuming too readily that they can speak for God. A thorough exploration of the expression across biblical material is offered by Werner E. Lemke, "The Near and the Distant God: A Study of Jer 23:23–24 in Its Biblical Theological Context," who concludes that we do best to understand this Jeremiah use as making the point that God's distance implies freedom and refusal to be manipulated and that nearness suggests an inappropriate sense of managing the deity, such as false prophets are accused of doing.

9. Lundbom, *21–36*, 205, observes that the classical prophets do not deal in dreams though they do make use of visions, which we may have difficulty distinguishing from dreams.

10. Lundbom, *21–36*, 214, sorts that vv. 33–34 are addressed to Jeremiah and vv. 35–40 are spoken by him to the false prophets. He also opines that the verb *ns'* generates two distinct nouns: oracle and burden. Additional punning when the false speakers are "given"/*ntn* and "cast off"/*nṭš* (215, 219).

11. For an interesting discussion of related factors, see R. J. R Plant, *Good Figs, Bad Figs: Judicial Differentiation in the Book of Jeremiah.* He is interested in issues of what we may understand as "deserving," how to categorize the various bases of divine choice. He also raises the question of the workings of this divine discrimination for individuals (e.g., Jeremiah, Baruch, Jehoiachin) and for groups (leaders, people). He makes a number of good observations, though to my mind, the nuances of who deserves what are somewhat of a red herring.

12. Brueggemann, *Commentary*, 217–19.

13. See Lundbom, *21–36*, 266, for explanation of v. 26 as in this tiny form, an *atbash.*

14. Brueggemann, *Commentary*, 220, calls the chapter "an odd and unexpected unit," resembling nothing to be found in the book so far.

15. In a study of this material, Mark H. McEntire, "A Prophetic Chorus of Others: Helping Jeremiah Survive in Jeremiah 26," 302, diagnoses narrative strategy here. Since we have already heard the whole speech as it was shared between deity and prophet and are aware of its apparent inability to change hearts, we are set to see something fresh here as it is actually delivered.

16. Stulman, *Jeremiah*, 240, notes that this is the first time in the book that someone listens to Jeremiah. I think he means listened positively, an amazing and underexploited observation.

17. McEntire, "Prophetic Chorus," 303.

18. On the group arresting the prophet, see Brueggemann, *Commentary*, 230.

19. Lundbom, *21–36*, 293, credits Jeremiah's testimony with changing the hearts of some, possibly some out-of-towners who might have been less shocked than the Jerusalemites themselves. Brueggemann, *Commentary*, 236, credits it to civic leadership, presumably as distinct from national leaders.

20. McEntire, "Prophetic Chorus," 303, again helps us by stressing how minimally we are actually given any criteria by which any make their decisions and how indistinct is the actual decision regarding the prophet standing before them, or the appraisal of those who side with him.

21. Contra most current critics, I see this as an example brought forward by participants, not an event happening within the narrated story.

22. The superscription says Jehoiakim but then refers to Zedekiah throughout the rest of the piece. Historians appear confident and in agreement that the episode reflects the years 595–94, thus occurring in Zedekiah's reign, and corresponding to

the "international" event referred to in the Babylonian chronicles. For discussion, see Lundbom, *21–36*, 307–8, and William Holladay, *Jeremiah 2: A Commentary on the Book of the Prophet Jeremiah Chapters 26–52*, 118.

23. Brueggemann, *Commentary*, 243. I assume he is finding extraordinary the bluntness of the claim, its breathtaking realism, shocking theology.

24. This option, theoretical at least for Judah, worries some commentators as being a nondeliverable choice. But for Judah to find a way to survive at home though certainly under imperial control seems, rather, the obvious route and basic default position. Not free, but not deported or destroyed—arguably the post 597 situation. That it becomes moot does not mean it was not viable at some moment when voiced.

25. Mark. W. Bartusch, "From Honor Challenge to False Prophecy: Rereading Jeremiah 28's Story of Prophetic Conflict in Light of Social-Science Models."

26. Commentators differ on the specific implication of what Jeremiah says, apparently proverbially. I think it is something like: Prophets do not need to warn about peace and scarcely have the opportunity to do so. If it happens that peace is about to break out, that blessed situation can be investigated. Bartusch thinks, rather, that peace requires validation by fulfillment whereas war does not ("From Honor," 461).

27. John Barton, "History and Rhetoric in the Prophets," 51–64. I think it is impossible to know how the thinking went, not necessary to assume it was all the same, but vital to ponder a variety of options.

28. Norman K. Gottwald, "Tragedy and Comedy in the Latter Prophets," 84.

29. Gottwald, "Tragedy and Comedy in the Latter Prophets," 92.

30. For a perceptive and clear discussion of various issues around the document, see Klaas A. D. Smelik, "Letter to the Exiles: Jeremiah 29 in Context."

31. Lundbom, *21–36*, 353, wonders who demanded dreams, but that seems an overly literal matter to query.

32. As is pointed out by virtually every commentator, false prophets need not be malicious but simply, from the point of view of the composers of the book and its main characters, mistaken.

33. They are accused of adultery with the wives of exile, whether this is more literal or metaphorical (or both) is difficult to say. The point is their fate, also to become a byword.

34. These clauses are not so clear in their interrelationship of reference. I am here following Lundbom, *21–36*, 363–67. Smelik, "Letter," thinks that the high priest (Jehoaida) has warned and protected Jeremiah (286).

35. Plant, *Good Figs*, 96, underlines the somewhat unusual evidence of split among participants, in chap. 26 and in 29 as well.

36. Brueggemann, *Commentary*, 264, says, "The primary work of the book of Jeremiah is to speak Israel into exile," thus indicating that such a task is not the only one

37. See Lundbom, *21–36*, 368–76. He also indicates intertexts between this material and certain other prophets as well as noting internal intertexts.

38. Fretheim, *Jeremiah*, 414. He notes the ways the material echoes some of the Abraham material.

39. A *mise-en-abyme* is a literary trope borrowed from heraldry, where somewhere on an elaborate shield the design of the whole is reproduced in a smaller space. Here the Rechabites' discernment of creative adaptation of their heritage in the midst of a situation that seems not to have been envisioned in their past serves as a model for what Judah's resettlers must do.

40. There is considerable recent and creative scholarship on Jeremiah 36: Consult Pamela J. Scalise, "Baruch as First Reader: Baruch's Lament in the Structure of the Book of Jeremiah."

Chapter 6: God's Desires Contested

1. By implicit, I mean that Zedekiah's predecessors are spoken of in the past, and the collapse of the city is not yet complete. Though I am naming these seven occasions as discrete and separable from each other, there is no clear chronological order among them; we may have two takes on the same moment, and in some instances, one incident rises from another in such a way that it can be considered the same event rather than a separate unit. Most who comment on this set of material with the aid of literary tools note the resistance of the material to chronology and suspect that in at least some cases it is multiple view of one event, as does Robert P. Carroll, *Jeremiah: A Commentary*, 627–28 and 672–79. This process may resemble options for studying self-portraits of Van Gogh with his bandaged head: The least important thing to ponder might be the chronological facts behind the portraits—not an easy position for modern biblical studies to take.

2. The figure of Zedekiah has had considerable attention from historical critics intent on the fate of the last-anointed king of Judah. Though as before, the details of history are not the focus of this book, still for his reign we can count on backdrop of the last ten years of Judah's quasi-independence, that is from the first deportation of King Jehoiachin until the second exile (ca. 597–587), and most urgently, during the months-long siege at the end of that period. That the general circumstances can be known does not help much with specific details of any scene, which I will take to be more fictive than factual. For an excellent literary study, see Mark Roncace, *Jeremiah, Zedekiah, and the Fall of Jerusalem*. Brief but brilliant is Mary Chilton Callaway, "Telling the Truth and Telling Stories: An Analysis of Jeremiah 37–38."

3. See Else K. Holt, "The Potent Word of God: Remarks on the Composition of Jeremiah 37–44," who says, 169, though without a lot of close corroborative work, that the king and prophet confront, reflect, and complement each other, mutually assist each other. Roncace, *Jeremiah, Zedekiah, and the Fall of Jerusalem* calls attention to the conflation of the pair several times, e.g., 62, 108, though also without developing it to the extent I am doing.

4. William Holladay, *Jeremiah 2: A Commentary on the Book of the Prophet Jeremiah Chapters 26–52*, 213, specifies that the court of the guard is in the palace and

characterizes it as a sort of honorable protective custody, a point I have difficulty accepting.

5. Callaway, "Truth," 257–58, calls this "language of confinement." Roncace, *Jeremiah, Zedekiah, and the Fall of Jerusalem,* 50, sorts the terminology.

6. Holt, "Potent Word," 164, sees the nested confinements as signifying, rather than Zedekiah's choices enacted, the effort to confine the world of God.

7. Lundbom, *37–52,* 55, notes that it is difficult to catch the tone of Zedekiah: testing? fearful?

8. Roncace, *Jeremiah, Zedekiah, and the Fall of Jerusalem,* identifying prophet-king confrontations as a type-scene and suggesting that there are some thirty biblical occurrences (24) calls it anomalous for the king to help the prophet (64).

9. Twice king and prophet communicate through intermediaries. In both of those cases, the king asks for a word from God hopeful for the fate of Jerusalem, apparently prompted by the withdrawal of besiegers (21:1–2 and 37:3). Once Jeremiah indicates that he had communicated with Zedekiah, though no prompt of the king is noted and we do not witness the encounter (27:12; 34:2–22). Another of the scenes involves teams of surrogates: four men accuse Jeremiah to the king and demand that he be imprisoned; and four men (reading with the emendation of "three" for "thirty" [see Holladay, *Jeremiah 2,* 267]), also at the behest of the king, release him from where he had been placed (38:1–13). Only three of the exchanges are face-to-face: where the king asks Jeremiah why he talks as he does (32:3–5), where Zedekiah asks whether an oracle has been spoken (37:17–20), in their final scene (38:14–28).

10. Walter Brueggemann, *A Commentary on Jeremiah: Exile and Homecoming,* 361, says that the "submit and survive" is, in Jeremiah, to be equated with obedience to God's will (though he also calls it pro-Babylonian, which I think utterly misleading).

11. I have found no one who anticipates my point that the narrative of land redemption is the response to the king's question. Consult Lundbom, *21–36,* 499–509, who does end up concluding that the action is symbolic; Brueggemann, *Commentary,* 300–2 discusses its various aspects. The work of Gerald L. Keown, Pamela J. Scalise, Thomas G. Smothers, *Word Biblical Commentary,* 145–47 notes how awkward the joining is, with no relation between question and answer; Carroll, *Jeremiah,* 620–21, calls it a story of how Jeremiah secures the future, but not because it is relevant to what the king has inquired about.

12. Again, I am unable to cite anyone to explain the odd and presumably false words of deity and prophet against the backdrop of the slave-non-release story. Consult Lundbom, *21–36,* 547–68; Holladay *Jeremiah 2,* 234–35; Brueggemann, *Commentary,* 324–26; Carroll, *Jeremiah: A Commentary,* 642–47, thinks it works better as "midrashic" than as historical.

13. Various scholars note the lack of realism: In a siege, how does Jeremiah anticipate leaving the city? Lundbom, *37–52,* 51, notes that details are arranged "in a fashion not corresponding to the march of events."

14. Surrogates abound: Zedekiah deals with Jeremiah through Pashhur son of Malchiah and Zephaniah son of Maaseiah (21:1), Hananiah (ch. 28), Irijah son of Shelemiah (37:13), Shephatiah son of Mattan, Gedaliah son of Pashhur, Jucal son of Shelemiah, and Pashhur son of Malchiah, Ebed-Melek and his three helpers (38:1–12). What Zedekiah asks in 21:2 is picked up in 37:3 in the mouths of his two emissaries: a request that the Babylonians withdraw from the city. This same contested topic of how seriously the Babylonian threat is to be taken occurs in the scene of the contested yokes, where Jeremiah lifts from Hananiah's prophecy words articulating the same hope of Zedekiah: that the Babylonian threat be ended (chap. 28); Jeremiah counters with his own prophecy—to deny the possibility (28:9, 16; 29:2–4, 11, 14).

15. Thomas W. Overholt, "Jeremiah 2 and the Problem of Audience Reaction," 262–63, notes that this biblical book has a far higher occurrence of quoted speech than do others and claims as well that Jeremiah the character is distinctively characterized by such a practice. See Roncace, *Jeremiah, Zedekiah, and the Fall of Jerusalem*, 40–42, for a discussion of ways often it is impossible to see whose speech it is, for various reasons. I am not engaging that problem here either.

16. Literary analogy: See Roncace, *Jeremiah, Zedekiah, and the Fall of Jerusalem*, and also A. R. Pete Diamond, "Portraying Prophecy: Of Doublets, Variants and Analogies in the Narrative Representation of Jeremiah's Oracles—Reconstructing the Hermeneutics of Prophecy," 111–13, for a sketch of how this narrative strategy works and some examples of how characters resemble others at particular moments (e.g., how Jeremiah and Jehoiakim recall and resemble Isaiah and Ahaz or Hezekiah). Analogy is useful, especially when it is not simply impressionistic and ephemeral but sustained over time. A momentary resemblance, even if startling in clarity, may not make a cumulative impression. Roncace, *Jeremiah, Zedekiah, and the Fall of Jerusalem*, 34, also suggests that the very name "Jehoiachin," wherever appearing, calls attention to the very subject under discussion: go to Babylon or do not, local or exile as the correct place to be.

17. Holladay, *Jeremiah 2*, 238–9, urges for legal texts Deuteronomy 15:1 and 12 and also Exodus 21:2 and Leviticus 25:40–41, while noting that the quote is actually a blend of these passages, offering a welter of intertexts with their possibilities.

18. If, as scholars speculate, the king and his elites freed slaves in times of stress so that their chances for survival would be improved, we see a similar thing explicitly with the situation of the king and prophet in 37:20–21.

19. Ebed-Melek is both bound (his foreign status) and free (his action) as he mediates. Roncace, *Jeremiah, Zedekiah, and the Fall of Jerusalem*, 85–86, comments usefully on facets of this minor character.

20. Roncace, *Jeremiah, Zedekiah, and the Fall of Jerusalem*, 31–32, 35, says that Jeremiah is showing the king how he can in fact satisfy both obligations if he submits.

21. Callaway, "Telling the Truth," 256, 259, makes a case for the distinctiveness of this scene, e.g., that the king is unaccompanied here; that his advisors are always

narrated negatively and he is without them here is adequate signal of something new on the king's part against most who do not sense a shift. For more discussion, consult Roncace, *Jeremiah, Zedekiah, and the Fall of Jerusalem,* chap. 3, specifically 95–115.

22. It begins in the ninth year of Zedekiah, the tenth month, and presumably finishes that year (two months), runs another year—the king's tenth year—(so twelve more months) and enters his ninth year and is in the fourth month: so at least eighteen months to date.

23. Roncace, *Jeremiah, Zedekiah, and the Fall of Jerusalem,* 96, counts differently.

24. See Holt, "Potent Word," 169.

25. Brueggemann, *Commentary,* 365, lays out a structure of this encounter.

26. Lundbom, *37–52,* 76, notes it as a technical request for a divine word.

27. Roncace, *Jeremiah, Zedekiah, and the Fall of Jerusalem,* 104–7 makes the case that Jeremiah's offers are more variable than I think really matters. There are details that change, but I cannot hear the basic choices as other than consistent, at least at a fairly general level of abstraction. See also Diamond, "Portraying," 99.

28. In purely literary terms, the two are talking about their seating on the *Titanic:* no really good options, though of course some better than others. Roncace, *Fall,* 109, says each tells a partial truth.

29. Lundbom, *37–52,* 77, calls the scenario a vision; Brueggemann, *Commentary,* 290, wonders whether it is a lament or a taunt song.

30. Roncace, *Jeremiah, Zedekiah, and the Fall of Jerusalem,* 98–100, shows how deceiver and deceived roles toggle in the person of the king.

31. Lundbom, *37–52,* 78, reads it as a veiled threat.

32. Roncace so charges: see one sort of argument in *Jeremiah, Zedekiah, and the Fall of Jerusalem,* 55, another developing on 111–13. But the very Bakhtinian strategies he cites suggest otherwise. (For the influence of Bakhtin, influential throughout this book, see Barbara Green, *Mikhail Bakhtin and Biblical Scholarship*). The king crafts an utterance, which quotes Jeremiah on an earlier occasion; the king anticipates the participation of his officers in the conversation between himself and the prophet and also intonates the complex utterance as a promise and threat and hands it to Jeremiah, who does not, in our hearing, take it up. His silence may be his own potent rejoinder. The narrator summarizes, but very generally. There is not sufficient clarity to say Jeremiah dissimulated. Jeremiah's utterance of what the king told him to say is ultimately unverifiable. See also Callaway, "Telling the Truth," 257, who thinks the prophet at least complicit with a misrepresentation of truth; but also by the reading strategies which introduce her article, it is not so simple.

33. See Alex Varughese, "The Royal Family in the Jeremiah Traditions," for a summary of Jeremiah's indictment of the house of David.

34. Arguably, once the Babylonians have taken the city, the old options change. My interest here is in literary artistry, not historical *realpolitik.*

35. It is generally agreed at least by biblical scholars that prophecy is largely time bound and cannot unproblematically be lifted out of context and be abstracted into

timeless truth. On the other hand, as Brueggemann points out, *Like Fire in the Bones: Listening for the Prophetic Word in Jeremiah*, 12–13: The pragmatic advice of Jeremiah about what his compatriots should do in the early 6th century is not simply about Babylon but also claims that God can bring good out of what looks like a terrible choice. Even Jeremiah's most specifically situational language is also deeply theological and hence reusable, though not literalistically. Karen Armstrong, writing in quite another context, *The Battle for God: A History of Fundamentalism*, 50, says that *mythos* "does not provide a blueprint for pragmatic political action but supplies the faithful with a way of looking at their society and developing their interior lives."

36. Brueggemann, "Next Steps in Jeremiah Studies?" 416.

37. John Barton raises excellent questions about what we can call the conflation of natural disasters (e.g., drought) and political ones (e.g., empire and war): "History and Rhetoric in the Prophets." Barton explains how the telescoping of viewpoints is a heritage of the ancient Near Eastern neighborhood where Judah lived though is not, arguably, a blend appreciated by our contemporaries. If it was not particularly convincing for Jeremiah's original audiences, the less so now.

38. Brueggemann, *Fire*, 37–39 offers some examples of what we are being offered by Jeremiah.

39. Brueggemann, *The Theology of the Book of Jeremiah*, 45.

40. It is interesting to think about Jeremiah's possible role in the first exile, that of 597. I construct him as intensively involved in that effort, though there is no biblical sign of it.

41. Gary E. Yates, "Ishmael's Assassination of Gedaliah: Echoes of the Saul-David Story in Jeremiah 40:7–41:18," 103–12, shows narrative correlations between the strife typical of certain Davidids. It is not a point to pursue here, except to suggest that not facticity but analogy may be the main point of the passage.

42. Commentators thinking in terms of realism or redaction stumble here, but realism is not the genre, and redaction may not be the best explanation of the apparent duplication or overlap of detail. Others comment in terms of the presumed impact of this special treatment for Jeremiah by the Babylonians, supposing it will have hardened suspicions about his loyalties. But as narrated here, the story does not make that point. Consult Brueggemann, *Commentary*, 372, for additional discussion.

43. Kenneth D. Mulzac, "Is Jeremiah 39:15–18 Out of Order?" Lundbom is useful as well, 37–52, 97–99. Robert Carroll, *Commentary*, 696–97, characterizes this small scene as a virtual midrash, built up from many places in the tradition.

44. Terence E. Fretheim, *Jeremiah*, 532–33, suggests three reasons: his danger moment is intense when the masters of the city change; his promise falls due only when it can be made actual; and his fate contrasts with that of others discussed here.

45. Mulzac, "Out of Order," 71.

46. John Hill, "Jeremiah 40:1–6: An Appreciation," 133: "This is the first explicit statement in the book that *Yhwh*'s judgment against Judah and Jerusalem has been realized by the Babylonian conquest of 587." If we are reading the narrative rather

than simply watching it confirm what we think can be established historically, it is easy to miss these subtle perspectival cues.

47. He needs to make the negative space clear.

48. For a carefully observed discussion of this material, consult Joel Weinberg, "Gedaliah, the Son of Ahikam in Mizpah: His Status and Role, Supporters and Opponents." Weinberg's aim is to tease out and demonstrate the historicity of the material, but his work also helps us simply note what is given us as part of background.

49. We know from other sources, archeology included, that some in fact did, but not according to the book of Jeremiah.

50. Brueggemann, *Commentary*, 389–403.

51. This timing is unusual, worrying commentators, but I do not think it is particularly important, except perhaps to suggest that some things have changed. It may be related to Jeremiah's relative lack of activity in this section: slower motion now throughout.

52. Brueggemann, *Commentary*, 390.

53. Brueggemann, *Commentary*, 391.

54. See the argument of Teresa Ann Ellis, "Jeremiah 44: What If 'the Queen of Heaven' Is Yhwh?" 475, that Johanan was earlier depicted as a reliable but unbelieved provider of information when he warned Gedaliah of the impending assassination.

55. Brueggemann, *Commentary*, 394.

56. For various other points linking Moses and Jeremiah, see Christopher R. Seitz, "The Prophet Moses and the Canonical Shape of Jeremiah."

57. For a detailed, well-observed, and analytical discussion of multiple issues impacted here, see Ellis, "Queen of Heaven." Notable among her other points but not able to be pursued is the observation that worship of a female deity is presented here without being sexualized or lampooned in sexual terms (488).

58. Ellis, "What If 'the Queen of Heaven." Look also at a brief article of Gerda de Villiers, "Where did she come from, and where did she go to? (The *Queen of Heaven* in Jeremiah 7 and 44)," who reminds us that language shapes as well as reflects reality.

59. Commentators seem comfortable with the general correspondence between what is prophesied and what happens, e.g., Lundbom, *37–52*, 169; Ellis, "Jeremiah 44: What If 'the Queen of Heaven," on the contrary, doing close and careful comparative work, is not so certain (483–87). That, again, is a historical question lying somewhat outside the concern of the present work.

60. Brueggemann, *Commentary*, 413.

61. Lundbom, *37–52*, 1167–68.

62. For a sampling of the discussion, consult Walter Brueggemann, "The 'Baruch Connection': Reflections on Jer 43:1–7," and Pamela J. Scalise, "Baruch as First Reader: Baruch's Lament in the Structure of the Book of Jeremiah," who take the discussion away to various other places. See also Marion Ann Taylor, "Jeremiah 45: The Problem of Placement."

63. As Scalise argues, "Baruch as First Reader," 305, the expression "great things" is never used in that context.

64. These chapters (46–51), introduced as God's word to Jeremiah concerning the nations and concluding with a similar note at 51:64, need here simply to have their main function made clear: They testify that those nations who think they may counter God's purposes will learn the opposite. Whatever temporary successes they may achieve will be reversed by God. The nations will prevail against neither YHWH nor Israel. No good figs in those baskets. Babylon is singled out in quality and quantity.

65. Lundbom, *37–52*, 533, notes that the numbers seem small; Brueggemann agrees, *Commentary*, 492–93. Given the insistence in Jeremiah that everyone goes somewhere off the land of Judah, eventually, that seems so.

Chapter 7: Getting Out

1. There is some sense among commentators (e.g., Jack R. Lundbom, *Jeremiah 21–36: A New Translation with Introduction and Commentary* [hereafter Lundbom, *21–36*], 231, 345) that the parsing of fates or choices must have been moot once they had been made so long ago. Why, when the book's production lies long past the key choice of going quasi-willingly to Babylon (or doing something else) is the matter so stressed? For another consideration, close to what I am arguing, see R. J. R. Plant, *Good Figs, Bad Figs*, 186. Robert P. Carroll, *Jeremiah: A Commentary*, 483, remarks perceptively that those arriving in Babylon ten years past the first group—and under far more brutal conditions, let us recall—will have found themselves at a disadvantage. Such circumstances are not so easily overlooked or forgotten.

2. Plant, *Good Figs*, 80, suggests that since figs appear more than once in a season, we understand these "good figs" as early, the first-born of the fruit to appear. Such a possibility makes even clearer that we are talking here about time.

3. See Terence E. Fretheim, *Jeremiah*, 345, for the observation that in the extant narrative, the scene is for the prophet.

4. Commentators split here as well as do characters. Is the point of reaction the old issue of inviolability (William Holladay *Jeremiah 2: A Commentary on the Book of the Prophet Jeremiah Chapters 26–52*, 106), the openness of the city's future and its dependence on actions of its citizens (Walter Brueggemann, *A Commentary on Jeremiah: Exile and Homecoming*, 233), or the claim that the deity is named as underwriter of the destruction (my sense)?

5. I am construing that the situations of both prophets and not simply the case of Micah are brought forward by this group of elders; cf. most others who think this Uriah note is a narrated event (e.g., Lundbom, *21–36*, 285).

6. Brueggemann, *Commentary*, 240 notes that his rescue is not the same as his vindication or validation. See also Mark H. McEntire, H. "A Prophetic Chorus of Others: Helping Jeremiah Survive in Jeremiah 26," for a good discussion of various issues.

7. Louis Stulman, *Jeremiah*, 240.

8. See also II Chronicles 36 and the Babylonian Chronicle (cited in Lundbom, *21–36*, 349): Lundbom summarizes that the Babylonian document claims that Nebuchadnezzar seized Judah's main city, captured its king, set up his own surrogate, and took tribute. We need not worry about whether the document exaggerates but simply note the tension between agents and their claims.

9. Note, with Holladay, *Jeremiah 2*, 141, the difference between what is offered here and what was promised to Pashhur in 20:1–6. John Hill, *Friend or Foe? The Figure of Babylon in the Book of Jeremiah MT* and more briefly in "'Your Exile Will Be Long': The Book of Jeremiah and the Unended Exile," suggests that the particular language implies that the life once envisioned in the land of promise becomes available outside it, with the effect that the exile never ends. I cannot quite follow him to that last conclusion, but the use of "land-language" for Babylon is indeed suggestive.

10. Stulman, *Jeremiah*, 259, cites Ronald Clements as calling this the pivotal center of the book, akin to Isaiah 40–55.

11. Every commentator makes a suggestion about the order of material and criteria for it, e.g., Fretheim, *Jeremiah*, 414–15; see also Mark Biddle, "The Literary Frame surrounding Jeremiah 30, 1–33, 26," and Bob Becking, "The Times They Are a Changing: An Interpretation of Jeremiah 30:12–17," 4 (expanded later).

12. George Ossom-Batsa, "The Theological Significance of the Root *ŠWB* in Jeremiah," makes the point succinctly.

13. The attributed speech is—as largely in chaps. 2–20 where we had it—mostly erroneous so that God corrects it. The tone is different here, since previously the clueless were about to get bad news (worse than they were saying), but here it is better than they are imagining.

14. Psalm 126 uses the dreaming mode to describe the sensation of those returning from exile.

15. Brueggemann, *Commentary*, 277–78.

16. Gary Yates, "New Exodus and No Exodus in Jeremiah 26–45," suggests that chaps. 40–44 be read over against these of 30–33: so no return from Egypt as there will be from Babylon.

17. Kathleen M. O'Connor, *Jeremiah: Pain and Promise*. Her point is taken up with a slight twist in the work of David Reimer, "Redeeming Politics in Jeremiah."

18. Scholars tend to hear this as a rebuke (e.g., Lundbom, *37–52*, 176–77); Carroll, *Commentary*, 749, stresses that the point is survival.

19. Lundbom, *37–52*, 502, appraises it as a report of a symbolic action, and perhaps we might say it is directions for a symbolic action.

20. The setting date is 594–93, between what we call the first and second exiles.

21. The date agreed to for this is 562, as Nebuchadnezzar dies and is succeeded by Amel-Marduk.

22. For a comparison with the final chapter of 2 Kings, see the charts in Steve Delamarter, "But Who Gets the Last Word?"

23. Becking, *From David to Gedaliah: The Book of Kings as Story and History,* scrutinizes all of this material in terms of its literary antecedents, in and outside the Bible, concluding that the amnesty of Jehoiachin is plausible. My question is a bit different.

24. Here the Joseph story does not seem directly useful, since as the book of Exodus opens a couple of generations past "the brothers," it is not so clear that the link with the deity has been maintained.

Afterword and Implications

1. The book of Jeremiah is filled with named but minor and evanescent characters, some sixty of them distributed unevenly throughout the book, inviting interpretation of various kinds. It was my plan to deal with them, but the plan was regrettably deferred. The subdiscipline of propsopography offers some fruitful ways forward, though it usually counts on historical information not (yet) available in biblical material. For an overview of these figures in Jeremiah, see Lundbom, *Jeremiah 1–20,* 876–81. For prosopography, K. S. B. Keats-Rohan, ed., *Prosopography Approaches and Applications: A Handbook.*

2. Walter Brueggemann, *A Commentary on Jeremiah: Exile and Homecoming,* 264.

3. Karen Armstrong, having studied and written extensively on world religions for some decades, urges that compassion is possibly the best candidate for God's most basic and cherished identity. See her work, *A History of God: The 4,000-Year Quest of Judaism, Christianity and Islam,* 285–89

SELECT BIBLIOGRAPHY

Ahlström, Göstra W. *The History of Ancient Palestine from the Paleolithic Period to Alexander's Conquest.* Edited by Diana V. Edelman. Sheffield: Journal for the Study of the Old Testament Press, 1993.

Allen, Leslie C. *Jeremiah: A Commentary.* Louisville: Westminster John Knox, 2008.

Armstrong, Karen. *The Battle for God: A History of Fundamentalism.* New York: Alfred A. Knopf. 2000.

———. *A History of God: The 4,000-Year Quest of Judaism, Christianity and Islam.* New York: Ballantine, 1993.

Barstad, Hans M. "Prophecy in the Book of Jeremiah and the Historical Prophet." In *Sense and Sensitivity: Essays on Reading the Bible in Memory of Robert Carroll,* edited by Alastair G. Hunter and Philip R. Davies, 87–100. Sheffield: Sheffield Academic Press, 2002.

Barton, John. "History and Rhetoric in the Prophets." In *The Bible as Rhetoric: Studies in Biblical Persuasion and Credibility,* edited by Martin Warner, 51–64. London and New York: Routledge, 1990.

Bartusch, Mark W. "From Honor Challenge to False Prophecy: Rereading Jeremiah 28's Story of Prophetic Conflict in Light of Social-Science Models." *Currents in Theology and Mission* 36.6 (2009): 456–63.

Becking, Bob. *From David to Gedaliah: The Book of Kings as Story and History.* Fribourg and Göttingen: Academic Press and Vandenhoeck and Ruprecht, 2007.

———. "The Times They Are a Changing: An Interpretation of Jeremiah 30:12–17." *Scandinavian Journal of the Old Testament* 12.1 (1998): 1, 4–25.

Bellah, Robert N. *Religion in Human Evolution: From the Paleolithic to the Axial Age.* Cambridge, Mass.: Belknap Press of Harvard University Press, 2011.

Biddle, Mark E. "The Literary Frame surrounding Jeremiah 30, 1–33, 26." *Zeitschrift für die alttestamentliche Wissenschaft* 100.3 (1989): 409–13.

———. *Polyphony and Symphony in Prophetic Literature: Rereading Jeremiah 7–20.* Macon, Ga: Mercer University Press, 1996.

Brueggemann, Walter. "The "Baruch Connection": Reflections on Jer 43:1–7." *Journal of Biblical Literature* 113.3 (1994): 405–20.

———. *A Commentary on Jeremiah: Exile and Homecoming.* Grand Rapids, Mich.: Eerdmans, 1998.

——. "Jeremiah's Use of Rhetorical Questions." *Journal of Biblical Literature* 92.3 (1973): 358–74.

——. *Like Fire in the Bones: Listening for the Prophetic Word in Jeremiah.* Edited by Patrick D. Miller. Minneapolis: Fortress, 2006.

——. "Next Steps in Jeremiah Studies." In *Troubling Jeremiah,* edited by A. R. Pete Diamond and Kathleen M. O'Connor, 200–22 . Sheffield: Sheffield Academic Press, 1999.

——. *The Theology of the Book of Jeremiah.* Cambridge: Cambridge University Press, 2007.

Callaway, Mary Chilton. "Telling the Truth and Telling Stories: An Analysis of Jeremiah 37–38." *Union Seminary Quarterly Review* 44.3–4 (1991): 253–65.

Carroll, Robert. *Jeremiah: A Commentary.* London: SCM Press, 1986.

——. "The Polyphonic Jeremiah: A Reading of the Book of Jeremiah." In *Reading the Book of Jeremiah: A Search for Coherence,* edited by Martin Kessler, 77–85. Winona Lake, Ind.: Eisenbrauns, 2004.

Christensen, Duane L. "'Terror on Every Side' in Jeremiah." *Journal of Biblical Literature* 92.4 (1973): 498–502.

Crenshaw, James L. *A Whirlpool of Torment: Israelite Traditions of God as an Oppressive Presence.* Philadelphia: Fortress Press, 1984.

Delamarter, Steve. "But Who Gets the Last Word?" *Bible Review* 14 (1998): 34–45, 54–55.

Diamond, A. R. *The Confessions of Jeremiah in Context: Scenes of Prophetic Drama.* Sheffield: *Journal for the Study of the Old Testament* Press, 1987.

——. "The Jeremiah Guild in the Twenty-First Century: Variety Reigns Supreme." In *Recent Research on the Major Prophets,* edited by Alan J. Hauser, 232–48. Sheffield: Sheffield Phoenix, 2008.

——. "Playing God: 'Polytheizing' YHWH ALONE in Jeremiah's Metaphorical Spaces." In *Metaphor in the Hebrew Bible,* edited by P. VanHecke. Leuven: Peeters Publishers, 2005.

——. "Portraying Prophecy: Of Doublets, Variants and Analogies in the Narrative Representation of Jeremiah's Oracles—Reconstructing the Hermeneutics of Prophecy." *Journal for the Study of the Old Testament* 57 (1993): 99–119.

Diamond, A. R. Pete, and Kathleen M. O'Connor. "Unfaithful Passions: Coding Women Coding Men in Jeremiah 2–3 (4:2)." *Biblical Interpretation* 4.3 (1996): 288–310.

Dobbs-Allsopp, F. W. *Weep, O Daughter of Zion: A Study of the City-Lament Genre in the Hebrew Bible.* Rome: Editrice Pontificio Istituto Biblico, 1993.

Dubbink, Joep. "Jeremiah: Hero of Faith of Defeatist? Concerning the Place and Function of Jeremiah 20:14–18." *Journal for the Study of the Old Testament* 86 (1999): 67–84.

Ellis, Teresa Ann. "Jeremiah 44: What If 'the Queen of Heaven' Is Yhwh?" *Journal for the Study of the Old Testament* 33.4 (2009): 465–88.

Floyd, Michael H. "Prophetic Complaints about the Fulfillment of Oracles in Habakkuk 1:2–17 and Jeremiah 15:10–18," *Journal of Biblical Literature* 110 (1991): 397–418.

——. "'Write the Revelation!' (Hab 2:2): Re-imagining the Cultural History of Prophecy." In *Writings and Speech in Israelite and Ancient Near Eastern Prophecy,* edited by Ehud Ben Zvi and Michael H. Floyd, 102–44. Atlanta: Society of Biblical Literature, 2000.

Fretheim, Terence E. "Caught in the Middle: Jeremiah's Vocational Crisis." *Word and World* 22.4 (2002:) 351–60.

——. *Jeremiah.* Macon, Ga.: Smyth and Helwys, 2002.

Friebel, Kelvin G. *Jeremiah's and Ezekiel's Sign-Acts.* Sheffield: Sheffield Academic Press, 1999.

Gitay, Yehoshua. "*Rhetorical* Criticism and the Prophetic Discourse." In *Persuasive Artistry: Studies in New Testament Rhetoric in Honor of George A. Kennedy,* edited by Duane F. Watson, 13–24. Sheffield: Journal for the Study of the Old Testament Press, 1991.

Gottwald, Norman K. "Tragedy and Comedy in the Latter Prophets." *Semeia* 32 (1984): 83–96.

Grabbe, Lester. *Ancient Israel: What Do We Know and How Do We Know It?* London: T and T Clark, 2007.

——. "The Lying Pen of the Scribes? Jeremiah and History." In *Essays on Ancient Israel in Its Near Eastern Context: A Tribute to Nadav Na'aman,* edited by Yairah Amit et al., 189–204. Winona Lake, Ind.: Eisenbrauns, 2006.

Green, Barbara. *Mikhail Bakhtin and Biblical Scholarship: An Introduction.* Atlanta: Society of Biblical Literature Press, 2000.

——. "This Old Text: An Analogy for Biblical Interpretation." *Biblical Theology Bulletin* 36.2 (2006): 72–83.

Haney, Linda. "YHWH, the God of Israel . . . and of Edom? The Relationships in the Oracle to Edom in Jeremiah 49:7–22." In *Uprooting and Planting: Essays on Jeremiah for Leslie Allen,* edited by John Goldingay, 78–115. New York: T and T Clark. 2007.

Henderson, Joseph M."Jeremiah 2–10 as a Unified Literary Composition: Evidence of Dramatic Portrayal and Narrative Progression." In *Uprooting and Planting: Essays on Jeremiah for Leslie Allen,* edited by John Goldingay, 116–52. London: T and T Clark, 2007.

——. "Who Weeps in Jeremiah VIII 23 (IX 1)? Identifying Dramatic Speakers in the Poetry of Jeremiah." *Vetus Testamentum* 52.2 (2002): 191–206.

Hill, John. *Friend or Foe? The Figure of Babylon in the Book of Jeremiah MT.* Leiden: Brill, 1999.

——. "Jeremiah 40:1–6: An Appreciation." In *Seeing Signals, Reading Signs: The Art of Exegesis,* edited by Mark A. O'Brien and Howard N. Wallace, 130–41. London: T and T Clark International, 2004.

———. "'Your Exile Will Be Long': The Book of Jeremiah and the Unended Exile." In *Reading the Book of Jeremiah: A Search for Coherence*, edited by Martin Kessler, 149–61. Winona Lake, Ind. Eisenbrauns: 2004.

Holladay, William L. *Jeremiah 1: A Commentary on the Book of the Prophet Jeremiah Chapters 1–25*. Philadelphia: Fortress Press, 1986.

———. *Jeremiah 2: A Commentary on the Book of the Prophet Jeremiah Chapters 26–52*. Philadelphia: Fortress Press, 1989.

Holt, Else K."The Fountain of Living Water and the Deceitful Brook: The Pool of Water Metaphors in the Book of Jeremiah (MT)." *Metaphor in the Hebrew Bible*, edited by P. Van Hecke, 99–117. Leuven: University Press, 2005.

———. "The Potent Word of God: Remarks on the Composition of Jeremiah 37–44." In *Troubling Jeremiah*, edited by A. R. Pete Diamond et al., 161–70. Sheffield: Sheffield Academic Press, 1999.

Jackson, Jared J. "Jeremiah 46: Two Oracles on Egypt." *Horizons in Biblical Theology* 15.2 (1993): 136–44.

Jindo, Job Y. *Biblical Metaphor Reconsidered: A Cognitive Approach to Poetic Prophecy in Jeremiah 1–24*. Winona Lake, Ind.: Eisenbrauns, 2010.

Keats-Rohan, K. S. B. ed. *Prosopography Approaches and Applications: A Handbook*. Oxford: Prosopographica et Genealogica, 2007.

Keown, Gerald L., Pamela J. Scalise, and Thomas G. Smothers. *Word Biblical Commentary*. Vol. 27, *Jeremiah 26–52*. Dallas: Word Books, 1995.

Kim, Uriah. *Decolonizing Josiah: Toward a Postcolonial Reading of the Deuteronomistic History*. Sheffield: Sheffield Phoenix, 2006.

Kövecses, Zoltán. *Metaphor: A Practical Introduction*. Oxford: Oxford University Press, 2004.

Lemke, Werner E. "The Near and the Distant God: A Study of Jer 23:23–24 in Its Biblical Theological Context." *Journal of Biblical Literature* 100.4 (1981): 541–55.

Lundbom, Jack R. *Jeremiah 1–20: A New Translation with Introduction and Commentary*. New York: Doubleday, 1999.

———. *Jeremiah 21–36: A New Translation with Introduction and Commentary*. New York: Doubleday, 2004.

———. *Jeremiah 37–52: A New Translation with Introduction and Commentary*. New York: Doubleday, 2004.

———. *The Hebrew Prophets: An Introduction*. Minneapolis: Fortress Press, 2010.

McEntire, Mark H. "A Prophetic Chorus of Others: Helping Jeremiah Survive in Jeremiah 26." *Review and Expositor* 101 (Spring 2004): 301–11.

Meynet, Roland. *Rhetorical Analysis: An Introduction to Biblical Rhetoric*. Sheffield: Sheffield Academic Press, 1998.

Miller, J. Maxwell, and John H. Hayes. *A History of Ancient Israel and Judah*. 2nd ed. Louisville: Westminster John Knox Press, 2006.

Mulzac, Kenneth D. "Is Jeremiah 39:15–18 Out of Order?" *Andrews University Seminary Studies* 45.1 (2007): 69–72.

Nissinen, Martii, ed. *Prophecy in Its Ancient Near Eastern Context: Mesopotamian, Biblical, and Arabian Perspectives.* Atlanta: Society of Biblical Literature, 2000.

O'Connor, Kathleen M. *The Confessions of Jeremiah: Their Interpretation and Role in Chapters 1–25.* Atlanta: Scholars Press, 1988.

———. *Jeremiah: Pain and Promise.* Minneapolis: Fortress, 2011.

Ossom-Batsa, George. "The Theological Significance of the Root *ŠWB* in Jeremiah." *Andrews University Seminary Studies* 39.2 (2001): 223–32.

Overholt, Thomas W. "Jeremiah 2 and the Problem of 'Audience Reaction.'" *Catholic Biblical Quarterly* 41.2 (1979): 262–73.

Paterson, Robert M. "Repentance or Judgment: The Construction and Purpose of Jeremiah 2–6." *Expository Times* 96.7 (1985): 199–203.

Peels, Eric. "God's Throne in Elam: The Historical Background and Literary Context of Jeremiah 49:34–39." In *Past, Present, Future: The Deuteronomistic History and the Prophets*, edited by Johannes C. De Moor and Harry F. Van Rooy, 216–29. Leiden: Brill, 2000.

Petersen, David L. "The Ambiguous Role of Moses as Prophet." In *Israel's Prophets and Israel's Past: Essays on the Relationship of Prophetic Texts and Israelite History in Honor of John H. Hayes*, edited by Brad E. Kelle and Megan Bishop Moore, 311–24. New Haven: T and T Clark, 2006.

———. *The Roles of Israel's Prophets.* Sheffield: Journal for the Study of the Old Testament Press, 1981.

Plant, R. J. R. *Good Figs, Bad Figs: Judicial Differentiation in the Book of Jeremiah.* New York: T and T Clark, 2008.

Polk, Timothy. *The Prophetic Persona: Jeremiah and the Language of the Self.* Sheffield: Journal for the Study of the Old Testament Press, 1984.

Premnath, D. N. *Eighth Century Prophets: A Social Analysis.* St. Louis. Chalice Press, 2003.

Reimer, David J. "The 'Foe' and the 'North' in Jeremiah." *Zeitschrift für die alttestamentliche Wissenschaft* 101.2 (1989): 223–32.

———. "Redeeming Politics in Jeremiah." In *Prophecy in the Book of Jeremiah*, edited by Hans M. Barstad and Reinhard G. Kratz, 121–36. Berlin: Walter de Gruyter, 2009.

Roncace, Mark. *Jeremiah, Zedekiah, and the Fall of Jerusalem.* New York: T and T Clark, 2005.

Scalise, Pamela J. "Baruch as First Reader: Baruch's Lament in the Structure of the Book of Jeremiah." In *Uprooting and Planting: Essays on Jeremiah for Leslie Allen*, edited by John Goldingay, 291–307. London: T and T Clark, 2007.

Schipper, Jeremy. "'Exile Atones for Everything': Coping with Jeremiah 22:24–30." *Journal for the Study of the Old Testament* 31 (2007): 481–92.

Seitz, Christopher R. "The Crisis of Interpretation over the Meaning and Purpose of the Exile." *Vetus Testamentum* 35.1 (1985): 78–97.

———. "The Prophet Moses and the Canonical Shape of Jeremiah." *Zeitschrift für die alttestamentliche Wissenschaft* 101.1 (1998): 3–27.

Sharp, Carolyn J. "Embodying Moab: Jeremiah's Figuring of Moab (Jer 48) as Reinscription of the Judean Body." Paper presented at the annual meeting of the Society of Biblical Literature, Atlanta, Ga., November 21, 2010.

Smelik, Klaas A. D. "Letter to the Exiles: Jeremiah 29 in Context." *Scandinavian Journal of the Old Testament* 10.2 (1996): 282–95.

Smith, Mark S. *The Laments of Jeremiah and Their Contexts*. Atlanta: Scholars Press, 1990.

———. *The Origins of Biblical Monotheism: Israel's Polytheistic Background and the Ugaritic Texts*. Oxford: Oxford University Press, 2001.

Smothers, Thomas G. "A Lawsuit against the Nations: Reflections on the Oracles on the Nations in Jeremiah." *Review and Expositor* 85.3 (1988): 545–54.

Strawn, Brent A. "Jeremiah's In/effective Plea: Another Look at נכפ in Jeremiah I 6." *Vetus Testamentum* 55.3 (2005): 366–77.

Stulman, Louis. *Jeremiah*. Nashville: Abingdon, 2005.

———. "Jeremiah the Prophet: Astride Two Worlds." In *Reading the Book of Jeremiah: A Search for Coherence*, edited by Martin Kessler, 41–56. Winona Lake, Ind: Eisenbrauns, 2004.

———. *Order Amid Chaos: Jeremiah as Symbolic Tapestry*. Sheffield: Sheffield Academic Press, 1998.

———. *The Prose Sermons of the Book of Jeremiah. A Redescription of the Correspondences with Deuteronomistic Literature in the Light of Recent Text-critical Research*. Atlanta: Scholars Press, 1986.

———. "The Prose Sermons as Hermeneutical Guide to Jeremiah 1–25: The Deconstruction of Judah's Symbolic World." In *Troubling Jeremiah*, edited by A. R. Pete Diamond and Kathleen M. O'Connor, 34–63. Sheffield: Sheffield Academic Press, 1999.

Sweeney, Marvin. *King Josiah of Judah: The Lost Messiah of Israel*. New York: Oxford University Press, 2001.

Taylor, Marion Ann. "Jeremiah 45: The Problem of Placement." *Journal for the Study of the Old Testament* 37 (1987): 79–98.

Tiemeyer, Lena Sofia. "God's Hidden Compassion." *Tyndale Bulletin* 57.2 (2006): 191–213.

Varughese, Alex. "The Royal Family in the Jeremiah Traditions." In *Inspired Speech: Prophecy in the Ancient Near East. Essays in Honor of Herbert B. Huffmon*, edited by John Kaltner and Louis Stulman, 319–28. London: T and T Clark International 2004.

Villiers, Gerda de. "Where Did She Come from, and Where Did She Go To? (The *Queen of Heaven* in Jeremiah 7 and 44)." *Old Testament Essays* 15.3 (2002): 620–27.

Walsh, Jerome T. *Old Testament Narrative: A Guide to Interpretation*. Louisville: Westminster John Knox, 2009.

Weinberg, Joel. "Gedaliah, the Son of Ahikam in Mizpah: His Status and Role, Supporters and Opponents." *Zeitschrift für die alttestamentliche Wissenschaft* 119.3 (2007): 356–68.

Willis, John T. "Dialogue between Prophet and Audience as a Rhetorical Device in the Book of Jeremiah." *Journal for the Study of the Old Testament* 33 (1985): 63–82.

Yates, Gary E. "Ishmael's Assassination of Gedaliah: Echoes of the Saul-David Story in Jeremiah 40:7–41:18." *Westminster Theological Journal* 67.1 (2005): 103–12.

———. "Narrative Parallelism and the 'Jehoiakim Frame': A Reading Strategy for Jeremiah 26–45." *Journal of the Evangelical Theological Society* 48.2 (2005): 263–81.

———. "New Exodus and No Exodus in Jeremiah 26–45." *Tyndale Bulletin* 57.1 (2006): 1–22.

INDEX

ABOUT THE AUTHOR

BARBARA GREEN is a professor of biblical studies at the Dominican School of Philosophy and Theology at the Graduate Theological Union in Berkeley, California. She is the author of several books including *Jonah's Journeys; How Are the Mighty Fallen? A Dialogical Study of King Saul in 1 Samuel;* and *Mikhail Bakhtin and Biblical Scholarship: An Introduction.*